**Rhys Alun Wilcox** was born in Luton on Decimalisation Day. He does not think that missing out on shillings by a few hours has affected his life in any way.

He started writing some time between his first and second birthdays and has never looked back. Literature took a more serious turn at Portsmouth University whilst reading Media & Design. There, he found he had a lot of spare time on his hands so wrote some plays for the drama society, tried his hand at stand-up comedy and conceived the idea for the *Blood Lust* series.

Most people think he thinks he's funny but this is wrong; he knows he's funny. It's not his fault that other people don't share his pragmatic understanding to fully appreciate his jokes.

He currently exists in West Sussex, with his wife and two children, where he attempts to complete at least another dozen novels in between parenting, procrastinating and dying. Not necessarily in that order.

He seems to spend most of his time not updating his website *www.thebloodlust.co.uk*.

### Also by Rhys A. Wilcox
Blood Lust
Blood Lust 2: The Carrion
Blood Lust 3: Revelations
Blood Lust: Sound Bites #1 - 10

### Also by Rhys A. Wilcox (but not in the *Blood Lust* series)
Aftermath

Rhys A. Wilcox

# Blood Lust 2.5
# L'Hunch Est Dos

RAW!

© Copyright 2010
**Rhys Alun Wilcox**

The right of Rhys A. Wilcox to be identified as the author of this work has been asserted by him in accordance with the Copyright, Designs and Patents Act 1988

**All Rights Reserved**

No reproduction, copy or transmission of this publication may be made without written permission. No paragraph of this publication may be reproduced, copied or transmitted save with the written permission or in accordance with the provisions of the Copyright Act 1956 (as amended).

Any person who does any unauthorised act in relation to this publication may be liable to criminal prosecution and civil claims for damage.
So ner!

ISBN 978-0-9561559-1-7

<u>For:</u>
My Dichotomous Monsters: NAW & LAW
The one eternally bound to my soul: MAW


<u>Major Props to:</u>
Luc Besson
Jean-Pierre Jeunet
Jean Reno
Ron Perlman


<u>Apologies</u>
The author would like to publicly apologise on behalf of his fictional character, Penelope Helsine, who, in an earlier text (yet later adventure) was taken to say, "Slam dunked him off the Eiffel Tower." This was an entirely erroneous comment to make as, at no time whatsoever, did she go anywhere near that landmark. The author does not know why she would have said such a thing and can only presume it was a deliberate, malicious action on her behalf in an attempt to draw more attention to her needs as a figment of the author's imagination. The author has seen to that good and proper in this tale and hopes it will teach her a bloody lesson to mind her mouth and not fuck about with the author's continuity in the future. Or past. Whatever.

The author would also like to apologise for any inaccuracies in his translations and would like to officially pass the blame onto the English education system that allowed him to do Drama CSE instead of a second language.

# BOOK 1

## 1 (*Dann*)

## Lasciate Ogni Speranza

The World was halfway through the nineteenth century, just recuperating from the shock waves of the Industrial Revolution. Attitudes had changed, politics had changed, modes of production had changed, religious dependencies had changed and the global society suddenly found itself evolving, out of control. For better or for worse was unknown at the time because it was happening too fast for many to keep a check on it and too fast for many to keep up. Those uncomfortable with the notion of progress were scorned as ignoramuses and their protestations were ignored.

There were still plenty of changes yet to come that would overshadow these events and cause many concerns to be forgotten. Wars were on the horizon. Wars that would pit one nation against the other, claim the lives of millions of innocents and change the World even more. For better or for worse?

But even such global events could be considered negligible when placed beside those of an individual. How can you relate to phenomena whose overall effects, no matter how revolutionary, will take place over years, when, in comparison, something may have happened last night that caused everything you used to believe in to change irrevocably?

A scientific man had encountered something that defied all known science. A pious man had seen something that defied the word of God, perhaps even His very existence. A dying man had discovered life. A cynic had found love.

It was Hamburg and the city was recovering from a vicious epidemic that had claimed the lives of many citizens. It came without reason and it seemed to have left just the same.

One of the many victims of the plague had been the home of this changed man. The apartment had been burned to the ground because of a slight misunderstanding. For some reason accusations had spread about this place being the source of the disease. The Residents Committee had turned up one night with the appropriate civic mandates - torches and pitchforks - and the majority law of the common people had been administered.

They had stormed the place and found no one. Whoever had lived there had left in a hurry and left empty luggage, clothes and money. There was scientific equipment lying around the place: vials, beakers, tubes and blood. Lots of blood in different states of composition: dried stains across the floor, smears down the walls, samples being cultured in Petri dishes, test tubes, buckets of the stuff and even a wineglass with warm residue at the bottom and lipstick on the rim.

Anything of value was the first to be taken, then anything that was easily removed, even if it had no obvious worth. Then the torches were laid upon the godless den of disease.

One retrieved item was a journal. The man who had taken it had thought that the leather covering might provide some remuneration but was disappointed when the pawnbroker told him it was not even real leather.

The broker paid a few Marks for the journal anyway. He started to read it, presuming it was some sort of work of fiction. Entries were filled with medical case notes, scientific developments, educational teachings and geographical travels. Although the book made for fairly interesting reading, it did not have any kind of cohesive narrative or character development.

The journal was read, piece by piece over a period of years. Whenever he had nothing better to do. Under normal circumstances he would have disposed of it but his wife was insistent of its removal from her house so that was reason enough to keep it. Another was that it had become a topic of conversation with many friends.

"What has the diary been up to recently?" someone would ask.

"He has begun mapping the nervous system of a dog," the broker would reply.

"What does that mean?"

"I have no idea."

Every now and again would come an entry of morbid fascination. Experiments conducted on human cadavers, which would generally provide no satisfactory results. The tests would be upgraded to living subjects. The pages would contain illustrations and, to add effect, a few drops of crimson.

Then he came to one of the last entries that detailed a trip to Hungary and its Emperor's need to find a cure for a plague that was beleaguering his nation. The reports were that multiple victims had died due to some sort of anaemic disorder. The journal stated, after many autopsies, that they had died because of a complete lack of blood.

The broker remembered the epidemic that had spread through his neighbourhood just before he had been given the book and began to wonder whether the author was just twisting historical fact to create a better literary effect.

As he became engrossed in these later passages, the evening closed in, lights were extinguished and his wife retired for the night. The broker continued to read with only one candle flickering over his shoulder.

The journal stated that no rational explanation could be found and therefore no cure could be suggested. The tone of the author became melancholic and nihilistic.

Then the broker came to a word that nearly froze his heart.

*Vampyre.*

There had been screams one night, outside his house. At the time, he and his wife had hidden in their attic, thinking it was a riot. In the morning they found out that the disease had become its most virulent and had passed on to some of his neighbours. People had been panicking, not because of the threat of violence but because they were dying. Among the screams had been this bizarre oral formation of a word 'vampire' exclaimed more as a declaration rather than a plea for help.

There was a loose insert at this point. He could not read it because it was written in a language he did not know but it had an official looking wax seal on it.

There were, on the few remaining pages, details how a human shell could continue living after its vitality had been removed but there was no scientific reason for it. It was immortality and it came at a cost; the need to feed on human blood.

During one experiment, the author stated that he had inherited a portion of these creatures' abilities and he was no longer ageing.

The broker was no longer so sure that this work was fiction. He managed to calm himself that it was just a literary device. The author must have lived nearby and would have been privy to the same events outside that he had. The author must have had an active imagination to weave the real occurrences around them into this bizarre mix.

Nevertheless, fiction or not, he wanted rid of the book but could not bring himself to destroy it. If the owner came looking for it then he wanted to be able to say it went somewhere else.

Despite the early hour of the morning, he threw his coat on and left the house. His journey along the darkened streets was one in which he found himself peering into shadows and looking over his shoulder a lot more than he normally would. He came to the house of an acquaintance and unabashedly rang the doorbell.

Eventually, a dishevelled old man answered the door attired in dressing gown and slippers and before he had the time to say anything, the broker apologised for the unsociable hour and explained everything.

The broker was given entry to the house and seated with a warm drink where he then went over the tale again. "... and with you being a librarian, I thought it would be better in your hands," he explained.

"I see," the librarian sighed with a wry smile. "Passing the blame, are you?" he teased. "Spreading the misery." He opened the journal to the pages that had caused so much consternation and read in silence. He inspected the loose insert then carefully replaced it. Upon reaching the journal's end he pursed his lips in concentration. "I'll take this book from you," he decided.

The broker was very pleased but his face changed when a thought came to him. "What of its subject matter?" he asked.

"Hmm? Oh, a work of fiction, of course," the librarian chuckled. "Walking dead, immortality, blood-drinking demons? Dear man, you need to stay off the strong cheese this late at night."

The broker laughed with embarrassment and apologised again.

"Yes, I know of a young Irish man who would be quite interested in reading this," the librarian commented as he ushered the broker to the front door.

"Thank you, Mr Leavis," the broker said and made his way home with a lighter sense of relief.

Yet, he still could not stop himself from double checking the occasional shadow.

## 2 (*Then*)

## Kisses for Blows

Things were going to change.

No. He had to correct himself.

Things *had* to change. Now more than ever before.

It was not as if things had never changed; it seemed that every other day someone was changing the rules. As soon as he thought they had found themselves a niche in life, something would come along and shift the objectives and make them re-evaluate everything. More often than not they found themselves having to re-evaluate themselves and how they felt they fit in the big plan.

Whatever that might be.

Or, perhaps, whatever it had been but was no longer valid.

Too many times they had looked sincerely into each other's eyes and nearly packed it all in. How many times did you have to say, 'It's not working,' before you stop trying to make it work?

Now it had to work. Now things were going to change and they were going to change in their favour. *They* were changing the rules and everyone else was going to have to re-evaluate *their* plans.

His real name was unknown, lost within the progression of many years not being able to use it. Anybody who knew of his reputation simply called him Professor although, they too, were becoming few and far between.

He had recently found that he was slowly but surely outliving his reputation and most people who might have used his name with revered awe were dead, which left him as a figment of fable or history. This meant if he tried to use his name against his reputation then he was either laughed at or physically threatened. It had got to the stage that he would answer to any name other than his given family name to save on complications.

He was probably in his late fifties although it was difficult to judge with just a cursory glance. If he would allow you the opportunity to study his appearance - and you were inclined to be that observant - then you would see a whole host of conflicting signs of age.

Most strikingly was his full head of pure white hair. The colour, obviously, signified a considerable age but then the heavy consistency of it might imply that he was much younger and had been cursed with premature discoloration.

His face displayed the undeniable weathering of time. When it was relaxed, it bore an expression of concentration. It might even have been worry. His brow would be furrowed as if lost in profound musing whilst his eyes would tighten as if he was focussing on some minute detail. Their corners splayed more age lines across his temples like a Japanese fan. It was his mouth that inferred a constant state of sorrow rather than deliberation as further erosion caused the corners to be downturned and morose.

To look directly into his eyes would make it seem that there was a younger man peering through a mask. They sparkled with vigour and vitality rather than being dulled by tiredness and deficiency. They also hinted at an extensive intellect and vast experience if you knew what to look for. Also, if you caught a look in the wrong light then they could indicate imminent and absolute menace.

There was his gait. He always walked with a walking stick and, although it was not an uncommon symbol of gentry, you would usually see him gripping the silver head as if his life depended on it. You might think that if he were to lose his grip then he would lose his balance. However, when he did move, it was with absolute control and deliberate strength.

Looking beyond the loose fitting three-piece suit you might have been able to see a well-toned, muscular body.

Finally, there was the way he spoke. A jumbled European accent denoted a knowledge of many languages or, at least, that he had spent long periods of time ensconced in a multitude of varying cultures. The words he chose were polite, articulate and to the point. He was obviously academically educated but he also tended to use old-fashioned sentence structures. Certainly there was something to be said for using correct grammar and diction but the evolution of language had spread the usage of colloquialisms, euphemisms and slang beyond the throes of lower classes and into the more refined realms of society.

Professor very rarely used colloquialisms and certainly did not use slang. If it seemed like he did then it was more likely to be a misunderstanding from the point of the listener than the orator.

Beyond all that was the present company he was keeping and, specifically, the young woman whose hand he was holding passionately. Although, again, the specifics of her age were difficult to pinpoint because of the gargoylish expressions of pain she was pulling, the deep red coloration in her face brought about by intense straining and the sweat that had soaked her hair and drawn it into lank curtains across it all.

The woman was dressed in a plain white nightdress, which was pulled up, over her incredibly engorged stomach. She was lying on a small cot with her knees raised and pulled apart and had a mid-wife positioned between her knees focussing on her exposed vagina.

It was New Year's Eve, 1899 and Professor had managed to secure himself a period of peace in a small Kentish village in England. The abode in which he and his partner were now dwelling was a plain hostelry at the back of a quiet inn. They had been residing there since the start of the second term of his partner's pregnancy, having travelled there from France.

"That's it, Eve," Professor encouraged. "You are doing wonderfully."

"Shut your fucking mouth, Eric," Eve screamed at him with a heavy accent. "Don't you fucking speak to me. Don't you say a fucking word."

Professor was taken aback and looked apologetically down to the mid-wife across from him.

"I suppose you must hear a lot of expressions like that during times like this," he said.

The woman returned a steely, disapproving stare and resolutely shook her head.

Eve gave another huge scream and bore down.

"I can see its head," the mid-wife declared and Professor attempted to move down a bit to get a better look.

"Don't you fucking move!" Eve bellowed. "You fucking stay right where you are. You ain't going nowhere."

"I only wanted to -"

"I told you not to fucking speak," she reiterated through gritted teeth as she strained again.

"Here it comes," the mid-wife stated. "It's crowned so just take a moment to regain your strength."

"Regain my strength?" Eve gasped. "What the hell for?"

"We have to get the shoulders through now," Professor told her and then regretted it.

"'We'?" Eve demanded. "Fucking, 'we'?"

"Push!" the mid-wife demanded and Eve bore her chin onto her chest and growled.

She cried with relief and threw herself back onto the bed trying to catch her breath.

The mid-wife clamped the bloody child's umbilical cord and cut it free from its mother's connection. She hung it upside down by its ankles and gave it a harsh slap across its buttocks. The baby squealed with displeasure and hacked up a mouthful of fluid.

"It's a girl," the mid-wife told them as she wrapped it up in swaddling. "Quite a small one too which is why you had it so easy."

Eve was too exhausted to react.

The mid-wife passed the bundle to Professor who cradled it carefully in his arms.

"A girl," he purred and stared into her blood-smeared, scrunched up face. Again, an anachronistic visage of contrary ageing signs; such a small body having the wrinkled face equivalent to an octogenarian.

Yes, everything *was* going to change for them now.

He looked at Eve to see how she was doing. She was still trying to catch her breath. Her eyes were closed and she panted heavily.

The mid-wife was washing her hands in a basin at the back of the room.

"What will you call her?" she asked.

"I like Agnes," Eve muttered. "What do you think, Eric?"

There was no answer from him so Eve opened her eyes to see if he was giving her an admonishing look or if he was just lost in the moment of awe. The mid-wife turned around to address them both and was surprised to see there was no 'both' to address. Professor was not in the room. Neither was the newborn baby.

"Eric?" Eve called out nervously and looked to the mid-wife in abject fear.

Professor was in a carriage that was rattling through the cobbled streets, heading out of the village. He still held the swaddled child close to his chest and pulled the towelling away to reveal slightly more of her face.

"Hello, Penelope," he said. "Things are definitely going to change."

# BOOK 2

## 1 (*Now*)

## Unpopularity

Penny had not really wanted to leave Leeds quite that urgently. She had rather thought she might be able to hang around with her friends for a bit longer, revel in their victory and celebrate being alive. Of course that would also have allowed her to dilute the time she was due to spend with her father. Not that she did not want to get to know him again but would have preferred to have been eased back into a relationship. Instead, everyone decided to get up and ship off, just like that.

So here she was, sitting opposite her old man on a train, desperately trying to think of something that might spark up a conversation that was not anything to do with thousands of people being horrendously murdered, vampires or why it had been over fifty years since they last spoke.

Ha! Last spoke. That was a good one. It was something like, 'Father, please! I beg you!' He had not actually spoken to her for about two weeks. She really could not remember what their last, proper, verbal exchange had been. The one before her last words had been a cacophony of embarrassed explanations, shouts of abuse and her struggles to prevent her father from killing the young man in question, all wrapped up in a fountain of clothes and burlap sacks.

Penny smirked and looked out of the train window at the blurred scenery. At the time there was absolutely nothing funny about it. No one wants to get caught by their parents during any kind of sexual exploration, absolutely not mid-coitus with an orphaned altar boy.

"Something amusing you?" Professor asked and shocked her back to her surroundings.

"No," she replied guiltily. "Well, yes, I was just thinking about Paris."

He waited for further elucidation but she returned her attention to the window.

He had not changed much in the last hundred years aside from allowing his white hair to grow longer, which he now had tied back in a ponytail. He still carried the same silver-handled walking stick but had swapped the suits for less restrictive, black roll-neck jumper and smart corduroy trousers. He had a neatly folded black raincoat in the empty seat next to him, being guarded by a black Fedora.

He had felt less uncomfortable than his daughter concerning the silence between them. He was using the time to study her. She certainly *had* changed quite considerably since the day of her birth and, despite their unnatural ageing processes, she had also changed a lot since the last time he had laid eyes on her.

When he had left her at the doors of the convent, she was still a little girl. She had long fair hair that he made her keep tied out of her face with a red Alice Band. Although, now he came to think about it, he could not remember her wearing it that day.

He used to make her wear glasses even though she did not need them. The spectacles simply contained plain glass but they added to an overall, unassuming appearance for her. He did not want her to draw attention to herself. She may have been older than her outward appearance indicated but that outward appearance was still of a very young girl and he wanted to protect her as much as possible. That meant protecting her from unscrupulous males, all the other males and any half-witted vampires that might pass her by with a cursory glance.

He had kept her in full-length skirts even though the fashions had been causing the hem to gradually recede up the ladies' legs and were, at the time, just passing their shins to rest at their knees. They were, in his opinion, ungainly and, moreover, impractical. The dress down to her ankles not only meant she had more coverage from wayward eyes but, with the addition of petticoats, allowed her extra volume to hide a variety of blades, stakes and vials. One unintentional mark of progressiveness on his part was his insistence that she wore breeches under her dresses as often as she could. She, of course, did not see it as setting a feminist statement but was just another punishment and embarrassment enforced by her father. Fancy having to wear boys' clothes! No matter that she could run faster without the restriction of her bustles; she would rather have run away in just her underwear.

Her dresses' material had been of light calico cotton but darkened with such a deep purple that they looked practically black in poor light. She thought people would think she was in constant mourning but she supposed she was, really, considering everything that had come to pass. His reasoning behind the depressing shade was that it allowed her to disappear into the shadows better.

Then there were her shoes that she was not sure about either. Yes, the Mary Janes, themselves, were the height of fashion across the boards of class and culture but it was the customised two-inch platforms Professor always had added that caused her the most consternation.

She was not a particularly tall girl so they did not do much for her stature but they did take some getting used to. He had them raised as it meant she had another inconspicuous place to store more weaponry.

All in all, if you were to look at her then all you would see was a young girl. Perhaps you might deduce that her slightly out-dated dress sense meant an over authoritative father - rather than a vampire hunter - was raising her. Ultimately, as was intended, she did not stand out for either her looks or her dress sense.

He looked at her and felt a slight pang of disappointment. Was her state of attire now a deliberate rebellion against the way he had raised her or just a sign of the progression of today's fashions? He had to admit that he had become completely out of touch with the interests of youth culture since her departure. Well, apart from a brief interest in the evolution of European Hip-Hop and its US influences during the eighties. Really, though, that was nothing more than a distraction and seemed that no sooner had he been humming along to *You Know I've Got Soul* than everyone was body-slamming to *Smelly Teen Spirit* or something.

Where had her hair gone? She used to have truly beautiful hair when she was smaller. It seemed so difficult for him to do anything with her that did not result in her looking truly stunning. Hence why the glasses had come into effect. But they had been cast aside along with her light-brown locks; she had her hair trimmed right back to only a centimetre all over her head. It was, quite frankly, scarily masculating. Along with an absolute lack of any kind of make-up, which he was actually quite relieved about. Had she been taking a contrary stance to his will then she would be made-up to look like one of those little girls' prostitute dolls that are all over the place. *Tartz*, were they called?

Maybe it was a sexual revolution then? She was unhappy with her life as being female? The hair, the lack of make-up and jewellery and the clothes she wore. Denim dungarees over a plain white t-shirt and large, black 'dock workers' boots.

"You don't like my boots?" Penny asked and he jumped to attention.

"I beg your pardon?" he replied.

"The way you were staring at my boots," she explained. "It looked like you don't like them."

"Not at all," he said. "I was just wondering what sort of heavy lifting you did at the university that necessitated you wearing them."

She rolled her eyes. "I happen to like them," she said.

"Why?"

It was all coming back now. This was more like it. Their last words. A constant need for her to explain her motivations. It could never just be, 'because I want to,' or, 'because everyone else does.'

"They are comfortable. They are practical. They are hard wearing. They really hurt when I kick someone in the head with them."

They stared at each other.

"I was only asking," he sulked.

"Oh, I doubt that," she muttered.

Yeah, she definitely could have done with a bit of settling in time before this.

"What were you reading?" Professor asked.

"Pardon me?"

"At your university? What course were you reading?"

"Oh, it was an advanced theology degree," she stated and watched his eyebrows try to shoot off his forehead.

"Theology?"

"Mm-hm. I got thinking about the vampires and all and tried to work out how they fit into the grand scheme of everything," she explained. "I never found any kind of reference to them in anything I studied so I had to keep on studying."

"I had never thought of that before," he said.

"If they really had existed since the dawn of time and are global then why have they never figured in any religious tomes in one form or another? Why have they only ever appeared in tenuous folk law and popular culture? How did they manage to stay so secret for so long?"

"I suppose any witnesses are either subsumed or outright killed leaving only speculation in their wake," he postulated.

"What about you? Didn't you ever try to take it public?" she asked.

"More often than you could possibly imagine," he sighed. "I was either ignored, ridiculed or condemned to death. By the time it was safe for anyone to see, there was never any concrete evidence left."

"But at least it's all over now, huh?"

"Yes," he said distractedly. "Why Leeds?"

"There are only two universities in the UK that run the course," Penny explained. "The other one is in Portsmouth and already had someone studying it."

"Only one person?"

"Yeah, it's not so much a degree," she said, "these places just allow the selected student unfettered access to all their library resources. There's no official qualification at the end of it; more like an industry recognition."

"What sort of resources did they have access to?"

Penny leaned forward conspiratorially and Professor flashed a secretive look around the carriage then joined her.

"It's a secret," she said and sat back.

He blinked a couple of times.

"Really?"

She nodded.

"You won't tell me?"

"Can't."

"Anything?"

She thinned her lips in thought. "Ancient texts. Really, *really* old stuff from all over the place. They are a knowledge based organisation that sit outside the bounds of religion, politics and industry."

"Why the secrecy?" Professor demanded.

"Because they have information that people from these other areas would kill for."

"To get their hands on?"

"To prevent from ever getting into the hands of anyone else."

"How on earth did you get yourself involved with them?"

"I've been in the schooling system for the last forty-five years," she explained. "It was bound to happen eventually. There's a finite number of courses that I'm going to be interested in taking. After my first doctorate -"

"First?"

She nodded. "After the first one, I had to go back to the beginning of the next degree. Eventually I got bored of going back to the start every seven years or so, so decided to see how far I could push one theme and settled on theology."

"Can't you tell me anything?" Professor begged.

She tutted. "Bearing in mind that I was only looking into the theological side of their resources, had I then 'completed' the course then I might have been allowed to get into another area. I can't tell you what I read and, unfortunately, the vampires came before I could finish the course."

She leaned forward again.

"Rumour has it that they have absolute evidence of who didn't kill Kennedy."

"Didn't?"

"Yup. Apparently he's not dead but sitting in some Texan retirement home rotting away for his indiscretions."

He waited to see if she would give him a wry, knowing smile but nothing came.

The train floated along for a few minutes more.

"What about you?" Penny asked. "What have you been doing?"

He returned her gaze with confusion.

"Apart from killing vampires," she added.

"Well, nothing really," he confessed. "Just staying alive from one day to the next."

She paused and wondered whether she should ask the next question.

"You never met anyone else?"

"I never had the time," he replied despondently then smiled. "Or the opportunity or the inclination."

He paused and wondered whether he wanted to know the answer to the next obvious question.

"You?" he asked and cleared his throat uncomfortably.

"Me? God, no," she laughed and noted with further amusement how his demeanour relaxed slightly. "I never had the inclination."

She returned her attention to the scenery and caught a glimpse of his reflection; did he mouth the word, 'Good'?

She quickly turned back but he gave no indication of having said or thought anything else.

"You had some interesting friends," he commented.

"They are some of the best I have found so far," she replied.

"Really?"

"Are you that surprised? Were they that bad?"

"No," he said defensively. "Just, interesting."

"Yeah? And how often do you have to update your address book?"

"Point taken," he acquiesced.

God, he was infuriating. So judgmental about everything and she was no longer willing to let him get away with it.

There was that silence again. So many things needed to be said between them but they needed to be said in a place where she had the chance to turn around and walk away.

"I was very surprised by Cameron," he said and she was about to bite again but thought about his words.

"Me too, actually," she agreed and they looked at each other with amusement.

"You didn't think he had it in him?" Professor asked.

"I'd never met him before; the others used to talk about him sometimes. They were all really critical of him; even Gillian. Well, especially Gillian if truth be told. I thought he was going to be some drugged up vagrant or something."

"And you didn't think that after you had met him?" he joked.

"He was a bit rude at first but then I had a talk with him and he seemed genuinely down on his luck."

"We usually make our own luck, Penelope," Professor lectured.

"True," she replied. "I would never have put him down to being a hunter, though."

"No," he said. "I didn't even think he would be chosen as hunted either."

"Oh that's harsh," she giggled. "Even vampires don't have standards."

"But there's always a difference between fine dining and MacDonalds, isn't there," he told her. "Which would you choose if given the choice."

"There's also such a thing as 'too much of a good time,' you know? Sometimes it's nice to rough it," she countered.

Professor was looking at her with mock amusement.

"What?" She thought about her analogy. "Oh, piss off, you," she spat playfully. "I did not fancy Cameron."

"Good," he said definitively.

"I can't believe that we were so close to losing everything," she pondered. "Had you ever seen them try something so bold? Or spread so quickly?"

"No," he replied. "I suppose it was bound to happen sometime and, perhaps, had happened before but we were never around to see it."

"But who could have stopped it if we hadn't been there?"

"Maybe someone else," he said. "Maybe no one. Maybe they would have won and humanity would have been doomed. We were probably just very lucky, that is all."

"Unlucky for some," she muttered. "Did I hear those people say about half-a-million died?"

"In Leeds alone," he replied. "There were countless numbers of his armies spread all around the globe. Who knows how many people have just disappeared."

"It's a horrific number of deaths. Too big a number to comprehend," she stated. "So many that it's so easy to not think about it."

"Have you not had any vampire encounters since -"

*Ack!* He did it. He broached the subject without thinking about it and now did not know what to call it.

Penny wondered if she should try to help out and offer a diplomatic phrase to ease his discomfort.

Nah!

"Since then," was all he could manage. He tried not to look at her when he said it and waited for a reprimanding.

She just gave him a few moments of reflection.

"Yes," she eventually replied. "There were a few but none of any consequence. I don't even think they had the chance to register me."

"Well, you were well trained," Professor commended.

"And I guess I should thank you for that?"

"Who else?" he replied smugly.

"Erm, since when did you ever teach me any martial arts?"

"I laid the foundations," he argued. "You have to give me credit for that."

"I suppose I do," she conceded.

They sat and stared at each other while the train trundled on persistently.

"Would you believe me if I said I was sorry?" he asked.

"Is it something you think you're likely to say?"

"Yes."

"When you get around to saying it," she advised. "Make sure you let me know what you're saying it for, okay?"

"I will."

This was going to be one fucking long train journey.

## 2 (*Adesso*)

## The Grand Hall

Had anyone seen him there, then they would have immediately known that he was not supposed to be there. There were, primarily, three reasons for this.

Firstly, he was walking around with no lights on. Now, unless he was actually looking for the fuse box to reset the trip switch, it would be a fair deduction to say he was deliberately keeping it dark so as not to be noticed. Also, there was no fuse box there.

Secondly was his furtive movement. Again, allowing him reasonable doubt might infer that he was trying not to make too much noise and wake anyone up. That would be fine but there was no one sleeping there.

Thirdly, and probably the real clincher, was that no one was allowed down there. So anyone there, seeing him, would know they were not supposed to be there and hence would deduce he was not also. There were no reasonable excuses for this one. Men had been killed for going down there. Well, they had not been killed for going down there; even for *them* that was an extreme punishment for that particular crime. No, men had been killed for seeing what was kept down there.

This particular man was less than a silhouette in the darkness. He was only noticeable as he moved along. When he stopped to wait for his eyes to become better accustomed to the gloom, he completely disappeared into the surrounding void of light.

Satisfied that he was completely alone, he struck a match against the wall to light a small candle which he held at waist height. All that could be discerned about the figure was that he was wearing a black, sackcloth gown of some sorts.

He wavered the light from side-to-side to better gauge his location and revealed rough, wet concrete walls on one side of him and racks of wooden shelves on the other. The room was nothing more than a corridor in width although the light could not penetrate the length of it.

There were a plethora of things on the shelves. There were boxes of varying sizes, some so large as to have necessitated intermediate shelves to be removed to allow them storage. Some were made of cardboard and there were dozens of ornate ones carved from wood and stone. There were some boxes that proved *someone* had been down here reasonably recently; they were office style archive boxes. They were however, like everything else, carpeted in a couple of centimetres of dust.

There were books, loose-leaf sheets of paper, manuscripts tied together with neat, red ribbon bows and pyramids of scrolls. There were numerous devices littered around. Some looked like they may have been designed to kill, some looked like they were built to hurt, and the really scary ones were so intricate that they looked like they were designed to hurt as much as possible, for as long as possible, with the intention of eliciting pleads for death by the end. Pulleys, winches and handles connected to chains, blades, hooks and vices. He came to such an object blocking his progress and had to clamber over to continue. As he passed his candle from one hand to the other it briefly illuminated an inscription, *Tomás estuvo aquí*, but his inquisition was not stirred.

Some of the contraptions were nothing more than ancient household objects like washboards, flat irons, pokers and an electric toaster. It was after here where the corridor opened for the light to diminish in all directions. He paused to focus to the gloom and could just make out the silhouettes of large balls stacked up to the ceiling and the floor looked like it had been laid with an oversized raffia carpet. Too big for the room, in fact, as it lapped up the edges of all the walls around it.

His light hovered unsteadily as his other hand rooted around in a pocket. It pulled out a piece of paper, which he unfolded and had a crudely drawn floor plan on it and, indeed, showed a room full of balls and crosshatches. His curiosity got the better of him and he inspected this room's floors coverage to discover it was a collection of brooms and the balls were actually fire pots and cauldrons.

He cursed himself for allowing himself to get distracted and continued his progression.

The corridor's width returned as did the shelving and miscellany.

The harder materials had now changed to cloths and parchments and he started to take more care to examine each article as he passed it. Eventually he stopped as the light focussed on a small, lustrous bag.

He gasped and accidentally blew out his candle.

There followed a muttering of unintelligible expletives and rummaging in pockets for the matches. A small flame flared from off the wall and was carefully placed on the candlewick. He repositioned it so the light fell on the shiny bag again. He edged forward and the ring of light crept up his chest to his chin.

It was an old chin: angular and wrinkled with fine white stubble all around it.

The light inched up to his mouth. His lips were tight and puckered but they were smiling.

The illumination was prevented from revealing any more of his features when it was blocked by something hanging over the edge of the shelf above. As he leaned further in, his forehead brushed against, what was, cloth and it jangled delicately from the contact. He drew away - which caused it to ring even more - and blew out the candle.

He stood in the darkness waiting for someone to come running to his position but no one came. Remember, *no one* was actually allowed to be down there.

There was a ruffling of sackcloth as he rooted for his matches again accompanied by another dose of exclamations under his breath.

Silence, then a resigned sigh, then a gentle 'click' and the corridor was swathed in brilliance as he waved a five-hundred watt torch down each way of the corridor to reveal any intended threat to his person. There was no one.

He directed the light in front of him to identify the source of the chimes and saw they were small, gold bells sewn around the hem of a blue robe. Between each bell were orbs of some description embroidered in blue, purple and scarlet yarn.

"Aaron," the man growled with irritation and reached out to take the garment. He hesitated, retracted his hand and bent under the cloth for the bag.

In this light, it was easier to see that it was a small, rectangular, green silk purse ornamented with a piece of green glass at its centre. He gave it a cursory shake as he picked it up and its contents rattled dryly. He pulled at the drawstring and directed its opening towards the shaft of light. He reeled as a waft of camphor assaulted his olfactory senses. As the pungent aroma faded he peered closer to the contents to see a loose collection of seeds.

His lips parted to reveal his plaque stained teeth clenched together. He barked a hearty laugh then slapped his hand over his mouth as it echoed along all directions of the corridors.

He quickly flicked the light off and swathed himself in darkness.

There was a gentle jingling and a muttering of curses.

## 3 (*Now*)

## The Dog and his Master

A distressed priest hurriedly walked along the tiled hall of the Vatican. Every now and again his pace would increase to throw a kind of skip into his gait. The various administrators, guards and nuns who he passed did not pay him any obvious attention although they all thought he looked very stupid.

*Why doesn't he just run?*

Robes flailed around him and his sandals slipped on the black and white chequered floor. Sweat poured down his face and, although he was only a young man, he looked as if he was on the verge of a heart attack.

He raced towards two large oak panelled doors and screamed a command so shrill that it was almost inaudible. It was indiscernible as to be any particular words but more of an oral representation of the man's emotional state of mind. The stripy guards managed to understand the implication behind the outburst and quickly hauled the doors open so the priest did not need to alter his pace to gain entrance to the vast hall beyond.

"Cunctus jus, sanctus patris?" he called out as the doors were closed behind him.

He continued his double-time march along this high ceiling room. The marble pillars flashed past him and he was either too preoccupied to notice the morning light that rainbowed through the stained glass windows that flanked the room or had simply been desensitised by over exposure to its wondrous glory.

"Sanctus patris?" he called again and started to look around him as he approached the end of the room and a large oak desk that resided at the top of a small flight of steps. "Es vos velieris quod quaestio?"

His pace slowed at the bottom step and he ascended cautiously.

"Patris?" he stuttered with trepidation.

As he climbed the second step he could see the top of the high-backed chair behind the desk. Made of the same dark oak of the table it was padded with burgundy velvet.

"Is est consequentia, patris," he said with less urgency and deliberation in his voice. "Patris? Commodo?"

Another two steps up and he could see that the seat was vacant. Another step and he could see that a document was half written but the penmanship of the last word trailed off the page as if the pen had been dragged away.

"Patris? Es vos effectus rideo risi risum mihi?"

He approached the desk and peered over it. His worse fears were realised as he identified the white robes of the Pope heaped on the floor like discarded washing. He then saw his face: aged, ashen and peaceful.

He ran around the desk and pulled the chair away. He rolled the old man on to his back and pressed his ear to his chest; there was the indication of slight respiration as his chest fluctuated gently.

The priest kneeled and marked the four points of the cross on his chest. The Pope burst out laughing and the priest threw himself backwards.

"Patris?" the priest enquired.

With that, a number of black robed cardinals entered the scene from behind the pillars that had acted as hiding places. They, too, were laughing.

"Aspicio vultus in vestri visio!" the Pope roared as he lifted himself up.

"Quid a caseus caput capitis!" one of the nearing cardinals declared and the others laughed harder.

The priest hauled himself to his feet shaking with anger and embarrassment. He swept an accusatory finger across them all.

"Cunctus vos!" he stated. "Haud abbas!"

The Pope and his advisors stopped laughing abruptly and stared at the priest as tears began to well in his eyes.

"Oooooooooh," they all mocked and started laughing again.

"Ah, Archbishop Wuh," the Pope sighed as he took his seat again. "You must learn to lighten up. We cannot all be so serious all the time."

"Patris -" the Archbishop began but was cut short by a raised hand from the Pope.

"Relax, Brandon," the leader of Catholicism ordered.

Archbishop Brandon Wuh was incredibly uncomfortable with the instruction and then remembered his purpose for being there.

"Something has been taken," Brandon blurted.

The Pope scrunched up the paper in front of him and dropped it in a bin by his side.

"Someone has been helping themselves to the branded stationery again?" the Pope asked and a few of the cardinals cleared their throats nervously. "I keep seeing our pencils turning up on Ebay."

"Your Eminence," Brandon urged. "Some *thing* has been taken."

Even though the air of joviality had been killed by the implications of petty office thievery, this reiteration performed a post mortem on their behaviour and gave the atmosphere an extreme Requiem Mass.

"How do you know?" the Pope demanded.

"Someone had left the door open," Brandon said.

"Do we know what is missing?"

"Something from the materials," Brandon reported. "There was a clear patch in the dust just under the ephod's robe."

There came a gasp from a couple of the cardinals and the Pope looked up at them sternly.

"What was it?" Brandon asked.

The Pope considered his options. Was it best to keep it a secret? How would they retrieve it if no one knew what it was they were supposed to be getting? Yet, if another person would find out what it was then that would be one step closer to the end of the World as they knew it.

"Leave us," the Pope instructed and Brandon stepped away from the desk.

"Not you," the Pope said and turned his attention to the cardinals. "You. Leave us."

There were general mutterings of dissent from most of the men apart from, as Brandon noted, the few who had shown recognition of the object. They were the first and quickest to exit the room.

When they were alone, the Pope sat back in his chair and stared at the young man.

Brandon was in his late thirties but when it came to the ranks of Catholic clergy he was positively still a boy. And when it came to things like this then he was certainly an innocent.

Brandon was a plain looking man. He had a round face with a high forehead and light brown hair parted at a peak. His lack of defined lips and fine eyebrows added to his plainliness. His only distinguishing feature was his cleft chin.

"Brandon," the Pope addressed him seriously, "it seems that you have been chosen to carry forward a Holy Quest."

Brandon took a step backward. "Why me?"

"It was your discovery and, should you fail in this mission, then you will discover its importance and why as few people should know about it as possible."

Brandon allowed the words to rattle around in his head until he had managed to work out their implications.

"Hang on," he said. "I'll find out how important it is if I fail? Surely I should find out how important it is to help me succeed."

The Pope sighed wearily. "I'm afraid that is not possible, Brandon. You see, as is the way with Holy Quests - and I mean proper Holy Quests, ones that have been approved directly by God to one of His ministers, not some Mid-Western American Christian housewife having a mid-life crisis claiming she saw an angel in her brownie pan. The way with *real* Holy Quests is that they have to be performed in the nature of Holiness and that is with absolute and total faith."

"So I have to do whatever you tell me to do without question?" Brandon paraphrased.

"Exactly," the Pope enthused and pulled himself to his feet. He walked around his desk, threw an arm around Brandon's shoulder and directed him down the steps towards the large doors at the end of the room.

"We (and when I say 'we' I mean 'God') needs you to retrieve this item without really knowing what it is," the Pope explained.

"Okay," Brandon said.

"And without anyone else knowing exactly what it is."

"Well, I won't be able to tell anyway," Brandon chuckled.

"That's the spirit," the Pope praised. "So, off you go, son. Do us proud."

The Pope gave Brandon a hearty slap on the back and made him stumble forward.

"But what is it?" Brandon asked.

"I just told you, you can't know."

"I realise that, but I do need to know what it is that I'm looking for, rather than actually knowing what it is," Brandon tried to explain, clearly confusing himself further. "Otherwise, how will I know if it is what I'm looking for if I see it?"

"Yes, exactly," the Pope agreed conspiratorially and tapped the side of his nose with his index finger.

Brandon stared at him.

The Pope waited.

"Well?" Brandon demanded.

The Pope sighed again.

"It is a silk bag with a fake emerald set in its centre," the Pope finally confessed.

Brandon scoured his memory.

"It does not mean anything to me," he stated.

"That is a good thing," the Pope commended. "Good for you and good for everyone."

They continued in silence until they reached the door. Brandon turned, took the Pope's hand and kissed his ring.

"Eminence, could the World really be destroyed if this bag's secret be revealed?"

"My son, if you fail then it would have devastating effects across the World," the Pope replied. "All hope for mankind will be lost."

"I will not fail," Brandon declared, turned and walked resolutely to the doors and waited. He knocked on them, they were pulled open and he walked out.

The Pope stared as the doors closed and listened to the clunk reverberate around the great hall.

"You should not sneak around so much, Cunningham," he said. "It can't be good for your health."

A shadow stepped out from behind a pillar. He was dressed in the yellow and blue striped uniform of the city's Swiss Guard Corps, the only difference being that his clothes weren't quite so flouncy as the standard attire.

"It is usually the health of others that suffers because of my stealth," he growled. Underneath his jaunty black beret was pure white hair. Under that were a pair of pink eyes inset a pallid face. A scar ran from his left temple down to his chin.

The Pope turned to him.

"You will go see that things are resolved," he instructed although there was a slight intonation that he was asking nicely at the same time.

The guard looked from the Pope to the door and then back again.

"Why allow him to go?" Cunningham asked.

"Because he will act without question," the Pope explained. "He will speculate the answer but never solve it. In speculating he will inject confusion into the minds of those who also search the truth."

"He will get in the way."

"Of them and you."

"And at the end?" Cunningham asked.

"What is God's will?" the Pope recited.

"Whatever," Cunningham replied and stepped back into the shadow of the pillar.

"Don't go out looking like that though, eh?" the Pope suggested.

"I wasn't going to," Cunningham sneered from his hiding place.

The Pope just stood in the middle of the hall in contemplative silence. Despite his brevity with Brandon he understood the seriousness of the situation. It really could mean the end of everything so a bit of martyrdom was not completely out of the question nor unreasonable.

"Oh, just use the door will you," he instructed with irritation.

Cunningham stepped out again with a petted lip.

"I couldn't go anywhere with you just standing there," he complained.

"I know, I know," the Pope said. "Don't worry about it. Just go and see that everything gets sorted."

Cunningham slouched towards the door and the Pope watched him as he crossed the floor like a stroppy teen. Something came to mind so the albino stopped and turned to him.

"I come and go as the breeze drifts -" he explained.

"Yes, I understand," the Pope interrupted. "I'm sorry I didn't comply to your use of theatrics."

This upset the guard even more and he stomped off.

"'Theatrics'? I am as silent as the butterfly but as devastating as the wrath of the Lord and you ..." Cunningham's voice trailed off as he neared the door, opened it, stepped out and slammed it behind him.

The Pope rolled his eyes and made his way back to his desk where he sat down and looked over his paperwork.

"They will be working at crossed purposes," a woman's voice told him.

He threw the paper down in exasperation and looked around him.

"Is there nobody here who doesn't creep around this place?" he demanded.

A nun was sitting, quite visibly, in a recess in the corner of the room. She was dressed in a long, black habit that looked as if it had been tailored to suit rather than the standard issue 'one size fits all'. It clung to her slim figure in a manner that was probably not appropriate. Her veil flowed majestically back from her forehead and over her shoulders. She was ninety if she was a day. Aside from the gold cord around her waist, there was a purple emblem embroidered on her right shoulder. It was an inverted letter A.

"Ah, Mother *Furca*," the Pope sighed. "And what would you have me do?"

"Send in the knights," she suggested.

"Templars? Are you joking?"

"One problem might resolve the other," she said.

"I'd never hear the end of it," he groaned. "Ooh, a call from his *Eminence*," he squealed.

"You would be as well to give Opus Dei a call," a man said from the opposite side, which caused the Pope to jump.

"Christophe, you nearly gave me a heart attack," he chastised.

"My apologies, Eminence," the man called Christophe said. He was dressed in formal cardinal choir dress of scarlet biretta and cassock. Again it should have been very difficult for him to have entered the room without being noticed by someone.

The Pope double-taked.

"What's with the formality?" he asked.

"I have just come from ... a thing," Christophe dismissed with an idle wave of his hand.

"Look, I don't care who gets involved, we just need it resolved," the Pope concluded.

A musical chime rang out to the tune of *Cor Jesu Trinitatis* and the Pope looked accusingly from one side of the hall to the other at each of his guests.

"Not mine," the nun stated and Christophe held his hands up to deny blame.

The Pope listened and located the ring to the top drawer of his desk. As he pulled it open the chime became louder and revealed a discreet mobile phone. He picked it up, pressed the call button and placed it to his ear.

"Hello?"

"Leave it to me," a gruff voice told him.

"Oh for -" the Pope cried. "Get off the line, Silas!" he shouted at the phone and disconnected the call.

"Both of you," he bellowed. "Get out, stop being so bloody clandestine and on your way out, tell the Black Monk that I know he's standing behind the door waiting for an appropriate time to make his dramatic entrance. I want that bag back."

The nun and cardinal met each other at a small door at the back of the hall and, as they opened it, a man fell through. He was dressed in a black habit and black Fila hooded jacket that hid his features.

The cardinal caught him as he stumbled in and redirected him out.

"I'll explain it to you as we go," Christophe said and the monk just nodded.

"How would you have offered your services?" Mother Furca asked. "You've still got seventeen years left on your vow, haven't you?"

The door closed but the Pope could still hear, "Two words. First word, four syllables. First syllable rhymes with chest - no - rib! Glib, sib, hib, fib - fib!"

The Pope dropped his head and allowed it to bang on his desk.

## 4 (*Allors*)

## The Little Shoe

The cruiser had docked into Calais and Professor disembarked with the baby carefully cradled in his arms.

He involuntarily shuddered as he walked down the gangplank. There was something unnerving about bobbing along above so much water. It was made considerably worse now that these passenger ferries were being constructed from metal. Even him, as a scientist, had trouble with the logic of that. It is metal, yet it floats? It was as if science had discovered a way of just switching off the logic receptors and that was all that was needed to make it work; the fact that people believed that it did.

Of course that was not enough to befuddle his sense of reason and he had actually been privy to science's next nature defying act; controlled flight.

Hot air balloons and dirigibles? Not a problem. Hot air rises while hydrogen and helium are lighter gases than air. That is scientific and logical. A mass of metal and wood lifting off by going forward quickly? What was that all about?

Then, as if to go out of their way to prove him right, he had heard of a flying demonstration taking place up in Sanford. He had taken leave from Eve for a day and headed off early to Leicestershire but had been disappointed to find that the flying device had broken before being able to demonstrate anything. Instead, the man, Pilcher, gave a display of his flying prowess in a glider called *The Hawk* which he promptly crashed. Apparently he had died a couple of days later from his injuries. It was a tragedy but he hoped that the World might learn a lesson from these results and know when too far had been exceeded.

Professor sighed with relief when his feet stepped on to the solid ground. He looked around the ambling masses for a familiar face but could not make one out amongst the throng.

The baby fidgeted in his arms and he looked into her face.

He had named her Penelope but for some reason he could not refer to her as much more than 'baby'. It - yes, 'it,' because the scientist in him was coming out again - had no real human characteristics aside from its physical attributes and it certainly did not display any gender specific qualities. Apart from the obvious.

It was an 'it' and that was all.

He had never really taken much interest in children during his life of studies. Child mortality rates were pretty low because they were generally too weak to survive. That was as much of the science as was needed to be known. Now, the reason why adults died was the more interesting topic. They must have a much more robust constitution to have survived childhood so whatever it was that shuffled them off this mortal coil was a force worth learning about.

That was the other reason why he did not use her name. She had only a fifty per cent chance of becoming a teenager and it seemed foolish to become attached to something that might have a short-term effect on his life. Love was, he had learned, a long-term investment and not one to be flittered around without care and consideration.

"Abraham!" a woman's voice called. "Over here!"

Professor looked up to the direction of the shout and saw a woman about a third of his age waving a deep red handkerchief at him.

"Is that him?" she demanded and started shoving her way through the crowd.

She was, by no means, a big girl but the way she cut a swathe through the tourists, sailors and dock-workers was like watching her wade through a corn field.

That was his investment. Right there. They were more than just physical lovers. They were connected spiritually, mentally and biologically.

Her face was flushed with excitement and he realised how long it had been since he had seen her. Her blue-grey eyes were wide in anticipation and she was biting the corner of her bottom lip. Her wavy, fair hair was tucked away under a black bonnet and, as she got closer, he could see that she was completely dressed in black.

He turned sideways to her so as not to crush the child as they embraced. They kissed for a long while and he sighed with absolute contentment.

She pulled away suddenly, causing him to stumble forward and blink himself back to earth.

"Let me see him," she said. Her accent was a strange twist of Eastern European and English but what was more interesting was the way her enunciation would be on a par with Professor's but every now and again, slip into a more lower class brogue. "What did you call him? Cam-"

"Her," he corrected and she looked at him with surprise and, if it were possible, even more excitement.

"Really? A baby girl? Oh, hand her over, Abraham. Don't make me wait another second."

He carefully passed the child across and she took the bundle as if handling a bowl full of chicks.

"Penelope," he introduced, "this is your mother, Mary."

"Oh, Penelope. I like that," Mary cooed. "She is just too adorable, Abraham. You are the prettiest little thing I have ever seen. We should have done this a long time ago."

"We'll see if you are still saying that when you are feeding her at three o'clock in the morning," he said.

She nudged him playfully with her shoulder. "You are such an old misery sometimes," she teased. "I don't want to ever sleep. I want to stare at her forever and ever."

Mary juggled her arms so she freed one hand and could trace her fingers across Penelope's delicate features.

A porter approached them.

«Sir, your luggage has been loaded on to the carriage,» he said.

«Thank you,» Professor replied and put his arm around his besotted companion to lead her to their awaiting transport.

Now *there* was something else; the horse and carriage. What was it about the imminence of the new millennia that was causing so many men to discover more violent ways of killing themselves? In about half-a-dozen different countries, all at the same time, men were adapting steam engine properties to propel horseless carriages.

Trains. Now there was a contraption that scared the hell out of him. Tonnes of iron hurtling along at thirty, maybe forty, miles per hour was just asking for multiple deaths.

"She has your scowl," Mary said and he noticed her manner had slipped into melancholy.

"What is it?"

"What if she does not love me?"

"Why shouldn't she?" Professor demanded.

"Because she is not mine."

"Does she know that?" he asked rhetorically. "Offspring of all animals imprint the first creature they focus their eyes on. Piglets think they're dogs, ducks think they are chickens and so on."

She was not looking at him but he knew that his words had not had their desired effect. Sometimes it was so hard for him to be compassionate because he always found his subject matter trailing off into the bare bones of life.

'Do I love you? Yes, even though we are just weak sacks of matter that are as insubstantial as water filled bladders whose lasting affect on this world will be forgotten within years of our passing.' It was not the most romantic thing he had said to her although, in his defence, he had just returned home from a particularly bad day. In fact, it was that very evening when they had suggested having a baby.

It was some months later when they decided they could not.

He supported her arm as she lifted herself up into the carriage.

"What I am trying to say is; although you are not her natural mother, that won't stop you from loving her like one," he explained. "Why should she know any different?"

Mary looked up at him as he seated himself opposite her and the smile returned to her face.

"And remember," he soothed and leant forward to place his hand on her knee, "that because of *us* there is a part of you in her."

The depression was completely lifted and she returned her attention to the baby.

"I will love you so much," she whispered.

Professor was quite surprised that he did not feel at all jealous of that statement. He was going to have to share his life's love now. To the extent that he may even be superfluous at times, yet it did not bother him in the slightest.

Things were coming together and things were already changing. She was happy again.

He had not seen her for over a year and, although it was a relatively short period of time for them, it had eked out forever. But now they were back together, it seemed like he had never been away. It seemed like time had gone back on itself to those years just after they had first met.

But even in the short time of a year, people can die and he had been worried about leaving her to fend for her self for that long.

"Why are you dressed in black?" he asked.

"It keeps the attentions of young admirers away," she replied casually without looking up.

He pondered the course of the conversation if he was to ask what had happened to necessitate the defence but decided to leave it. God knows the last year had been full of extra marital duties that she could dredge up if he started down that treacherous topic.

"How have things been?" he asked.

"Not too bad," she said. "I did miss you, though."

"Good," he responded with a warm smile. "As I did you."

Mary stared out of the carriage window at the passing scenery.

"What about her?" she finally asked.

"Nothing," he said flatly.

"Really? That simply?"

"What else could there be?" he asked. "Christmas cards? Visitation rights?"

"No," she decided. "You are right."

Penelope decided to open her eyes at that stage and stared into her surrogate mother's.

"Oh, Abraham," Mary gushed, "she is smiling at me."

"She is only a day old," Professor said. "It's more than likely to be -"

Penelope interrupted them with a long, deep, wet fart that vibrated through the swaddling and into Mary's lap.

The couple looked at each other with wide eyes and then burst out laughing.

"She is obviously more like you than you thought," Professor joked and she kicked him in the shin.

## 5 (*Maintenant*)

## Long Live Mirth

Inspector René Anjo was too old for this shit. He had, once, been an optimistic defender of public rights; an enthusiastic keeper of the peace; a smart, polite and conscientious gendarme. Now he was jaded by the mire of human excrement he found himself having to wade through on a daily basis. Both figurative and literal.

He was a big man - six foot four - and heavily set. The criminals had second thoughts before going up against him. They would normally just surrender, which he always thought was a bit of a shame because if there was one thing that a jaded inspector needed to do every now and again was have an excuse to beat seven shades of shit out of a few human excreta.

There was another part of their surrender that always amused him in that they were usually so busy weighing up their two options that they forgot about their third; run away. He never chased. He might call for back up and tell them where the suspect was heading but he could not be bothered to make the effort to go after them himself.

He was in his late fifties and looked like he had been sleeping rough. Half closed eyes implied a lack of sleep, his unkempt stubble was as long as the receding hair on his head and, in a relaxed state, his mouth hung open as if he was catatonic. He wore a dark brown suit that was probably about ten years old. The elbows on it were thinning and threads had been snagged in various places all over. His shirt was untucked at one corner and the top two buttons were missing. He had stopped wearing a tie years before his wife had left him.

He was being directed along the corridor of a museum of sorts; paintings and sculptures adorned both walls but he was less than interested in them. Although he looked forward, his head was hung low and his shoulders were hunched. He had already had the rough details of this case given to him over the radio and he was eager to get in, hand it over to someone else and then find a quiet café to have a couple of espressos and, maybe, a large glass of red wine.

A man was dead. There were a few other details but it was all speculation from the scene officers. Lots of, 'I think,' and, 'It could be.' He did not have time for that and had learned long ago not to let someone else's first opinion affect his.

«He is through there, Inspector,» the young gendarme told him and stopped. Anjo stopped after another couple of steps.

«You are not coming in?» he demanded.

«I -» the gendarme said and then started gagging.

«Go wait outside,» Anjo ordered and the gendarme did not wait for further encouragement.

That did not bode well.

Anjo took another two cursory steps forward until he could get a better view of the room through the arch. There were a couple of forensics officers taking photos whilst another gendarme was talking to a suited man and making notes in a pad.

No dead body, though.

He took another step forward so his foot was just before the archway's threshold and he could see further down the room along the nearest wall.

«Good morning, Inspector,» a soft, female voice greeted him from the floor.

He looked down to see the back of the woman as she crawled around on all fours at his feet.

«What are you doing, Matilda?» he demanded.

She looked up at him with wide, excited eyes. Her short, black hair waved around her head like a grass skirt. He hated her for this. She was a nice girl. She was a clever girl. She was a pretty girl. She was enthusiastic, polite and conscientious. She walked around with this doe-like expression as if everything was a new, incredible experience for her. Her first sip of mint tea in the morning was like a gastrorgasmic event every time. So when something truly exciting did happen she was truly disturbing to look at.

The pleasing effect generally caused by her round face, high cheek bones and permanent pout were drowned out by her over-dilated pupils that receded her dark brown irises to a mere band of separation from the sea of white.

«Mapping the crime scene,» she told him eagerly.

And it was for every one of these reasons that he hated her. She was a nice girl and he did not want to see her ending up like the embittered, miserable git he had become. He did his utmost to belittle her suggestions, rip apart her theories and be a generally unpleasant person to be around. In all fairness, that last part was not much of a hard task.

Matilda had become conscious of her appearance when she was a young girl. The other children certainly made it clear that she was little, scrawny and quiet but it was the adults who really scarred her ego. 'Matilda will have the pink one,' they would say or, 'Matilda will play with the dolls.' Yes, it had been the grown-ups who perceived her as 'a girl' just because she looked like one. They were shoving fairy puppets and dolls that wet themselves into her arms when all she wanted to do was play football in the street, climb trees and throw stones at glass bottles on the building site.

Now she was a grown-up herself, she could decide her own path but physically, none of that outward appearance had changed. No matter how much she exercised she could not bulk up her body to rid herself of her petite frame. So she had to take jobs that would compensate and when the opportunity arose to work beside Inspector Anjo - she would sometimes get goosebumps just thinking about his name - then she leapt at it.

She knew of his gruff exterior and no nonsense attitude; that did not bother her in the slightest. Had he been easy on her then that would have been more of a shock. Years of living with herself had prepared her for the departmental onslaught of mocking and tomfoolery. She was happy because of his impeccable record for case closures.

What she had not thought about was there was a difference between closing and a case and actually solving it.

He could talk down to her and test her investigative skills as much as he wanted because she knew it meant he was just toughening her up. Preparing her for the harshities of the job when she went it alone. She would never let him down by being scared off by a few negative criticisms.

Now that he was completely in the archway he could see clearly into the room but, still, there was no body.

She got to her feet as he turned to ask, «What crime scene?» and it was then that he noticed the bright red puddle on the white tiled floor. She had not been randomly scuffling around on the ground but had been marking the border of a pool of blood.

No body though.

His eyes wandered to the corner of the room where he could see the source of the flood; rivulets winding their way down the marble wall. He looked up to see a man nailed to the ceiling's crossbeam. His body was stained with his leakage and there was a collection of lacerations across his chest.

«Dear god,» he muttered.

He did not know what was worse.

The ghastly scene before him?

«He was one of the museum's security guards,» Matilda told him.

Or was it the thought that there was someone out there whom would go to the trouble of murdering in this way?

«His name was Brian Gagnant, thirty five. Married with two children.»

Or was it the implications? Someone going to this much trouble to kill usually implied there would be more.

«It was only him on the night shift for this wing and was only discovered this morning when his relief came on duty.»

And the carvings? That usually meant a clue of who would be next. Even worse, it could mean a ritual killing, which would lead to covens and the like. These groups usually had two or three members from high positions in society.

«I am estimating that it all started at about ten o'clock last night and he died around seven hours later.»

It took that long and no one heard him call out. That meant that the murderer had been in the room all night with him. Up until the point when Brian would have passed out and then carried on dripping until dead.

Whatever. All that he saw was a marathon of legwork and a mountain of paperwork. That could have been the most horrific aspect if it was not for the fact that Brian was actually smiling.

«There is a symbol marked out in his blood on the floor,» she reported, «and a nine digit number marked out in blood by his head.»

Something was wrong with Anjo. He took a step closer to peer at the lacerations on Brian's chest.

«His feet were nailed individually through the ankles and his left arm pinned up through his wrist allowing the hand to hang free. His right hand was pinned back through the palm.»

The cuts looked ordered, like words but he could not make anything out.

«The writing is upside down,» Matilda told him and he twisted his head to the side.

*Ce dernier clou était un salope.*

He spun on his heels, his face was burning red with rage.

«Who is responsible for this?» he roared. «Do you think I am fucking stupid?»

Everyone was too taken aback to reply verbally but they all managed to shake their heads.

Matilda tried to calm him with her hand on his arm but he just shirked it off. «No, Inspector,» she said. «The writing was self-inflicted.»

«That is ridiculous,» he snorted. «How can a crucified man write on his chest. How can he write, 'That last nail was a bitch'?»

She raised her eyebrows at him then picked up a stepladder that was resting on the floor against a wall. She propped it against Brian's right hand and climbed up. At the top she indicated for Anjo to get a better position to see behind the crossbeam. The nail had been forced right through.

«The nail has chest hairs caught in it and the angle of the letters is consistent with him scratching with the nail in his palm. He wrote, 'That last nail *IS* a bitch.' Present tense not past.»

«What? And the murderer would just stand here and wait for him to finish?» Anjo demanded.

Matilda descended and waited until she was on the floor before saying, «No murderer.»

Anjo contemplated exploding again until that awry sensation reminded him of its presence.

«How?» was all he could ask.

«There is nothing here to indicate another person,» she told him. «No disturbance, no DNA, not even any signs of things being cleaned. If there was anyone here then it had to be a ghost.»

«How can you crucify yourself?» he asked wearily. He had realised what that nagging sensation was and he was about to get rid of it once and for all.

She mimed a hammer tapping at her feet then stabbing something into the palm of her right hand. She stabbed something into her left wrist, which she then hammered, and then slammed her right arm back with her fist clenched. She was crucified.

«What is the force that a man would need to drive a nail through a beam that thick with his bare hands?» Anjo asked.

«There are a few holes up there that indicated several attempts,» she said.

That thing that was wrong with him? That unusual feeling? It had taken a little while for him to realise what it was because he had not felt it for a while. He was genuinely interested. Yes, the case was gory and depraved but at some level he had to respect the person who could engineer something like this.

«Good work,» he said and headed for the arch.

«Inspector? What?»

«Good work, Matilda,» he reiterated. «Write it up and close it. If you need me -»

«Sir, we cannot leave it like this,» she sated.

«As you said, Matilda, no one else, self-inflicted, suicide.» He continued with his escape.

«But what about the other things?»

«No 'things,' Matilda,» he ordered.

«I believe he was forced to suicide,» she revealed. «Isn't that worth investigating? Discovering the extortionist?»

Anjo stopped and sighed. «Was the extortionist handing Brian the nails?»

«No. There was no one there.»

«Then close it,» Anjo spat and walked.

«The numbers!» Matilda squealed. «I think they are some sort of code.»

«I do not care, Matilda,» Anjo cried.

«They are like Fibonacci, but out of sequence. They will probably -»

«No things, Matilda.»

«The symbol in the blood!» she hollered. «He did it as an afterthought. Drew it by peeing on the floor. It looks like a heart inset with a diamond.»

He stopped and marched back. Matilda's eyes widened with apprehension and they nearly made him lose his nerve.

«Matilda! No things! Do you understand? Suicide! Case closed!»

«One thing, Inspector?» she asked timidly and he nodded. «Does it mean nothing that his left hand is pointing at the painting of *The Last Sup* -»

«No. This means nothing,» he told her.

«Or that there was a letter from him that reads, 'PS. Cancel my milk. PPS. Find Robert L -»

«That was two things,» Anjo growled. He was desperate to get away, he had found an inkling of an out and he wanted through it. He had one last chance to get to this over zealous girl. Charm.

He calmed himself then smiled. It actually hurt a bit.

«Matilda,» he sang and she looked around her nervously. «You came to me because you wanted to know how to do this job properly, yes?»

She nodded.

«This isn't the cinema,» he told her. «That man is really dead and his family will want to mourn. It would be so much better to let them get on with it rather than draw out their grief with tenuous conspiracy concoctions. Get him down and ship him off to the coroners. Get the room cleaned up and clean up all the 'things,' you understand? Tell the press it was suicide and that he was found 'hanging' in the room - it's not a lie. We don't want a media frenzy thinking we have some fundamentalist serial killer on the prowl.»

She allowed the words and their meaning to sink in. It also gave her enough time to realise he had finished.

«Okay,» she said.

He nodded to her and turned around. As he marched toward the exit he allowed that grin to spread across his face again.

He dropped it. It still hurt.

The gendarme folded his notepad closed.

«Thank you for your time, Mr Curé,» he said. «Here is a number to call should you be able to think of anything else.»

«Of course,» Mr Curé replied and took the small card being offered to him. «I will do anything I can to assist in the horrible matter. I shall be in my office if I am required for anything else.»

He turned and hastily exited the room via the furthest portal from Brian. He shook his head as inner thoughts threatened to make him scream out in frustration. So many things to think about. The whys and hows of Brian's death alone were enough to send him mad but then there were also the matters concerning the museum itself.

The mess! My god, the mess. He did not have a chance to get close enough to check the exhibits but he prayed that no blood had got onto them.

The place's reputation was at stake. That wing would have to be closed down and it was one of the most popular. He pondered that there might be a way in which they could use the death to boost their intake. Maybe they could 'accidentally' let people past the doors to clearly see the corner.

They would definitely have to commission some art student to do a piece in honour of the man.

He turned a corner and nearly fell over Cardinal Christophe who had changed into a less obvious black cassock.

«My apologies, Monsignor, I did not see you there,» he spluttered.

«It is quite all right,» Christophe replied. «I should not really be lurking.»

«Ah, yes. The police.»

«Is there something interesting happening?» Christophe asked innocently.

«A man has been crucified. One of the security guards.»

Christophe's expression changed from interest to concern. «Excuse me, will you? I need to make a telephone call.»

«You can use my office phone,» the man suggested but Christophe was already heading towards the exit.

Mr Curé walked in the opposite direction to another junction where he saw a skinny nun admiring a Sumerian sculpture of a naked man.

«Er, hello? Sister?» Mr Curé called. «I'm afraid we are not open to the public yet.»

Mother Furca turned around to glare at him. She turned so he clearly saw the embroidered upturned 'A'.

He stared at it in awe then remembered himself and bowed dutifully.

«Forgive me, Matriarch. I was not expecting you,» he simpered.

«You may self-flagellate after I am gone,» she told him.

«Thank you mistress. How may I honour you? Hieros Gamos?»

She paused, puffed her cheeks and raised her eyebrows while considering the offer.

«Not just yet,» she decided. «What is happening through there?»

«A man was crucified.»

«You did this?»

«No, Mistress, it was performed on a cross beam, not a furca.»

«Who might have done this?»

«They say he did it himself.»

Her habit disappeared from his downturned view and he dared to look up. She was gone.

He sighed with relief and quickly trotted over to his office door before any other religious ministers could waylay him. He entered his sanctuary and slammed the door shut behind him.

There was a man sitting in his seat with his back to him. Mr Curé could not make out many details of the man but he did have pure white hair and was wearing a yellow and blue striped woollen jumper.

«Hallo? Can I help you?»

The man spun around in the seat to face him. His eyes were pink and he had a long scar down the side of his face. He held a black, wide brimmed beret in his lap.

«I have been expecting you, Mr Curé,» Cunningham said. «I wish to know everything.»

Cunningham's appearance was usually intimidating enough but the tone of his voice added extra weight. As did two of his Swiss Guard (Special) Corps associates who stepped forward from Mr Curé's flanks.

Mr Curé wanted to back away but there was nowhere to retreat to. He seemed to try to collapse inside himself but the two guards grabbed an arm each and stretched him out again.

Cunningham pulled himself to his feet and placed a gold plated pistol on the desk. It was smoother than any gun Mr Curé had seen before. It was as if all of its corners had filed down to make it easier to draw and holster. It had two engravings on it: one was a bizarrely designed, *90two*, while the other was, *C. Deut 33:11. P.*

«Everything,» Cunningham emphasised.

In the corridor outside Mr Curé's office was a man in a full-length, black habit and black Fila hooded top that hid his features. He wandered along the hall a bit, stopped then dipped his hands into his pockets. He pulled out a museum brochure, opened it and checked the pages. He looked up and down the corridor then back at the pamphlet which he rotated ninety degrees.

"Merda," he growled then slapped his hand over his mouth. He looked around him again and ran towards, what he hoped, was the nearest exit.

It was the stairwell to the basement.

## 6 (*Maintenant*)

# The Place de Grève

The journey had not taken as long as Penny had feared.

Something had awoken her and she did not even know she had been sleeping.

An image of Sean Connery in *From Russia With Love* was dissipating from her unconscious as reality seeped in. It was a lovely recurring dream she always had that left her feeling warm, squooshy and, to a degree, sexually satisfied. She stretched and groaned with pleasure, then reality completely filtered in and she remembered she was on the train, sitting opposite her father.

She opened one eye to see Professor staring inquisitively at her. She tried not to make it obvious that she knew she had been caught - damnit! - with her pants down (albeit unconsciously) but she stalled halfway through the stretch and then pretended badly in an attempt to recover.

"Are we here already?" she enquired as calm as she could manage. She could not help but think her face had turned bright red with embarrassment and that everything she had been imagining might as well have been projected on a cinema screen above her head.

"Already?" he asked. "You've slept for almost two hours. Had I known your company was going to be this riveting then I would have bought an *earPod*."

Penny slumped in her seat in frustrated annoyance and 'ugh'ed loudly.

"It's an *iPod*," she snapped and he just shook his head at her.

"My point is not one of product placement but to draw issue to how rude it was of you to go to sleep."

"I didn't *go* to sleep," she argued. "I *fell* asleep. There's a difference; one is a conscious effort to escape, the other is brought about by necessity or is forced upon a person by external influences."

"And that means what?"

"I'm still knackered after Leeds and there wasn't enough stimulation to prevent me from falling asleep."

"Ah, my fault," he deduced.

"No," she replied defensively. "Not specifically your fault, just everything that was going on lulled me. Sorry."

He smiled at her. "Actually, I only just opened my eyes a second before you did," he confessed.

"I can't handle this taste for wit that you've developed," she grumbled.

"Well, you can blame your friends for that," he retorted.

They gathered their luggage, bundled off the train and made their way across Gare du Nord to the exit.

"Well, this place hasn't changed at all," Penny commented as she looked around at the half-circled windows that lined each side of the enormous terminal. There was something stirring within her that, at first, she presumed was just travel sickness but as they made their way to the front of the building, each passing cast iron support pillar caused the sensation to intensify slightly.

Was it just nausea or was it some emotion she had kept locked away for all those years? She hated to say it but she was home. Really home. No matter what had happened here to make her leave, or run away - however you wanted to describe it - this was the place where she had been raised during those arduously long and painful formative years.

All she had to do was get closure on all the bad stuff or simply disassociate it with Paris and she could, quite possibly, actually enjoy their time together here.

"Are you all right?" her father asked.

"Just reeling from a waft of nostalgia," she replied light-heartedly.

"Where do you think we should stay?"

"It depends on who's paying."

"I think I owe you more than monetary compensation," he said.

"Yes, but we can start with monetary and work our way up," she suggested. "So I thought about l'Hôtel de Ville."

"On the Place de Grève?"

"What is now called de Place de l'Hôtel de Ville," she told him.

"It shall always be 'de Grève' for me and, really, not an area I would like to revisit," he complained. "And anyway, it's not even a hotel," he said and completely missed her sniggering to herself.

They were out of the terminal by this time and descending the stone steps. Professor hailed a taxi.

"How many times did they try to execute you there?" Penny questioned innocently.

Professor stiffened as he realised that she was fully aware of the reason for his reticence.

"Five," he growled.

"During what decades?"

"You know very well that it was in the period of one week," he snapped and reeled around at her causing her to jump back. Still smiling though.

«Good afternoon, sir,» the taxi driver interrupted cautiously. «Shall I take your bags?»

Professor calmed and turned his back on his antagonistic daughter. «Yes, thank you,» he replied and got into the yellow cab. Penny trotted down after him and had to cross to the other side of the car to get in.

«Hi,» she said to the young driver. «The Ritz, please.»

«Ah, very nice,» he replied enthusiastically and dashed ahead of her to open her door. «My name is Daniel, and if there is anything I can do for you?»

«We will let you know,» Professor said gruffly and the two outside pulled mock, grumpy faces at each other then smiled.

Penny lowered herself into the car, Daniel closed the door behind her then finished loading the boot. He jumped into the front, spun around in his seat with his right elbow resting next to the headrest and smiled at them.

She had not stopped smiling since they had greeted. It was not that she actually fancied him, although he was by no means unattractive. His skin was smooth and healthily tanned, his brown hair was cropped neatly all over and his blue eyes sparkled with vitality. It was his voice that was making her smile. Ah, French boys and their accents. She remembered how much she loved talking to a French boy who could talk articulately and intelligently. Each word would be enunciated like a delicate kiss and rattled off so quickly that they tickled against her ears like butterfly wings.

«You are not Parisian, Daniel?» she asked.

«No, I am here doing a favour for a friend,» he replied and she noticed her father fidget impatiently.

«Isn't it illegal to work outside of your licensed district?» Professor demanded.

Daniel grinned at him and flashed his eyes. «Only if you get caught,» he said.

«Somewhere South,» Penny pondered. «The Mediterranean tan and the accent would suggest, Marseille.»

Daniel was playfully awe-struck. «I'm impressed. You could tell just from that?»

«And your license,» she said and indicated his credentials on the dashboard.

Daniel wagged a finger at her.

«How fast do you want to get there?» he asked.

"Where?" Professor demanded but Penny 'shushed' him.

«Take your time,» she said and noted the resigned disappointment on his face.

«Yes, there is no need to impress us with your driving expertise,» Professor instructed. «Your tip will be quite safe as long as we remain so.»

«Ah, you mistake me for some of these nine to five drivers,» Daniel said. «I don't expect gratuities because this is the job that I have chosen to do and the job that I get paid to do.»

«So you won't want a tip?» Professor asked.

«Only if it's a really big one,» Daniel joked.

He returned to face forward, started the car and the engine roared with power.

«It sounds like it might need tuning,» Professor mocked.

«You do not know your cars, then,» Daniel said peering at the old man through the rear-view mirror.

"Leave him alone," Penny chided her father. "He is just being polite."

Daniel pulled forward as soon as there was the slightest gap between passing traffic for him to squeeze into. Professor and Penny were thrown back into their seats from the acceleration.

«Sorry,» Daniel apologised to them. «Paris drivers are the rudest in the world. If I sat there waiting for one to let me out, we would be still here at sunset.»

Penny pulled herself forward to sit between the front seats and get a clear view of everything that passed them by.

«What about you, miss?» Daniel asked.

«Hmm?» she asked dreamily.

«Where is home for you?»

«There's a good question,» she replied. «I've been wondering that myself for a few years.»

«Your accent is very good,» he commended.

«Oh, I was raised here so the French is second nature,» she said.

«I meant your English accent.»

«Ha! I see. Yes, I have spent a long time there, as well. That's why I'm not sure where 'home' is.»

«My home? It is where my family and friends are,» Daniel professed. «Not where I come from or where I am.»

«That is very deep for a taxi driver,» Penny suggested.

«I am so much more than any old taxi driver,» Daniel boasted.

«I can see that,» she agreed and pointed towards an open wallet on the passenger's seat. The black, leather purse was displaying a police badge.

«Ah! That's not mine,» he said. «It's my friend's.» He leaned over, scooped up the offending object and tossed it into the glove compartment. «Stupid Émilien,» he grumbled.

Daniel turned north from the terminal building and Penny frowned.

«Do you know where you are going?» she enquired as politely as she could.

«I know where I'm going,» Daniel replied. «The Ritz, right?»

"What?!" Professor squealed.

«Place Vendôme, yes?» Penny assured.

«If you say so,» Daniel replied. «I know where it is, I'm just not sure of the most direct route to get there. I thought we might take the scenic route. You said there was no hurry.»

«True enough,» she sighed and redirected her attention to the sights around them.

Daniel seemed to make the most effort to pass as many tourist attractions as he could. It felt strange that the pillars at the station had provoked more reaction than any of these monuments did.

There was the domed Sacré Cœur directly in front of them at the top of the Montmartre. The Basilisk barely evoked a second glance because she was too busy watching the people trudging up and down the three hundred-odd steps.

Daniel turned west along Boulevard De La Chapelle and she could just make out Moulin Rouge off a northern road. Again it was not a place that carried any fond memories because she had been 'too young' to witness the celebration of hedonism that it used to promote let alone sample it. It seemed that the place had just become a garish, commercialised cover-version of a classic rock song. Something that used to embody sentiments of meaning had been turned into a Pepsi advert.

Daniel picked up speed causing the people, buildings and trees to blur into a stream of colours. She had never seen her home city like this. Nothing could go this fast when she had been a girl. When she had been a younger girl, that is.

She was dimly aware of her father making noises of urgency as the car veered through the traffic and zipped past orangey-red traffic lights.

She turned her attention to the sky that sailed along on a much gentler current.

Clouds are clouds, though, and could not invoke any memories to adhere her to the now.

«Could you slow down, please,» Professor requested and she looked to see what his concern might be. Although not specifically going fast, Daniel was certainly managing to go faster than the flow of traffic around him. He deftly weaved his car into the tightest of spaces in an attempt to keep moving.

Ahead of them was l'Arc de Triomphe, which caused a wry smile to spread across her face.

Daniel saw a space in the orbiting traffic but had to adjust his speed to time the docking correctly. Unfortunately for Professor's stomach the adjustment was to go faster.

«Oh, heaven help me,» Professor gasped as the taxi sidled between two trucks with mere inches to spare at either end. The rear lorry pressed down hard on his horn. Daniel just threw his hand up in the air and shouted, «Aaay!»

«I hate this roundabout,» Daniel said whilst dodging through the traffic either side of them. «See? That was where we needed to go but can I get over?»

Father and daughter looked out of the window to see the Champs-Élysées whiz away.

«It's okay, though,» Daniel enthused, «it'll come around again.»

"I hate cars. Always have. Never trusted them," Professor complained.

«You have lots of roundabouts in England, huh?» Daniel called to him.

«I'm not English,» Professor replied.

«You're not French either,» Daniel noted.

«Dutch.»

«I'm sorry,» Daniel said.

«Dutch,» Professor said louder.

«I heard you. I'm sorry that's all,» Daniel iterated with a laugh.

Professor gripped the back of the boy's seat to stop the centrifugal forces squashing him into Penny.

She tried to support him by pushing against his shoulder and managed to get him back into his seat. She looked out of her window in time to see the *Tomb of the Unknown Soldier* under the arch. She wondered what sort of state he would be in if he would be dug up now.

«Stay on target,» Daniel hollered and swung the steering wheel around. The car veered across the seven lanes of traffic to make the exit this time. A chorus of harmonising car horns were heard in their wake.

The Champs-Élysées held little interest for her. Although it had always been a fairly cosmopolitan area, it seemed to serve very little purpose. The restaurants were far too expensive for the everyday tourist and the boutiques' wares were astronomical prices for things that no one could ever genuinely profess to need. It was the gathering place for the middle classes to watch the upper as if at a zoo, the very rich to show off how much money they had and the poor to beg from the others. Of course it did actually serve the purpose of giving any 'intellectuals' somewhere to observe all walks of life and justify their own universal superiority complexes.

Place de la Concorde became more defined in the distance and *there* was the real twinge of excitement in her. It was like seeing your street sign after a long, hard day. It held meaning that was beyond 'nearly home' but when just 'home' could be used. Home was now tangible even if it could still not be seen. It was there. Here. Now.

Daniel traversed the structure with the same control as before and then Penny saw the Louvre beyond. This was home. This was the place she would come to and spend hours learning about foreign lands, human psychology, anatomy and frailty. It was where she could escape from him.

A sharp turn to cross in front of the oncoming traffic and Daniel headed towards Place Vendôme to finally stop the car abruptly in front of their intended hotel.

«I knew it was around here somewhere,» he said with a cheeky smile.

"That was probably one of the worst rides I have ever experienced," Professor commented. "Even your friend, Cassandra, drove better than him."

«I may not speak the language but I do recognise the tone,» Daniel told them disappointedly. «I'm an excellent driver.»

Professor did not retaliate because he was too busy getting out of the car as fast as possible and wobbling to the pavement.

Daniel jumped out and rushed around to Penny's side to open her door before she could.

«Allow me,» he charmed.

«Why thank you, kind sir,» she replied jokingly and raised her hand for him to take. He did so and she pulled herself out.

«I hear this place has rooms for eight thousand Euros,» Daniel said as he fetched their bags. «The cheapest rooms are about six hundred.»

«Yes, thank you,» Professor said testily and called the doorman for assistance.

Daniel turned his back on Professor and handed Penny a small piece of paper. «Here's my card if you want to go anywhere. Although, I'm only here for another day or so. Hopefully.»

«Thank you, Daniel,» she said and gave him a kiss on each cheek. «You have given my return a most pleasant start.»

«Here,» Professor said and held out a fifty Euro note. «Don't worry about the change.»

«There's a gratuity that I will be honoured to accept,» Daniel told them and bowed to Professor. «Enjoy your time here.»

«Driver!» the doorman bellowed and Daniel turned around. «This gentleman needs to get to the airport as quickly as possible.»

A short man in an expensive suit dashed out of the hotel carrying a briefcase.

Daniel shrugged his shoulders. «I can get you there in twelve minutes,» he stated casually.

The man stopped in his tracks and looked from Daniel, to the footman then to Professor. They all laughed apart from Daniel who just blinked at them.

«Impossible,» the doorman declared. «It is twenty miles away and you will be hitting rush hour before you reach the A1.»

«Twelve minutes,» Daniel said again and held the door for the man to climb in.

«If you do it in under thirty, I will pay you two hundred Euros,» the man wagered.

«And if you can get back in thirty, you can collect another fifty from me,» the doorman chuckled as Daniel climbed into his seat and started pulling on a pair of leather gloves.

A bellboy had come out to the street to take up Professor's and Penny's luggage. They were all heading into the building when the car started to make an unusual whirring noise.

«Welcome to The Ritz,» the bellboy announced as they entered the foyer. There came an almighty screech of tyres from outside and a blaring of multiple horns. It was quite likely that a barely audible voice was screaming, «Heaven help me!»

«Is this your first visit?» the bellboy continued unperturbed.

«My first time staying but not my first visit,» Penny told him.

«I remember when this used to be the Hotel de Gramont,» Professor commented. «Although it has changed quite considerably since then.»

It was everything that luxuriant splendour could be imagined: a pristine marble room; Louis VX marquetry furniture; expensive lush rugs underfoot and all heavily garnished with sparkling gold adornments. It was opulence turned up to eleven.

The bellboy directed them up to the reception where a middle-aged man and two young women were serving. The man had a gold name-badge on that simply said 'John'.

«Good afternoon, sir,» John addressed them pleasantly. «Have you made a reservation?»

The question was asked in the manner of knowing what the answer was going to be. He was already tapping into his computer ready to check their details.

«No,» Professor replied which caused John to actually stagger back a step. «We have just arrived in Paris and were hoping -»

«I'm afraid we are completely full, sir,» John apologised after composing himself.

Professor leaned into the desk slightly which made John take an extra step back.

«Even the Da Vinci Suite?» Professor asked.

John smiled. «You are mistaken sir, there is no Da Vinci Suite here. Perhaps you are thinking of a different hotel.»

Professor stared at him and shook his head.

«Perhaps you are referring to the Da Vinci package,» one of the women suggested. «It includes a tour of the Louvre and a free copy of *The* -»

«No,» Professor said calmly. «I am referring to the Da Vinci Suite that is here.»

The staff were genuinely perplexed and their discourse was attracting the attention of a few other people.

«I do not know how I can help you, sir,» John apologised. «I cannot give you a room if there are no rooms to give and I certainly cannot give you a room that does not exist.»

Penny pulled at her father's elbow as she noticed a couple of security men draw towards them.

"We can go somewhere else," she whispered.

«Perhaps the manager -?» Professor asked.

«Sir, I have worked here for over thirty years,» John explained. «I have had intimate dealings in every department and covered every inch of the Ritz. I have studied the history of this building and the company as a global entity and I can assure you that there is not, and never has been, a Da Vinci Suite here, or in any other Ritz in the World.»

«Is there a problem, John?» a smartly suited woman asked from the side of the reception. She was flanked by two large security officers and, although she was not wearing a uniform, she was wearing a gold name badge that said 'Jacqueline'.

«No, Miss Patron,» John stated. «This gentleman is requesting a room without a reservation.»

«I see,» Jacqueline acknowledged and then turned to Professor. «I am sorry, sir, but you really do need a reservation. This is a particularly busy time for us and -»

«I was enquiring after the Da Vinci Suite,» Professor informed her.

«And I was trying to explain to the gentleman that there is no such suite,» John argued.

To her credit, Jacqueline's reaction was barely perceptible. Certainly even less so when John drew everyone's attention to him with his response. But Professor had noted it and smiled politely.

She returned the smile and shook her head. «I am terribly sorry, sir, but John is absolutely correct. We do not have a suite by that name. Perhaps you should try the Westin around the corner?»

«Thank you, we will,» Professor said, then turned to the receptionists. «I apologise for troubling you all.»

The bellboy bent to pick up their luggage again but Professor stopped him.

«That is quite all right. We have been too much of an inconvenience already. We can manage.»

The bellboy looked up at John for some sort of support and he urged the junior staff member on.

«Allow the gentleman on his way,» Jacqueline instructed so the bellboy stopped in mid grab.

Professor and Penny picked up their bags and walked out of the hotel.

"Well, that was disappointing," she muttered to herself.

"You will learn to trust your father again," he told her cryptically.

He started to walk along the front of the building then stopped as they reached its boundary. A small, insignificant door opened behind him and Jacqueline was behind it.

«This way,» she urged.

Professor stepped through the small alcove without hesitation whilst Penny took a moment for confusion to pass. Jacqueline shut the door behind her.

The door was an opening to a very narrow alley that ran along the edge of the hotel and its neighbouring building. It was not actually inside anything but the front had been bricked up to the height of the two structures and roofed in a matching style.

After locking the door, Jacqueline had to squeeze past the couple to get to the front.

«Please, follow me,» she said and started walking.

"What's going on?" Penny demanded.

"You are not the only one who has secrets," he replied.

"Oh, I'm pretty bloody sure of that," she agreed.

The alley stopped at another unobtrusive door, which the manager unlocked, opened and stepped through.

Father and daughter followed and entered a dramatically shrunken version of the main lobby. Jacqueline stepped around the back of a reception desk that was nothing more than a podium. Behind her was the cage door to a lift.

«I apologise for the welcome,» she said. «It has been a while since anyone has requested the Da Vinci Suite.»

«It is quite all right,» Professor replied. «There is no apology necessary. It was rude of me not to have called in advance but it had not even occurred to me until we got into Paris.»

Penny considered interjecting with a few, 'Whats, whys and hows,' but decided to save them until a bit later.

Jacqueline opened a book on the podium and scanned a column of writing. «In fact, I have never had the pleasure of a guest here in my career. I had considered that there was no one left who knew of its existence.»

«It was a very bizarre mandate that maybe we should consider altering while I am here,» Professor said and Jacqueline looked up at him with surprise and excitement.

«You think so?»

«The rule was that these locations would not be passed on to anyone,» Professor cited. «Not even inherited, so it was bound to happen, eventually, that only the Keepers - your good selves - would know but, technically, never be allowed to use.»

«And, of course, only know of our own,» Jacqueline added.

«Precisely,» Professor agreed. «So, if at some stage you would dig out the pact then I'm sure we might see about starting afresh.»

Jacqueline hesitated.

«I am very old,» Professor told her and she just nodded. She passed a blank piece of paper and a pen to him. He pulled the lid off to reveal a silver fountain pen. He put it on the paper, signed, 'Leonardo,' then pushed the paper back.

Jacqueline took the signature and compared it down the page in front of her.

«Professor Helsine?» she asked and he bowed to her. «Welcome to the Da Vinci Suites. I hope you will enjoy your stay and if there is anything I can do for you then please contact me. Here are my private numbers.» She handed him a business card with three telephone numbers on it. «And here are your keys.»

«Thank you very much, Jacqueline,» he replied, taking the card and pocketing it. «Call me when you have the time to go over the pact.»

She nodded and pulled the cage door open for them. Professor raised his hand forward for Penny to lead the way and then he followed. Jacqueline slid the door closed behind them. Professor pressed the only button present and a distant clank resounded from above them. The lift started to ascend with a soothing whirr.

When the reception area had disappeared beneath them Penny huffed. "What the hell?" was all she thought she needed to say. She was wrong.

"What?" Professor asked.

She rolled her eyes at him.

"You do that a lot, did you know?" he commented. "Is it a nervous twitch, or something?"

"An irritating twitch," she corrected. "Can you explain what that was all about?"

"It is an arrangement that was made a long time ago involving a select group of important socialites who found themselves -" he pondered the correct terminology, "- required to make an amalgamated effort to ensure the safety of humanity."

Penny just raised her eyebrows.

"At that time we offered a safe haven to any who might wish for one," Professor continued. "César Ritz obviously held the best option for everyone."

"And the thing about it having died out?"

"The pledge was made a *very* long time ago," Professor reiterated. "We decided, that by the time we were dead, the threat would be gone and there'd be no need for the secrecy. This - by all accounts, attic - was designed specifically as a temporary safe haven and nothing more."

The lift jolted to a halt. Beyond the cage door was a short passage and another plain door with a spyhole in it.

Professor yanked the lift door aside, they approached the door and he opened it with the keys he had been given.

Penny was shocked at the room before them. Firstly, it was the Ritz, for crying out loud. One of the most luxurious hotels in the World. Secondly, it was, as her father had described it, 'an attic'. It was supposed to be a hidey-hole for desperate people in times of need when they had no where else to turn so her expectations had been dramatically reduced. What lay before her would have had Louis XIV whistle in appreciation.

"'Attic,' my arse," she reproached and pushed past him.

The floor space must have been big enough for a football pitch and was a reflection of the main reception. Bright white marble flagstones had been laid with thick, patterned rugs dotted around. Penny stopped, self-consciously untied her laces and yanked her boots off.

"The floor is warm," she noted as she placed her socked foot on the stone floor.

"I should hope so," Professor replied as he shut the door and marched into the room.

The walls were seven feet high and plastered with fourteenth century artwork (Penny presumed they might be prints but would not put money on it). From the top of them were the windows, angled inwards and supporting the high ceiling, making the surface area of the roof less than the floor. Their three-hundred-and-sixty degree exposure allowed light to stream into the room from every position that the sun would be at.

Golden chandeliers hung down from intermittent points, lower than the windows, and matching candelabras were placed regularly around the room on desks and mantle-pieces.

The room was completely open-plan, had, what looked like, a dining room and three living rooms dotted through the middle and was bookended by a study at either end.

Penny dreamily walked past a bureau that rested against one of the walls. Its antiquity had been sullied by the presence of a flat-screen monitor, wireless keyboard and mouse and a cordless, slim telephone. Then she noticed one of the framed paintings was not what it seemed.

At first, the sheer size of it had caused her to overlook it. Then its blackness made her think it was some kind of open door. A third, longer look saw that it was mounted halfway up the wall and it was then, that she presumed it was a framed painting and the angle of light had caused the shadow. The computer terminal nudged her memory and told her it was actually a television screen.

She traced her finger across the desk's surface and revelled in the feel of the varnished grain.

Then something irked her and drew her out of her awe-struck state of hypnosis. Something did not add up and she looked at her fingers that had stroked the furniture. No dust.

"Well, someone knows about this place," she muttered.

Professor was making himself right at home and had tossed his coat over the back of a divan. "Explain," he instructed.

"The technology?" she questioned. "The state of cleanliness? I don't think the manager would be up here every day with a duster and Mr Sheen or hauling up an eight foot wide TV."

"Mr who?" Professor demanded. "Is that the make of television?"

"Gah!" she exclaimed.

Professor shrugged his shoulders. "Even secret sects need housekeeping," he suggested.

"I'm glad you take your elite order that seriously," she mumbled and continued to explore the room.

"What elite order? There's no-one left but me," he told her and plonked himself down into one of the six couches.

The room tucked around a corner to become a kitchen and second dining room. Again, everything had been liberally hosed down with marble and gilt. A black, nine ring gas cooker was the kitchen's centrepiece and a large American style fridge-freezer stood guard at the far end, watching over the room like a chrome, Herculean bouncer. She checked the cupboards and was only marginally surprised to see them fully stocked. She noted that every perishable product was still within its 'use by' date and thought about mentioning it to her father but considered he might not have the faintest idea what one was. She allowed her brain to change gear, idly pulled the fridge door open and calmly pulled out a can of Diet Coke.

As she pulled the ring-pull she noticed one more door across the other side of the dining table.

She did not want to acknowledge the paranoid thought that tapped at the back of her conscious but knew she would have to have it confirmed or denied.

She wandered around the table, took a cursory glance at her father as he studied a slim remote control, and threw the door open without hesitation.

It was dark inside so she felt the wall beside her for a light switch and flicked it up. It was a bedroom. There were no windows to allow any natural light in. There was a vanity unit to one side, another couch and two soft chairs, a door, a four-poster king size bed, chest of drawers, door, then desk and office chair.

She had resigned herself to the evidence before her but, again, felt a need to try to prove herself wrong so approached the first door.

It was just a walk in wardrobe that was bigger than the downstairs of her previous house. She closed the door, sighed and went to the second door.

That was an immense bathroom of marble and gilt: a walk-in shower cubicle, a huge bath with jacuzzi jets, a toilet and a bidet.

Despite the room's extravagance, she closed the door quietly and with despondency and made her way back to the main living area.

She strolled up to the back of her father's seat and watched for a moment while he still played with the remote control.

"There's only one fucking bed!" she screamed and he threw himself forward, instinctively grabbing his cane and drawing the blade from it before he could realise where the assault was coming from.

She just pursed her lips at him then returned to the kitchen in search of some alcohol to go with the Coke. Her father was left reeling in the middle of the room wondering whether he had been right not to impale her.

"I didn't design the room," he implored.

"But you chose it," she replied.

"Couldn't we -?"

"Absolutely not. Under no circumstances."

"I'll take one of the sofas then," he said.

"Yes," she told him as the fourth cupboard searched revealed a well-stocked selection of spirits. She grabbed a bottle of whiskey and a glass then returned to the living room.

"So, explain to me how a room of this size can remain secret from the outside world," she ordered.

Professor slipped his blade back into its housing and sat down again, keeping a wary eye on his daughter and the bottle of sixty year old Macallan that she handled like a £1.99 bottle of Soave.

"It's based on some designs by Da Vinci, on themes of perspective." he told her. "Hence its name. This suite is sunken below the level of the hotel's roof. Only the windows offer an extra foot of height, which is imperceptible to anyone from the ground. The angle of the windows allow natural daylight into the suite all day long and the angle of light shining out during the evening will only shine upwards, again making it indistinguishable from surrounding street lights to any common observer."

"What about satellite?" Penny asked as she sipped the neat liquor from her crystal glass. She grimaced and topped it up with the Coke.

Professor closed his eyes to hide the desecration taking place before him.

"Anything that would see from above or equal height around would only see the grill-like structure that the design of the windows make."

"Building plans?" she asked and showed more appreciation for the dilution of quality.

"If anyone would be bothered to take the time to find detailed building plans and examine them against the place then, yes, they may uncover the anachronism," he told her testily, "but then I would be forced to murder them."

Penny choked on her mouthful of drink and then saw the self-satisfied grin on her father's face.

"Gotcha," he told her. "Now give me that bottle before William Grant returns from the grave to wreak vengeance upon your uncivilised palette. I will find you a cheap bottle of 'hooch' should you wish to mix that muck with it."

"And I suppose he was in your covert group, too," she mocked as he took the bottle from her.

"He has a very nice cottage in Dufftown," he told her dryly and she decided it was best not to retort.

"So," she declared, "can we ring down for room service or do we have to cook our own?"

"What do you think would be suitable to go with your thirteen thousand pound bottle of whiskey?" he asked dryly.

Penny knew that he was not joking and thought about spitting out her last sip would it not have been an even bigger waste.

For some reason, despite being totally thrown by the price tag, her brain had not filtered her next statement before delivering it.

"I quite fancied McDonalds," she said and then slapped her hand over her mouth.

Her father nearly threw the bottle at her.

# BOOK 3

## 1 (*Maintenant*)

## A Bird's-eye View of Paris

James Mineur had just turned forty and, for the first time in his life, he was proud to say that he was ecstatic.

He had been happy before, on plenty of occasions and, on some of them, he may have described himself as being ecstatic but he knew now that it had been a completely erroneous definition.

*Now* was him being ecstatic. And he was not actually doing anything specific. Things had changed, that was all. Something so insignificant in relation to the rest of the world had turned his life around in the passing of one night.

He wanted to do something special tonight. Something that would go down in the annals of his life to declare, 'Yes! I did that.'

Nothing that was dangerous because he was not that way inclined. 'Extreme,' as they say. He was a fairly unassuming man who enjoyed unassuming pleasures. Cheap treats. Trips to the cinema, a posh meal at a restaurant or a trip somewhere.

Maybe that, then. Did he dare throw caution to the wind, jump on a train and just go somewhere? Just leave everything behind for a few days? He would call his work and parents to tell them he was gone and, if he should lose his job over it, then that was fine with him too. Things had changed so much that he was no longer sure that he even wanted to work there any more.

Yes. He was going to do it.

It was not far to the station and he walked so quickly that he nearly started jogging. He thought about Nice or Monte Carlo; somewhere warm with lots of beautiful people.

The few witnesses who were willing, or able, to make a statement said that the man seemed to be in a hurry. That sort of thing was not unusual at that time of day. It was after the rush hour and you normally got to see the occasional office worker running to catch the earliest train they could.

But then he just stopped in his tracks and shifted his balance between each foot as if having remembered something and not being able to decide whether he should go back for it or not.

One woman said that he had nearly scared the life out of her when he stopped like that. She thought she was about to get mugged, or something, but then saw the strange expression on his face. It was like he was thinking lots of conflicting thoughts at once.

A few more people had noticed the attention the man was drawing so had decided to observe the show as well. Most now thought he was a street performer of some kind and that his facial expression was a mock of a clown mask.

Then, in another instant, his mind was made up and he marched out into the busy road.

A low sports car hit him in his knees, ripping his legs in half, knocking his body over the bonnet and roof. The car's brakes were engaged and it came sliding to a halt further down the road.

James hung in mid air, spinning on all axes until he smashed into a fast moving coach. He shattered the windscreen and the driver only acted instinctively. He tried to avoid any further collision by pulling on the steering wheel and mounting the pavement. Half a dozen of the onlookers were indiscriminately crushed under its wheels. The coach stopped after it had ploughed through a café window.

More cars slammed on their breaks but they were all travelling too fast and too close together. At first it was a just a matter of one vehicle harshly rear-ending the one in front but the stockpile became bigger and each proceeding car came to more of an abrupt halt. The later cars were flattening those in front, causing drivers and passengers alike to be thrown through windows and into the building carnage. Drivers steered into clear lanes only to discover they were heading into the oncoming traffic and the pile-up spread across the width of the road.

Eventually the impacts quietened and the traffic came to a stop.

It would take a long while longer for the screaming to end.

James was lying on the counter of the café. His torn legs were bleeding heavily and his body was rent out of shape but he was still alive.

A waitress raised herself from her position of shelter to see him coughing up blood and staring at her imploringly.

She stood there with a gateau in one hand and a knife in the other and started slipping into shock.

He reached out and grabbed her hand, tightening her fingers around the handle, making her drop the cake and bringing her back to her senses.

«I shall call an ambulance,» she stuttered but he just pulled her closer.

She thought he might have some last words to say but as she got nearer he twisted the blade to point at his head.

She tried to pull back but he would not relinquish his grip. He kept pulling her closer and the more she fought the slower the knife approached his ear.

The tip of the blade entered and she screamed for help. He pulled harder and she felt a pressure give way from within his aural canal. Then her foot slipped on the gateau and the knife plunged into his head up to the hilt.

Then he let go of her.

She fell back to the floor, screaming hysterically, trying to get the psychological sensation of the handle out of her palm.

Anjo was actually one of the first to arrive. He had found an out of the way bistro a couple of streets away when he heard the noise.

He had jumped to his feet before really realising it. Then he had realised it and cursed this estranged feeling that was making its way back into his life.

He did not want to care any more. He did not want to be interested any more.

It was almost a relief to see that it was just a road accident. Okay, so it was a fucking huge road accident with lots of people seriously wounded or dead but at least that meant it was not more paperwork for him.

There now, that was more like him. He thought about smiling again but remembered the discomfort from before and also this did not seem like the appropriate time to grin.

He called in for assistance to be told that every available resource was already on its way. He then walked along the street assessing the wounded and advising those who were helping. He saw the coach and it looked like most people were being helped off having only suffered mild injuries. Then his policing kicked in and he saw that this vehicle must have been one of the major attributers to the incident.

*Don't care*, he told himself. *Don't be interested*.

The shop sign had been dislodged over the door so he stepped through the window to see the young waitress curled up in a foetal ball behind the counter and James' body on it with the knife sticking out of his ear.

*Why did you have to be interested?* he complained to himself.

A quick look at her told him that she was in no state to tell him or do anything. The man was fucked up beyond all recognition.

«Inspector Anjo?» Matilda called from outside.

«In here,» he bellowed and she eventually entered the building to stand on the opposite side of the counter.

He watched her with growing disdain and discomfort as she looked closely over the man's body.

«Coffee?» he asked her and reached for the hot pot from the filter machine above the waitress's head.

«No, thank you,» Matilda replied distractedly.

As he brought the pot over, the handle disconnected itself from the glass, which plummeted to the floor. It shattered loudly and sprayed hot coffee everywhere, waking the waitress from her catatonia. She started screaming again, jumped to her feet and ran towards the front door.

«Wait!» Anjo hollered but it was too late, the waitress ran through the open door, straight into the felled shop sign and bounced back into the room, knocking herself unconscious.

Anjo and Matilda stared at each other for a bemused second then she went back to her analysis of the body.

«I am surprised to see you here,» Matilda commented.

«Not as much as me,» Anjo replied.

«Why would you want to walk away from something as big as this?» she asked him. «I do not understand. Wasn't it you who solved the *M&Ms* murders?»

«No,» he growled. «That was a team effort.»

«That you spearheaded,» she reminded him. «It *was* you who deciphered the colour code?»

«That is true,» he conceded. «It was also me who lost three excellent officers and a best friend on that case, to that psychopath.»

She nodded in silence but stared at him.

«What?» he demanded.

«Is it that easy to fall from your path?» she asked.

«Easy? What's easy about watching someone you love drown in a vat of chocolate?»

«Easier than watching someone while drowning in a vat of chocolate, I would think,» she suggested.

He wanted to be furious, to throw things around and scream her. Tell her that she did not know what it was like to go out on the streets every night and know that tonight was the night that you would end up in a black bag with a tag around your ankle. But it was not *that* feeling that was the worst part, it was the sense of disappointment at the end of each day when it did not happen. That deep depression he would feel knowing that he was going to have to feel like that again tomorrow.

He wanted to do all that but the irritating feeling came back.

«Why did you say 'this'?» he asked and regretted it.

«When?»

«Why would I want to walk away from something 'this' big? What's 'this'? It's a traffic accident not homicide.»

She shook her head at him again and indicated for him to come nearer the body. He leaned over to look at the other side of the counter and saw that the man had drawn a picture in the blood by his hand. It looked like an outline of a mouse's head. Two ears joined in the middle then swung down to a point for its nose. But then it went a bit odd and an upturned 'v' was traced above the lowest point.

«What is it?»

«The same design that the museum security guard drew,» Matilda told him and he groaned. «I think it is a heart with a diamond inside.»

«Please, no more cults,» he prayed to anyone who might care to listen.

«Does it mean something to you?» she asked.

«No. Not the symbol itself but the practice of leaving messages,» Anjo said. «It usually means there is a secret. Someone is either trying to protect it, destroy it, reveal it to the world or keep it to themselves.»

«So we need to find a connection between the two victims,» she deduced.

«Aah, there will be no connection,» he predicted. «Nothing will join these people together, that is how secret societies work the best. But someone knows about their membership.»

«I will do background checks on them anyway,» she said and he shrugged his shoulders. «And the clues at the museum?»

«Maybe he liked the picture, maybe it's just his phone number or maybe he was just psychotic,» Anjo grumbled.

«And the note?»

«The 'PS'? What was the name?» he asked.

«Robert LeClerc.»

«Yes, find out who he is.»

He was being drawn back in and it did not feel nice. He had been resisting the lure of investigative work for so long that he did not even need to resist, he had managed to wedge himself into a nook of disinterest. But now he had leaned so far forward to see if he was still being pulled that he had overbalanced and the resulting force had yanked him off his feet. He was hurtling along out of control. The least he could do now was put his arms out and pretend he was deliberately trying to fly.

## 2 (*Allors*)

## Turn Vagabond

Professor and Mary were strolling along the bank of the Seine with Penelope wriggling happily in her pram. Mary was pushing it and was the embodiment of a proud mother. He walked beside her, tapping his cane on the cobbles with every other step.

It was a warm, summer's day so the baby's covers had been pulled back to allow her complete freedom of movement. Many of the people who would pass them would pause to look into the pram and coo at her. She would respond favourably from the interaction by wiggling on her back a bit faster or gurgling; mainly she would just smile.

"If she smiles any more then I fear her jaw might dislocate," Professor joked as an older lady poked her head under the bonnet and made, 'Shoo, shoo, shoo,' noises at the girl. As she drew away they could see Penelope's toothless smile had widened considerably.

"Any second now," he said.

«You have a most beautiful granddaughter, sir," the old lady remarked.

«Daughter,» Professor corrected and the woman's smile quickly dropped. She looked with concern from him to Mary and back again. Mary grinned and bowed her head to try to hide her mirth but still slipped her arm to tuck under his.

«Disgusting,» the woman spat and marched away.

Mary giggled while Professor pursed his lips in annoyance.

"What business of is it of hers -?"

"Oh, leave it Abraham," Mary advised. "You are old enough to be *my* grandfather let alone Penelope's. Some people just do not know how to deal with that."

«Love does not consider age to be a limitation of its reaches,» he shouted at the dwindling figure.

«Dirty old man!» the woman hollered back which caused Mary to laugh aloud.

Professor was speechless. "I should just tip her in the river and be done with her," he eventually snapped.

"She is just jealous," Mary soothed. "She would wish she had a virile young man to dust away her cobwebs."

He scrunched his face with distaste and demanded, "Mary, why do you still insist on using such vulgarities?"

"Because it's the only thing I can do to get you flustered, Abraham," she explained. "And anyway, I thought I was being quite reserved. I was going to say, 'unblock her plumbing,' but thought better of it."

"Well, I suppose I must thank you for that."

They continued their amble, arm in arm, and were turning to cross the Pont Neuf towards Île de la Cité when they passed a beggar woman huddled up on the floor.

«Please, sir?» she asked as she held out her dirty hands to them. Her head was tucked onto her chest either through subservience or fatigue.

Professor dipped his hand into his pocket and pulled out a coin. He placed it in her palm and she looked up at him with appreciation.

As their eyes connected, there was a moment of recognition; mostly from her, though, as he just looked away and continued their progression across the bridge.

"Eric?" she stuttered but this elicited no response from him. Although he was not deliberately ignoring her, he just continued his stroll and conversation as if not hearing.

"Eric!" she called louder and began to pull herself to her feet. He must have heard her that time but he still had not reacted. Maybe she was wrong.

"Eric!" she shouted and this time the couple stopped to turn around.

But no, it was not a reaction to the name - which still had not registered on his face - but to her angered scream. Now he had turned to face her, she could see him quite clearly and, yes, it really was him.

She was in shock now. She wanted to leap on the man and hug him but, moreover, wanted to scratch the flesh from his face with her ragged nails.

There it was. His incomprehension waned as her features filtered through to his memory and connected with the name she had called him. Her hair was greasy and matted, her face was bruised and filthy, her clothes were not much more than bound rags but he could see that it was Eve: his wife for a year and the natural mother of Penelope; the woman he had left in Kent and considered out of his life forever.

"Eric?" she whimpered. "Is it you?"

An irrational fear had gripped him. He was very angry at himself for allowing this situation to occur but more so for presuming that it may never happen and, so, being very unprepared for it. He was embarrassed by the social implications of this beggar, and possible prostitute, addressing him so casually in public. Thankfully the bridge was clear of any other pedestrians. He was also very ashamed. He had been caught in the act, so to speak. He had pretended to love this woman for a year, he had pretended that he made love with her and he had pretended that he would look after her. He had taken her from her homeland, which was poor but stable, then dumped her on foreign soil with nothing. No money, no friends, no family and no child that she had been carrying.

"Eve, I -" he began but Mary stepped forward to embrace her.

"You poor girl," she soothed and led her along the bridge, ahead of Professor. "You must be so confused. Tired? Hungry? Let's sort all that out and then try to make sense of this."

As they passed the pram, Eve peered in and saw Penelope writhing in pleasure. Emotions came flooding back.

"She is yours?" Eve asked.

"She is," Mary confirmed.

Eve looked over her shoulder at Professor who was now following, pushing the pram. She started to panic. She huddled into Mary's shoulder.

"I must warn you," she whispered. "I - we had a baby together, nearly two years ago, and he stole her from me."

They took a few more steps in silence.

"Do you think I might be mad?" Eve asked.

"No, it must have been a horrible couple of years for you."

"I only say this in case he plans the same for your baby," Eve said.

"I could not have babies," Mary confessed.

"But you said -"

"Oh, by all accounts she is my child but I did not give birth to her. She is the one he took from you."

"How can that be?" Eve questioned and stared back at the pram. "Are you mocking me? She is still a babe and yet mine would be walking and talking."

"That is part of the reason for him taking her," Mary explained. "You would not understand."

They were approaching Île de la Cité so Mary nonchalantly steered their course to the opposite side of the bridge where a large willow tree created a shaded corner.

"What is your name?" Mary asked.

"Eve."

"I am sorry for what has happened," Mary said sincerely. "Ab - Eric is a very clever man but he is still just a man and did not treat this situation with the right care."

"He is an insensitive and selfish man," Eve commented fiercely.

They dipped their heads as they brushed through the green waterfall.

"On the contrary," Mary argued. "He is actually a very sensitive and caring man. That is where he went wrong."

"What do you mean?" Eve asked and, for the first time since crossing the bridge, considered that something was not quite right.

Mary whipped the woman around and, with one hand, forced her against the bridge wall. Eve's body bowed from the impact and as she tried to call out with pain, Mary slapped her other hand over her mouth and continued to push, causing Eve to pivot over the wall; her head bent backwards and her feet left the floor.

Eve looked out from the corner of her eye and saw the Seine rushing along beneath her. She looked back at Mary whose face was impassioned yet set with determination.

Eve whimpered so Mary removed her hand.

"I will not tell anyone," she cried. "I will leave France. I am only here trying to get home. I will not say anything, I promise."

"No," Mary said. "That's my promise."

Mary leapt onto the stomach of the prostrate woman and balanced on her fulcrum. Eve watched with catatonic fear as Mary's eyes changed from their hue of blue to a deep red and her canines extended from her gums.

Mary whipped her face into the woman's neck and bit deep. She wrenched out a chunk of flesh and spat it into the river below. Eve inhaled sharply and was about to release every negative emotion she had just experienced in the last ten minutes and all those that had been pent up since Penelope's birth.

Mary punched her in the throat, crushing her trachea and oesophagus, making it impossible for her to breathe let alone make another sound. She returned her attention to the open wound on Eve's neck and began to drink back the gobbets of blood that fountained out.

Professor stepped into the cover as Mary pulled her head away.

"Any mess?" Mary asked through gasps of air.

He just shook his head while staring at the convulsing body of his ex-wife.

"Ensure the deed," Mary instructed.

Without hesitation, he twisted the silver handle of his cane and pulled an epee from its housing.

Eve managed one more imploring look at him before he brought the blade around and down upon her neck, neatly decapitating her.

Her head dropped into the Seine but, before it made a splash, Mary had hopped down and tipped the body over after it.

She watched its graceful descent and coalescence with the current. She looked up at Professor and he inspected her face. Her eyes had reverted to their normal hue and her closed lips did not hint at her dental extrusion.

"You have something on your chin," he told her and pointed to the corner of his own.

She wiped her thumb across the relative point on her chin.

"No, the other side," he told her.

The spot of blood was picked up with a second sweep of her hand. She inspected the smear on her thumb then popped it in her mouth.

"That was a bit earlier than anticipated," Professor commented as he watched her straighten her clothing.

"But very welcome," Mary replied. "That was nice."

"Yes, all right," he accepted. "Let us continue in case anyone from the banks saw something and come to investigate."

They stepped out from their arboreal hiding hole straight into the path of the old woman from earlier. Professor was brushing leaves from his jacket and Mary was still straightening her petticoats.

«Disgusting,» the woman blustered. «A man of your age.»

«Oh, you know you would love the chance to get a good futting,» Mary unashamedly laughed.

The woman stepped up her pace and Professor shook his head in disdain.

"Do you still want to look at the church?" Mary asked him.

"Mary," he sighed, "it is more than just -"

"Or shall we head back to retire early," she proposed and stopped him in mid-flow.

They checked the pram and Penelope had fallen asleep. That seemed to make the decision for them so they turned around and headed back along Pont Neuf the way they had come.

## 3 (*Maintenant*)

## From Charybdis to Scylla

The evening was drawing in and the number of tourists was thinning. Notre Dame is truly a majestic sight, a spectacle of gothic architecture steeped in history and lore but is also another example of the church's past eagerness to spend more on their houses of God rather than on His tenants.

The huge doors were being closed as Archbishop Brandon Wuh ran across the courtyard. He had decided to continue his mission undercover so had swapped the cumbersome cassock for jeans, shirt and a jacket but, as is the way with religion and normal clothes, they did not look right on him. His blue jeans were pulled up slightly too high, his white shirt was tucked in and revealed that he was rather portly, he had no belt, he wore brown shoes and a black jacket.

«Father Frollo,» he called to the priest behind the doors. «A moment please!»

«I am sorry, we must close for the day,» the priest replied. «We open early tomorrow morning.»

«It is most urgent that I speak to someone now,» Brandon called back as he bounded up the stone steps. «I am from the Vatican. I have been sent by The Pope, himself.»

The priest paused at this declaration and kept the door ajar, waiting for Brandon to reach the top.

«Yes, and I am Saint Fiacre,» the priest told him and shut the door.

Brandon thought about protesting through the thick doors but realised that his noise would be blocked by the wood or the priest's disbelief. Brandon also thought about praying for some assistance but knew that would be a futile gesture and the resort of a desperate man. He slumped down onto the top of the stone steps, staring despondently over Place du Parvis and the milling people with their plans and sense of purpose.

He had thrown himself into the deep end and was only just treading water. He did not know which way to head towards and was not even sure why he had come to Paris. A quick analysis of the time of the robbery and the train timetable had suggested this way. The purse was stolen in the early hours of the morning and the Paris express was the first train out of Rome. It seemed logical at the time but once here, the thief could have gone on to anywhere and that was why he felt it necessary to recruit some help.

If he could not get the local God Squad to believe him then who? Then he remembered a chance meeting with a German man who was trying to get a Papal Sanction for a sect that had been formed out of Cologne. Brandon had taken his name and number and said he would get back to him but never did. It is a strict precedence of the Vatican not to accept any more crusading factions unless they have a track record of killing heretics and hoarding religious artefacts. It was hard trying to find anyone who actually qualified at all these days.

He should have at least called to say so, though.

The more he thought about it, the more he realised he may have an ally; an organisation who may be willing to lend their resources to him without asking too many questions because of their desire to be accepted.

Who knew how far into society their links went? This purse was some sort of religious artefact which meant it only held any real worth within the realms of religion. It might just take one phone call and he could get his answer.

Elated, he jumped to his feet and rummaged inside his jacket pockets for his address book. He found it, opened it and flipped to the 'g's.

He then produced his mobile phone and started to dial the number he had found. He listened and prayed (figuratively) for a connection.

It rang.

It was picked up.

„Allo?", a gruff female German voice called.

"Sprechen sie Französisch?" Brandon asked.

„No", the German replied.

"Italiener?" Brandon hoped.

„No", the German replied.

"Englisch?" Brandon begged.

"I speak some English," the German said. "Who are you and what do you want?"

"My name is Archbishop Wuh and I am hoping to be speaking to a Henry Tauler about his 'friends'?"

The voice immediately changed its tone to a warmer, lighter brogue.

"Ah, ja," she cried. "Please wait and I get Henry for you."

"Thank you very much," Brandon said and sighed with relief.

Brandon could hear some hollering in the background and then some laughter.

"Hello, Eminence," a male bellowed.

"Oh, I'm not -" Brandon started but then decided this was not the best time to go into semantics. "This is Henry Tauler?"

The other end went silent. "*I* am Henry Tauler," Henry told him suspiciously.

"Good, good. I am sorry that it has taken me quite so long to call," Brandon said.

"I am very glad that you have," Henry interrupted. "I had thought that you would not. It has been so long. But I had suspected that it might be that way."

"It was very rude of me not to call but I did not want to speak with you without having something to say." Brandon analysed the conversation so far and decided it was not going well. Two men were trying to talk to each other in a language neither really understood. It was probably best to stop the chit-chat and get on with it.

"You have something to say now?" Henry asked.

"Yes. I have been instructed by the Pope to issue a Holy Crusade to your organisation. The successful completion of which will guarantee you a Papal Sanction."

Henry inhaled slowly and loudly, then went silent.

"You wish for us to kill the Muslims?" Henry asked.

"No!" Brandon shrieked. "No, not at all."

"Okay." Henry sounded almost disappointed. "We have some next door. That is all. It would be easy. While you were on the telephone."

"No. We need for your organisation to recover a Holy Relic," Brandon explained.

"Ah, that sort of crusade. Any one in particular?"

"Yes, it's -"

"Wait, I will get a pencil."

There followed the sound of shouting, rummaging and then heavy breathing.

"Ready," Henry declared.

"A small silk purse with a glass emerald in the centre," Brandon said.

"A. Purse. With. Emerald. In," he read as he wrote.

Brandon thought about his sentence.

"A *silk* purse with a *glass* emerald *on* it," he reiterated. "Stitched on it."

"Ja, ja. This is what I have written," Henry said dismissively. "And what is your time scale?"

"As quickly as possible."

"Was ist Das? One, two, maybe three hundred years?"

"Nein - no! Maybe three days!"

The request did not seem to phase Henry.

"And this thing is where?" he asked.

"Possibly Paris," Brandon said. "I am hoping your network might be able to get some information."

"Mm-hm, we will ask around," Henry told him. "I should contact you on this number?"

"Yes."

"And you are in Paris now?"

"Yes."

"I will be there in the morning."

The line disconnected.

Brandon's first feeling of elation had slipped into doubt and now he worried that not only was he going to fail to save the World but he was also going to get a right bollocking for his phone bill when he got back.

## 4 (*Maintenant*)

## Three Human Hearts Differently Constructed

The office was minimalist to say the least. Even 'minimalist' was too extravagant a word to use in this room but to say 'bare' would imply that it was bereft of anything. To see the room you would know that an incredible amount of care and attention had gone into making it look as empty as it did.

The walls were immaculately painted in something like 'white with a kiss of lilac haze' whilst the floor was bare floorboards. But not the kind of floorboards you would see if you lifted your upstairs carpet. No, you could see that these floorboards probably cost more than the entirety of your upstairs.

There were three glass and brushed-steel tables. Each desk had a large leather swivel chair behind it, a sleek black handset cast in a lopsided silver pyramid that declared BeoCom 6000 (each costing more than your downstairs) on it, and black, widescreen VAIO notebooks.

Only one of the desks were occupied. Like the room, he should have been described as being plain but to really look would show that he had been very precise to look as inconspicuous as he did.

He was dressed completely in black. A tailored D&G suit jacket was draped over the back of the chair he was reclining in, his light cotton shirt had its top three buttons open and his feet were crossed wearing a pair of polished Gucci boots. He had his hands folded behind his head and his eyes closed behind a pair of Prada spectacles.

His name was Hugh - you knew that because his name badge told you so and how 'entranced' he would be to assist you - and he was in his forties. His skin was healthily tanned and a closer inspection would notice a fine foundation around his cheekbones. His blonde hair was immaculately styled into a short, rolling quiff.

His computer screensaver was on, displaying a black haired comic book superhero character, wearing a black uniform with a white 'splash' effect around his neck and on his right hip. He was continuously racing from one side of the screen to the other, either running or flying.

His phone gently rang and he inhaled sharply from the surprise of being woken. He blinked, looked around the office and cleaned around the inside of his mouth with his tongue. He leaned forward to reach for the handset but checked his chin for drool first.

He picked the phone up and put it to his ear.

"Hello," he said calmly with a soft American accent, "you've called Clairvaux Holdings, my name's Hugh, how can I help you?"

He listened patiently to the person on the other end.

"That's right, sir. You sign all your assets over to us and we, in essence, liquidate them for you and hold the funds. All future income is also signed directly over to us. This allows you to declare a monastic lifestyle, makes you exempt from all council and governmental taxes."

He listened again.

"Technically, no," Hugh replied. "We do not offer a rate of interest because that would make us a bank which we are not, however we do pay off any existing debts you may have when you sign over to us and, of course, will tend to your lifestyle needs as and when is required. This applies to you and your entire family."

"Yes, sir, everything you currently own will belong to us," Hugh said. "Everything that comes into your possession will also belong to us. We will, of course allow you to be a custodial of the property until such time comes that you may need to make a pilgrimage and then we will be able to find you lodgings elsewhere."

"All over the world, sir."

"Yes, we have property in the Bahamas."

"No, we will not hold your children obligated to our cause when they reach adulthood but they will have to bear in mind that there will not be any inheritance due to them from your passing. We have found that many families stay with us for many generations as we do look after our members."

"Yes, sir, I can send you brochure. If I can take your details?" Hugh tapped the mouse pad and the screensaver cleared to show the screen's wallpaper of two muscular, topless men riding one white stallion across a beach. He double-clicked a desktop icon, which brought up a form. He started filling in the spaces.

"That'll be in the post for you this afternoon," Hugh told the phone. "Thank you for calling."

As he hung up, the office door opened and two older men entered, laughing between themselves. Both were equally as impeccably dressed and groomed but they wore crisp white shirts and black silk ties. One was in his fifties - his name badge said 'Geoffrey' - and the other - 'Jacques' - was late seventies.

They both had dark brown hair with geometrically perfect side partings. Geoffrey was slightly skinnier than his associate, his angular face made him look like he was sucking his cheeks in all the time. He was carrying a small cardboard tray with a folded paper bag and coffee cup.

Jacques was just plain old but he was holding it with dignity. He had a broad chest and flat stomach that implied either regular exercise or he had yielded to a girdle.

Hugh eyed them with disdain and they stopped their conversation mid-flow.

"Where have you been?" he demanded.

"Mochaccino, dear boy," Jacques replied in a deep, gravelly, well-accentuated English accent and tapped at the gold Rolex on his wrist. It matched the plethora of rings he had across his knuckles.

"You just walked out and left me to man the place on my own?" Hugh whined.

Jacques raised his eyebrows at Geoffrey and marched over to his desk. Geoffrey wandered to Hugh's and placed the tray down.

"I got you an almond croissant, too," Geoffrey said. His voice was softer but no less the tone associated with affluence, education and good breeding.

Hugh looked at the offering and his offensive pose lapsed. His shoulders dropped and he raised his eyes.

"Thank you," Hugh said.

"You're very welcome," Geoffrey replied with a bow and wandered over to his desk.

"Anyway, you were asleep before we went and we didn't want to disturb you," Jacques added as he logged into his laptop.

"I was not asleep," Hugh argued defensively. "I was thinking."

"You were snoring, Hugh," Geoffrey commented.

Hugh's eyes and mouth widened with shock. "I do *not* snore," he stated adamantly.

"Then you must have been thinking about truffles, then," Jacques suggested.

His phone chimed out the theme to *The Saint*. He allowed it to play for a few bars before picking it up.

"Yes?" he called into it. "Yes, it is. Who is this?"

Hugh and Geoffrey looked at each other quizzically and then back to Jacques who was eagerly beckoning them to his desk.

Geoffrey jumped to his feet and dashed over while Hugh scooted across the room in his chair. When they had both arrived Jacques pressed a button on the handset and placed it on his desk.

"I have just put you on the speaker," he told the caller. "Would you mind repeating that."

There followed a weary sigh from the other end of the line.

"Is this absolutely necessary?" the female caller demanded. She had a Continental accent.

"If this call is what I think it is then, yes," Jacques told her. "I think it's absolutely imperative for my colleagues to listen in and besides it will save my voice from having to repeat it all."

"Very well," the woman groaned. "This is Mother Furca of the Sisterhood of Ordered Ascension."

Hugh and Geoffrey let out a long, 'Ooh.'

"Oh, I knew this was going to be more difficult than it was worth," she muttered.

"All right, all right," Jacques calmed the men. "Go ahead, Mother Superior."

She took a bolstering breath of air then said, "We need your help. An artefact has gone missing and it is important to have it returned as quickly as possible."

"Ooh, a real crusade," Hugh gushed.

"Who is 'we' and what do we get out of it?" Jacques asked.

"We are the Vatican and you would get our eternal gratitude," she snapped severely.

The three men looked at each other.

"Cup of tea, anyone?" Geoffrey asked.

"Well, what would you want?" she demanded.

"Public absolution of all charges," Jacques suggested and ignored the sneer that rode up Hugh's face.

"Oh, please," she groaned. "All the charges were dropped ages ago. It's only through your own decisions that you've decided not to come out yet."

The three men looked at each other.

"I cannot go to the Pope and get him to broadcast that you are not a bunch of heretics and sodomites," she stated. "It's outdated, nobody cares and everyone knows it's not true."

"I beg your pardon?" Jacques blustered.

"The charges," she emphasised. "Everyone knows the charges aren't true - weren't true. It was just that silly king."

"How does the Bank feel about this?" Geoffrey asked.

"The Vatican Bank?"

"No, bloody Barclays Bank," he snapped sarcastically. "Of course the Vatican Bank."

"They will be unaware of your involvement," she stated.

"Until we get involved," Hugh added.

"They will be unaware of your connection," she reiterated. "As far as they're concerned you will be acting independently."

"So, really, we can't be seen handing the artefact over to you when we get it," Jacques deduced.

Mother Furca went quiet.

"Are you still there?" Jacques asked.

"Yes," she spat. "Very well. You may keep it but I must have your assurance that it stays undercover."

"You have our word," Jacques declared. "What is it?"

"The purse," she said softly.

It was the men's turn to fall silent.

"What? *The* purse?" Hugh asked.

"Yes, *the* purse. Of course *the* purse. I wouldn't be calling you if I was after just *a* purse, now, would I?"

"Well, I know it's not *a* purse because you would've said just 'a' purse but you didn't, you just said 'the' purse and not *the* purse hence why I wanted clarification that it was *the* purse and not some other purse," Hugh squabbled.

"The purse, *the* purse? How many purses do you know of?" she demanded.

"It's not a matter of how many I know, it's a matter of not knowing how many you know!" he screamed.

"Please, Hugh, it doesn't matter," Jacques stated.

"She started it," Hugh huffed.

"*The* purse," Jacques confirmed.

"Yes," she panted through a clenched jaw. "We believe it's somewhere in Paris."

Geoffrey checked his watch. "We can be there first thing in the morning."

"Good luck," Mother Furca said dryly and hung up.

The men pondered for a moment.

"It could be a trap," Geoffrey suggested.

"How so?" Jacques enquired.

"Why is the bequest coming from her and not him?"

"Like she said, maybe he doesn't know yet," Jacques hypothesised. "In which case it's even less likely to be a trap."

"If we get this Holy relic, we'll be reformed," Hugh said. "We'll have something to regroup around. And if it really is *the* purse then what better symbol?"

"Geoffrey, prep the plane," Jacques instructed. "Hugh, pack the bags. Be at Stanstead for six a.m."

## 5 (*Maintenant*)

### Monsieur the Cardinal

Cardinal Christophe was relaxing in his hotel suite. He had just finished his dinner and was dabbing the corners of his mouth with his napkin.

He stood, stretched, wandered over to a sofa and dropped into it. He picked up his mobile phone from the armrest and began fiddling with the buttons.

"'P' or 'S'," he said to himself as he scrolled through lists of names in the phone's address book.

He stopped pressing the down button, pressed the up twice and then pressed the call. He put the phone to his ear and inspected the cuticles of his free hand.

There was a ringing tone and then the other end was picked up.

«Hallo?» a male voice called.

«Hallo, may I speak to Pierre, please?» Christophe asked.

There was a brief silence.

«There is no one of that name here,» the voice replied.

«Yes, yes, yes, I know. I would like to speak to Pierre, please,» he told the voice rather than ask this time.

«No!» the voice declared more adamantly. «There is NO Pierre here.»

Christophe took the phone away from his face and sighed.

"Bloody covert groups," he grumbled. «Please, I wish to speak to Pierre concerning the Priory.»

«The what?»

«The Priory,» Christophe squealed. «Pierre? The Priory? Am I going to have to - gah - The Priory of Sion. I wish to speak to Pierre about -»

«There is no Priory of Simon here,» the voice stated.

«Not 'Simon,' Sion!»

«Oh, the Priory of Sion!»

«Yes, the Priory of Sion,» Christophe gasped. «Can I -»

«There is no Priory of Sion here,» the voice interrupted.

Christophe's face warped into a ball of fury. «Look, I'm the first person to commend any organisation on its ability to exist beneath the radar of modern media but -»

«They have moved,» the voice stated.

«I'm sorry, what?»

«They have moved,» the voice repeated. «They are not here any more. They had to move down the road.»

«Oh, I am sorry for disturbing you,» Christophe said.

«It is okay, it happens sometimes.»

«Do you have a forwarding number for them?» Christophe asked.

«No, but I believe they are listed,» the voice told him.

«Listed?»

«Try directory enquiries.»

Christophe disconnected the call then dialled one-one-eight-eight-nine-nine. He put the phone back to his ear.

"Yes, hello. I would like the number for the Priory of Sion, Paris, please?"

He waited.

"No, not 'Simon,' Sion. That's right."

He waited.

"No, no. That's their old number. Do you -? Yes? Okay, I'll try that. SMS? Yes, that would be easier thank -"

His text message alert went off in his ear with an almighty bleep. He threw the phone down and wiggled his little finger in his aural canal.

"Bastard!" he screamed at the phone.

He picked it up again and checked the recently received message. He pressed some more menu options and then the call button.

The phone went back to his ear and listened to the ringing tone.

«Hello,» a soft female voice said.

«Hello, may I -» Christophe started.

«Thank you for calling the Priory of Sion. If you have a touch tone phone, please press your star key now.»

A moment's confusion left him flustered but he managed to press the star and listened again.

«If you are calling about membership to the Knighthood of Catholic Rule and Institution and of Independent Traditionalist Union then please press one.

«If you wish to speak to someone about restoring your church to Latin liturgy, press two.

«If you are calling to complain about a division of the Priory or the Knights Templar, please press three.

«If your call is concerning any other issue, please hold the line and an agent will be with you shortly.»

*The Girl from Ipanema* started playing in his ear and he rolled his eyes. The music cut out after a while and he became alert again.

«Thank you for calling the Priory of Sion,» the recorded voice told him again. «Your call is important to us but all our agents are busy right now. You are in a calling queue. Please hold the line and you will be dealt with shortly. You are currently in -»

A man's voice cut in and said, «twelfth.»

Then the woman returned to say, «place. Some calls may be recorded for training purposes.»

*The Girl from Ipanema* returned for all she passed to say, 'Ooh.'

"How can they be so busy?" Christophe demanded.

The music stopped.

«You are currently in -»

«- twelfth -»

«- place.»

"Why are you telling me I am in the same place?" he screamed at the phone. "Tell me I am moving not that I am going nowhere."

The music stopped.

«You are currently in -»

«- twelfth -»

«- place.»

"Sacred mother of Mary!" he cried. "Who can be calling the Priory now? How can eleven other people be calling you? How many agents do you have to be busy enough to keep eleven other people waiting before me? What the hell do you people do?"

The music stopped.

«You are currently in -»

«- thirteenth -»

«- place.»

Christophe was not sure he had heard it right. He was about to change the direction of his rant that at least, at last, he had moved but was pretty sure that he had actually dropped a place. He pressed the disconnect button and then redialed. As the woman's voice started asking if he had touch-tone he was ready to jab the star button although it did not deter her spiel and she continued, «press the star button now.»

He expelled an unintelligible expletive and quashed the asterisk under his wrathful thumb.

The woman started through her list again and Christophe pressed one. He just wanted to talk to someone.

The woman's tone became slightly less breezy and more sincere.

«I am sorry but these offices are closed at the present. Recruitment office hours are between eight am and eight pm. You may call back then or leave a message for an agent to call you back.»

He wanted to explode into pyroclastic rage but did not have time.

Beep.

«Hello? This is Cardinal Christophe of the Vatican? It's only six minutes past eight. Is there somebody still there? Are you screening? Can you please pick up because it is incredibly important that I speak to someone about a holy quest. More of a crusade really. I realise this might not be the correct department to call but I did try the other line first and didn't get a response so I thought - anyway, my number is -»

Beep.

«Hello?» Christophe called dubiously but was met with nothing to confirm any suspicions one way or the other.

He disconnected and went through the process again until he reached the answer machine.

«- leave a message for an agent to call you back.»

«This is Card -»

Beep.

The level of his frustration had peaked beyond anything describable. He was practically catatonic. His brain was on the verge of complete shut down and it took him a few seconds for his jaw to unclench and his mind to stop conjuring Inquisitor scenarios.

«This is Cardinal Christo -»

Beep.

To print the words he expelled at this stage would be to damn anyone who read them. Remember that scene in *The Evil Dead*? The bit when they just played the tape that caused the Candarian demons to rise? That moment was like this but you only had to read these words that Christophe said to condemn your entire family line under the eyes of his God.

As soon as he had stopped, he pressed redial. Pre-empted the touch-tone and the department selection process.

«I am sorry,» the woman said. «We have been unable to process your request. Please wait for an advisor to help you.»

«Hallo?» a male voice asked.

Christophe was completely taken aback. He had readied himself with a swift fifteen-second retort for the answer machine again and was now faced with a real person.

«Hello?» he replied.

«You were having problems with the buttons?» the man asked.

«I'm trying to speak to Peter about the Priory,» Christophe blurted.

«This is Peter,» the man said. «Who is this?»

«Cardinal Christophe of the Vatican,» Christophe declared. «We are in need of your organisation's assistance.»

«What do you want?» Peter asked.

«We need to utilise your extensive network to locate a stolen artefact,» Christophe told him.

Peter went silent for a second.

«If we do this then we would want something in return,» Peter stated.

«Naturally,» Christophe agreed. «A Papal Sanction? Funding? What?»

«Firstly, we would demand that a number of the Pope's addresses to be delivered in Latin.»

«Well, he has said that himself so that would not be a problem.»

«Secondly, an official memo sent by the Pope to all state heads encouraging the reinstatement of Latin into local liturgy.»

«Riiiiiight,» Christophe replied dubiously.

«On letter-headed stationery,» Peter emphasised.

«I'll work on that.»

«Thirdly, we would demand that our organisation be publicly renounced by His Eminence.»

«What? You want the Vatican to deny your involvement?»

«To deny our existence,» Peter explained.

«You wish for his Eminence to add to your double-bluff conspiracy? You want to remain in the shadows?» Christophe asked.

«We find our efforts are less impeded the more discredited we are,» Peter stated. «We have been putting great efforts into proving our non-existence.»

«Very well,» Christophe sighed.

«That includes going ex-directory,» Peter added.

«Of course,» Christophe agreed without trying to hide his sarcasm. «The greatest trick the devil ever pulled, eh?»

«What?»

«Never mind.»

«David Blaine?»

«It really doesn't matter. I was thinking out loud. Is there anything else?»

«Not at this time,» Peter said cryptically.

«Look, I'm not having you lot holding us to ransom so if there's anything else then you need to bring it to the table now,» Christophe shouted.

The line went muffled and Christophe could hear people mumbling in the background.

Peter came back. «There is one more thing. We have a lot of brothers who claim to be descended from the Merovingian and it is causing a few problems.»

«Not for me!» someone shouted in the background.

«So what do you want us to do?» Christophe asked, not sure that he wanted to know where this was going.

«Could you send someone over to do some DNA testing?»

«Yes. Of course. That would not be a problem,» Christophe said with relief.

«Of course it would mean getting access to the tomb of Chilperic the second Noyon,» Peter stated.

*Ah, here we go,* Christophe thought. «Why not his son? The faux king?» he asked.

«There was never any proof of his lineage,» Peter stated.

«Childeric was Merovingian!» the background voice declared. «You cannot exclude him as he is my lineage!»

«Shut up!» Peter told him.

«Operor non irreverens meus prosapia!» the voice bellowed resolutely in Latin.

«You're making it up!» Peter stated.

«I will get someone out to Noyon,» Christophe interrupted.

Peter took a moment to compose himself then said, «So, you want the silk bag back?»

«Yes, how did you -?»

«We are the Priory and our network reaches out into all areas.»

«You know where it is?»

«No.»

«But you know who has it.»

«No.»

«Then how do you know it's gone?» Christophe demanded.

«Someone has posted an 'I want it now' on *Ebay*,» Peter said. «Someone called *niger_monachus*.»

Christophe fell back in the sofa in exhaustion.

«Just get it back,» he groaned.

«Thank you for not calling the Priory of Sion,» Peter said. «Someone will not be available to return your call as there is no one here.»

Christophe hung up.

# 6 (*Maintenant*)

## The Mysterious Monk

There was a man in a black habit and black Fila hooded top that covered his features. He silently entered a glass telephone booth at the side of the path.

He dipped his hand into his pocket and looked over is shoulder to ensure no one had followed him. He pulled out some money and turned back to the telephone, lifted the receiver and fed some of the coins into the slot.

He dialled a number and inspected the inside of the booth while waiting for the line to connect. There were a number of brightly coloured cards advertising the services of 'new' and 'just turned 16' blonde, girls who would like to talk to him.

That caused a moment of hesitation and he was just about to put the receiver down when the other end was picked up.

«Hallo? This is Opus Dei, how may I help?» a friendly female asked.

The Black Monk's lips pursed to form a word but then retracted to a grimace.

«Hallo?» the woman called.

He tried again but just exhaled.

«I know someone is there,» she said somewhat testily. «I can hear you breathing.»

He opened his mouth and emitted a grunt.

«Pervert,» she stated and hung up.

He looked at the receiver in his hand then slammed it back on the phone.

"Affanculo!" he declared in Italian, then stood there in a moment of incomprehensible shock.

## 7 (*Maintenant*)

## Claude Frollo

The priest shook his head in dismay for the future of the human race. The things these people would say just so they could get an extra five minutes taking photos of the stained glass windows that probably would not process anyway.

He had thousands of people complain to him year in, year out, that the lighting conditions in there were terrible for basic camera equipment. Even when the sun came streaming through, cast a rainbow of divine splendour across the pews and it almost felt like Heaven itself was manifesting in the room. Did the tourists marvel at this natural phenomenon? No, they clicked, flashed and videoed and tried to catch the miracle on film and watched it through tiny view holes and completely missed the point. The first time they would see it is when they got home and processed their photos or watched their film and said to themselves, 'Oh, that didn't come out very well. The effect was much better there. These things never seem to capture the moment properly, do they?'

Most people are not there for the moment when it happens. He wondered how many miracles have been missed because the chosen one could not get the lens cap off quick enough.

Something made him stop in the middle of the cathedral. There had been an unusual noise and he waited to see if it returned.

He was about to shrug it off when it happened again, a mournful sob being carried on a breeze. There was a movement from the corner of his eye but when he turned there was nothing there. Not even anything for something to have hidden behind.

Even though he was sure he was alone, he could not help himself.

«Hello?» he called and his voice broke on the second syllable.

Would he have felt better if someone had replied? If someone had said, 'I am here for you, Claude,' or something similar? At least he would have known that there was someone there. The fact that there was no response to his call did not mean there was no one there. It could just mean that that someone was still not answering.

A movement from behind him created a draft against the back of his neck and he wheeled again only to see the candles flicker. He shivered as the temperature dropped a couple of degrees.

That was the other thing about churches; yes, they were spectacular in the daylight but at night they became as creepy as He- as anything.

There was a definitive noise of solid movement that came from the confessional booths. As he got closer he could see a pair of feet from under the door.

«Hello?» he called more assuredly and opened the door.

Inside was a little old man. He was dressed in a thick raincoat and held a gnarled walking stick in his hands. His white hair had deserted his scalp a long time ago and he had made no effort to compensate elsewhere. He had a thin band of his remaining blades running from ear to ear. His angular chin was peppered with two-day-old stubble and his lips were tight and puckered. His eyes were closed and his head was leaning on the back wall. The priest rolled his eyes.

«Mr LeClerc,» he urged but got no response. He gave the man a prod with his finger. «LeClerc,» he barked a bit louder and the man snuffled to attentiveness.

He blinked and allowed his surroundings to come into view. Eventually he focused on the priest before him.

«Frollo?» the man asked.

«Yes,» Father Frollo replied wearily.

«It is I, LeClerc,» LeClerc told him.

«I know who you are, Robert,» Frollo said. «I am wondering why you are still here.»

«Argh,» LeClerc growled. «I slept again?»

Frollo nodded at him and offered a hand of assistance to pull him from the booth.

The old man accepted the help and pushed up against his walking stick. His body was twisted over, almost doubled.

«Why do you spend so much time here, Robert?» Frollo asked as he held on to the man's arm, waiting patiently for him to find his balance.

«Ha, in these Godless times you would make people stay away?» LeClerc teased.

«There are those who need God's touch,» Frollo said, «but there are also those who are firmly on the right path.»

LeClerc nodded sagely to himself.

«You know I do not have family, Frollo,» LeClerc said. «I have no real home. This place reminds me of happier times.»

«Ah yes,» Frollo remembered. «You were an altar boy here, is that right?»

«I was an orphan, taken in by the church. This place was my home,» LeClerc told him.

«Do not allow yourself to get depressed, Robert,» Frollo soothed. «Things are not all that bad. You *do* have a home and you have friends.»

«I do?» LeClerc asked with surprise and then understood. «You and God, I suppose?»

Frollo laughed. «Well, yes, of course. But, no, I meant those people I have seen you in here with. On many times.»

«You have noticed me with them?»

«Robert, you are not so old as to have slipped into the background completely,» Frollo remarked. «Although I think that is what you would like. You have been coming here for so many years that you have become one of the permanent features to me. If something changes from the usual then I do notice, yes.»

LeClerc sighed.

«Then I am truly sorry,» he said.

Frollo's smile wavered slightly and he frowned at the man.

«Whatever for?»

Frollo's mind was filled with rage, guilt, pain, envy, hatred, spite, loss, betrayal; every negative emotion that had a name and a few hundred that did not. But encompassing all of them was an overwhelming feeling of love; unadulterated, unconditional and unequivocal devotion and that was the worst part. How could something so wonderfully pure be conjoined with such negativity? It was unbearable.

He had taken himself up the four hundred steps to the top of the South Tower and threw himself off. The towers were only just closing so there were still a few tourists watching the sun set over Paris.

LeClerc was sat on one of the pews in the church and listened to the screams coming from outside. He was distractedly playing with something in his hands, flipping a small silken bag over to reveal the inset, green gem then tossing it over again.

He came to a decision, stood and hobbled into the aisle where he stretched and straightened his body. He tucked his walking stick under his arm and strolled purposefully to the front of the church where he veered off and entered the vestry.

# 8 (*Maintenant*)

## Earthenware and Crystal

It took a few minutes for Penny to show her father how to use the remote control and then she had to stand there and listen while he complained that, out of two hundred and fifty channels, how was it he was getting adverts on every one? Eventually he found German channel *RTL* airing a collection of '80s' Hip Hop which held his attention. She used the opportunity to unpack her stuff and freshen up. While he took his turn, she had a quick search on the internet for any news about Leeds but there were only stories of speculation and cover up. She thought about sending emails to her friends to find out how they were but considered it might seem a bit desperate after being away for only a couple of days.

Even though she *was* desperate, she did not do it. There was no telling that they would be thinking about checking email after everything that had happened and if there is one thing worse than sending messages out begging for attention, it is not getting any replies.

When he was ready, they left their room via the narrow passage to find somewhere mutually agreeable to eat. Her opening bid of *McDonalds* had been raised with *L'Arpège* but then withdrawn when he considered her attire. She upped her bid to *Planet Hollywood* and she thought he was going to have a heart attack. Since they had started walking east along the bank of the Seine, they decided to continue to Île de la Cité. A police cordon caused them to divert their route and, after winding down a couple of back streets, they came to *Le Vieux Bistro* that overlooked Notre Dame and a flashing display of police and ambulance lights.

The restaurant served traditional French cuisine so while Professor was quite eager to order the boeuf bourguignon, Penny was put out by the lack of hamburger options so ordered the same.

Their conversation was stilted again. It seemed that they only ever had a fully flowing discourse when they were bickering at each other about trivialities. They were only ever comfortable in each other's company when they were staring death in face. She hated to think what their sentiments would rise to if they dared to broach a serious topic of debate. Like politics, perhaps, or religion or why it had been so easy for him to desert her for so long.

"Is it nice to be back?" she asked him.

"I haven't been away so much," he replied. "I'm not sure that Paris means as much to me as it does you."

"Really?" Penny asked in surprise. "You managed to live here for quite a few years didn't you?"

"I did," he said and then corrected himself. "We did. It was a city that was easy to lose yourself in. Whether we were hiding from the prying eyes of society or running for our lives."

"I thought they always ran from you," she said.

"No, not always. You must remember the Catacombs and what we uncovered there?"

She shuddered. "Ugh. Don't remind me. That place was disgusting. I'd never seen them like that before, or again since."

"They had been living in perpetual darkness for centuries," he explained. "It was only natural that they would -"

"I asked you not to remind me," she growled. "They were just plain creepy and still give me nightmares."

A waitress brought over a bottle of red wine that Professor tasted and approved of. She poured half a glass for him and was about to stop at the same level for Penny when she gave her a nod of encouragement to keep going.

Professor rolled his eyes at his daughter's lack of finesse while she just glared back with petulance.

"What do you remember about your mother?" he asked.

Penny was taken aback by the sudden personal invasion.

"Nothing," she answered too casually. "You always said that she died when I was still a baby."

"You were a 'baby' for nearly five years," he stated. "I'm surprised nothing managed to ingrain itself in all those years."

Penny started to pick at a bread roll while she thought.

"My memories get so muddled," she said. "I'm not sure what was real and what images belong to the right ones. I think I remember you being so very happy."

He frowned ever so slightly.

"When it was just you and me," she continued, "you were always so strict and jobsworth, you know? I don't remember having any fun with you. It was all vampires and trying to wipe them out. But I sometimes have these dreams where you and I are in parks and on boats and we are laughing so much."

"Those aren't just dreams, Penelope. We did all have a lot of fun together but when she died my joy died with her."

"I am sorry," Penny sympathised. "I wish I had known her better."

Professor inhaled sharply to hold back the impending tide of emotion.

"She absolutely adored you," he said. "I often thought she loved you more than me."

"What a silly thing to think," she scoffed.

"Why? Why wouldn't she? You were everything that embodied unconditional love. Complete dependency. If there was ever a being that could make someone feel absolutely needed then it's a baby. You deserved to be loved more than me and I did not begrudge that. I knew that it do not mean that she did not love me at all, just not as much. And as much as she did was more than enough for me."

Penny could feel herself welling up. It was bad enough when you had to listen to someone lamenting over lost love. It was bad enough when you had to listen to someone telling you how much they really loved you. It was the worst ever when you had to listen to someone doing both and all you wished for was that you could know what it felt like to have those emotions.

This was all too soon. They had not even been here a day. They had not even had their starters yet. But then again, when was the right time to bare your soul? To allow the floodgates to open and let it all come pouring out? It was always too easy to say, 'This isn't the right time. I'll say something tomorrow.' The next thing you know, fifty years had passed and it still was not the right time. There is very little point making confessions to a grave stone; it does not help anyone.

"I have an image of someone but I'm not sure if it was her or not," Penny confessed.

"Go on," he urged.

"I remember curly hair, lots of it, pouring over my face like a waterfall. It's light brown but looks like gold when the sun shines through it. Blue eyes and a laugh that swells my heart."

She looked up to see he had a tear rolling down his cheek.

"Oh, god, I'm so sorry," she blurted.

"Don't be," he told her and wiped the tear away with his napkin. "The pair of you would play that game for hours; her dangling her hair in your face and you trying to grab it. It is a wonderful image to carry with you, Penelope, and I am so glad that you felt able to share it with me. Thank you."

"There is a downside, too," she said, unsure whether she should sully the moment. "Sometimes - with the nightmares - she appears to me like them."

"'Them'?"

"The vampires," she said. "Red eyes and sharp teeth."

They sat in silence for a few seconds until Penny chuckled.

"But even when she looks like that, she's coming to save me and I'll embrace her," she said.

"I suppose it could mean -"

"I shouldn't try to analyse it," she interrupted with a laugh. "Sometimes dreams are just that. And what with everything we've been through it's not surprising that bloody vampires end up infecting everything. They managed to destroy practically everything in reality so there's no reason why they shouldn't try to fuck up my mind as well."

"Language," Professor scolded.

"Well, that didn't last long, did it?" she grumbled.
"Quite," he agreed.

# BOOK 4

## 1 (*Allors*)

## Delirium

Professor marched into the living room to see Mary bent over on the floor. She was dangling her hair into Penelope's face who was having ecstatic giggling fits as the strands tickled her naked body and refused to keep still long enough for her to grab.

He smiled at the two of them. Penelope was still an infant but was on the verge of walking. Every day had been an exercise in coercing her to walk from Mary to him and then back again. It very rarely happened though. As soon as one of them stopped supporting Penelope, she would just drop to the floor and crawl across the gap. They would pull faces and make noises that just amused her to no end so when she was required to try again she would just drop to all fours for the reaction.

"Look, your father is here," Mary told Penelope without looking up. "Would he like to join us in a game?"

He stepped forward. "What are we playing?" he asked.

"Just the usual," Mary said. "Get your clothes off and lie down," she instructed and his advance faltered. He tutted at her when he realised she was joking.

He knelt down beside her and looked at the baby. Still 'just a baby'? He was unsure. The three of them did have such good times together, it was hard not to think of Penelope as anything but an extension of the woman he loved.

There, now. Penelope. That was not as hard as he expected, was it?

He lightly tickled his fingers over his daughter's shoulders and down her ribs. Penelope squirmed under his ministrations and giggled again.

"She will be five soon," Mary commented as she watched the bonding. "Five years, Abraham. Can you believe it?"

"Has the time gone that quickly?" he asked as he tickled Penelope's neck. She scrunched her shoulders up and trapped his fingers. The more he wriggled his fingers to free them the more it tickled her and she screamed with laughter. He could not help himself but chuckle as well.

"On the contrary," Mary said. "I cannot believe that it has *only* been five years. It feels like we have all been together forever. I can barely remember how it was before we had her."

"Good," he replied curtly. "I do not want to remember those days."

"So you do not regret her?" Mary asked.

He turned to face her. "When I see the joy she brings to you? I could not deny you that, no matter what misgivings I may have."

"What misgivings?" Mary demanded.

"None," he said jovially. "I actually have none."

"Good," she said, "because I didn't want to have to slap you."

Penelope had used the opportunity to roll herself over and crawl across the carpet.

"Watch this," Mary said. "We've been practising."

"Why have I got this feeling of impending doom," Professor groaned. "You haven't been teaching her any of your colourful colloquialisms, have you?"

Mary just eyed him with disdain while she wrestled with Penelope to get her pinned into a nappy.

"Just you wait and see," she sniffed as she finished her wrapping.

"Penelope," Mary said and the baby stopped fidgeting and looked at her mother. "Vampires, darling."

Mary took her hands away to allow Penelope to roll onto her front and crawl off. She scrabbled across the floor and disappeared behind a chair.

"You taught her to hide?" Professor asked. "Well done, I think."

"No, you silly old sod," Mary cried. "She's not hiding, she's -"

They both looked up at the window above the chair Penelope was behind.

"It's early, isn't it?" Mary demanded.

"No, it's past eleven," he told her.

She hurriedly gathered her dresses and got to her feet.

"Why didn't you say something?"

"I was about to," he said, "but I got distracted."

He pulled himself up just as there was a knock at the door.

"We're too late," she said.

"How many?" Professor demanded.

"I can't tell," she said. "That many."

"Damn," he snarled. "We knew this day would come."

"But not today," she replied and looked over at the corner chair.

Professor crossed the room, picked up his cane and drew his epee from within.

"Not today," she growled and he looked up. Her eyes were ablaze with red fury and her teeth were clenched as her canines slowly lengthened from her gums.

She picked up a poker from the fireplace and charged through the window into the street. There followed an unearthly scream and a couple of flashes of light.

The front door burst open and two large vampires stumbled in, tripping over the wooden fragments and each other.

"Please stay there, Penelope," he prayed in hushed tones.

The first one lumbered into the room causing the doorframe to splinter as he brushed against it. Professor lunged at the oversized demon but it was considerably faster than its size implied. It parried the thrust with its arm and swung across with its other knocking Professor across the side of the head. Even though he had carved a chunk of flesh from its forearm, it had not emitted even a grunt. This was going to be a tough battle.

Professor tucked in his shoulder and rolled across the floor to put some distance between him and his aggressor.

The vampire did not hesitate in its advance and now the second one had entered the room. Its attention was directed towards the corner chair.

"No," Professor ordered and tried to intercept but the first blocked his passage with another hefty swipe of its arm. The blow caught Professor directly in the chest and sent him hurtling into the brick fireplace.

The second vampire reached the chair and pulled it aside. Penelope jumped from her sudden discovery but found the sensation of shock to be very amusing and she giggled.

The vampire growled at her, baring its fangs and furious red eyes but, again, she just laughed.

Professor had lost his sword so reached out for the first thing that came to hand. A brass dustpan. He swung it at his harbinger of imminent demise and used the thin edge to slice across its eyes. The pan blinded it and allowed him to scrabble out of the way before it crashed into the fireplace.

Professor shoulder charged the second vampire but it barely shifted, meanwhile he rebounded onto the sofa.

The first vampire got to its feet; the slash across its face sealed shut and its eyesight returned. It bore down on Professor and pinned him into the cushions. His left arm was propped up, blocking the vampire from sinking its teeth into him but the way that it trembled indicated that either his strength would give up soon or it might just pop out of its socket. His right arm was trapped under the vampire's flank. He was able to punch the monstrosity in its side but it did not achieve anything.

He looked to the corner of the room to see the second reach down for Penelope.

"Mary!" he screamed. "The baby!"

The streets flared again and then she returned through the destroyed window – a dark angel of maternal fury – tackled the second vampire and the pair rolled across the carpet into the end wall.

It was no good. There really was nothing that they could do. Neither could come to the assistance of the other. Neither could gain an advantage over their opponent and, when the inevitable time came when they would be overpowered, the other vampire would help its brethren. And then they could take their time with the baby.

On top of that there were still the vampires outside who would be on their way in to sway the odds even further.

Mary was sat on top of her adversary but holding his hands at bay.

«Penelope,» she cried. «Vampires, darling. To your father.»

It had to be the most wondrous sight he had ever witnessed.

Penelope's eyes lit up as she realised that she was going to be able to finish her party trick. Not only that, but she was going to be able to perform it directly for her father. She leaned over behind the chair then emerged holding a stake in her hand. She tried crawling forward but found the process a bit cumbersome. She lifted her hand to the chair and pulled herself to her feet. Then, with the stake firmly held in her other hand she took a trepidatious step forward.

Professor could not help but smile. There were too many fathers in the World who missed these important moments, either because of work obligations or just simply because they had their backs turned.

Penelope moved her other leg forward; her eyes were set firmly on her father and her face was beset with pure concentration. She took another step and, with that one, she was free of the support of the chair. She teetered on the brink.

He did not dare take his eyes off her for fear that he might cause her lapse in focus. His smile spread even further and she bathed in the warmth of his encouragement. She took two more steps.

He lifted his hand out to her and she reached forward with her free hand. Another step but a look of worry spread across her face as her balance was failing. She was toppling forward and she tried to stop herself falling with her trailing leg. Her momentum got the better of her and her other leg pulled forward. She was almost running to his outstretched hand and she grabbed it to keep herself up. He curled her up in his arm, tucking her under his armpit. He took the stake and thrust it into the vampire's side between its fourth and fifth ribs.

It howled with rage and pain as the stake pierced its heart and reared off Professor. He rolled from the couch, scooped up his daughter and screened her from its blast of dying light. He grabbed the stake again and threw himself onto the chest of Mary's enemy, plunging the point through its sternum.

He averted his daughter's gaze as it erupted.

He picked up his sword, child and love and they charged out the back of the house, into the night streets as the first of the vampires from outside entered their building.

He looked into the face of his child. Penelope was still smiling at him and he had never been so proud of anyone, ever. He had never felt this way before. He was bursting with such emotion that he could have cried.

## 2 (*Maintenant*)

## Notre-Dame

Anjo and Matilda stepped through the maze of emergency vehicles to the steps of the cathedral.

«Who was first on the scene?» Anjo demanded and a female gendarme made herself known.

«There are witnesses who state he just jumped from there,» she declared and pointed up to the south tower.

«There was nothing else?» he asked. «No notes of any kind?»

«Not that have been found yet,» she told him. «That priest,» she pointed to an aged cleric being questioned by a gendarme, «says he was in the cloisters at the time of the incident and was not aware of anything happening until we knocked on the door. Father Frollo - the victim - had locked up as per normal and then committed suicide. Just like that.»

Anjo snorted with derision. «If only it was ever that simple. Keep asking around.»

«This is not the same,» Matilda declared after carefully looking over the body.

«It is,» Anjo argued. «Another person with no reason to kill themselves has done so in a very inconvenient manner.»

«Inconvenient for who?» Matilda asked.

«You are not funny,» he said. «Why take the time to climb four hundred steps and kill yourself amongst so many people who could potentially stop you?»

«A cry for help?»

«Nonsense. A cry for help is to look like you're trying without really trying. When you throw yourself from two-hundred feet your intention is to die, not to hope that someone might catch you.»

«Shall we talk to the other priest?» Matilda asked and pointed to the bald, old man stood at the top of the steps.

Anjo watched the crooked man as he talked to one of the officers.

«Not know,» he decided. «Get hold of these statements tomorrow and we can come back later if anything comes to mind.»

«What now then?» Matilda demanded.

«Back to the station and set up a network. We need to find out a connection and predict the next move before it happens.»

## 3 (*Maintenant*)

# The Inconveniences of Following a Pretty Woman through the Streets in the Evening

Penny hated to admit it, but it had actually been a very pleasant evening. Despite the return to their roles of 'admonishing father' and 'obstreperous daughter,' after such heartfelt revelations it turned out to be only a brief setback. Their conversation picked up and they spent the rest of the meal discussing the World and their experiences thereof.

Penny had discussed Italy: Rome and then Florence, where she first developed her interest for intense learning. From there she went straight to Britain where she studied in London for a couple of decades before heading to Edinburgh and then ending in Leeds.

He awed her with tales of his travels from Europe, through Africa, around western Asia and back into Europe again.

Her tales regaled the architecture and unique culture of each city as she searched for a meaning to her existence, then held a footnote of vampiric activity. His was a ceaseless struggle of domination over the hordes of undead in an attempt to root out its source, which happened to occur in different places.

Both of them seemed to be looking for the same answer but it was always beyond their reach. To the extent that they did not even know if they were looking in the right place. And here they found themselves, brought back together by, what? Fate? Coincidence? Inevitability?

At least his quest was over. His demons had been conquered and quelled. All that had happened for her search was that any first hand accounts were no longer viable prospects. Not that you could ever get a first hand account from a vampire without being its entrée.

Could she just drop it? Find something else? Could she be happy to replace her craving for answers in the shape of her father? Why not? After all, the desire for knowledge came when he had gone so why should they not equal each other out?

The food was excellent, the company was stimulating and the wine did its job very nicely indeed thanks. Perhaps being a catalyst to the stimulating part.

Yeah, she did not give a shit how much each bottle was costing because it was tasting good and making everything all right.

Professor paid the bill and they left the restaurant. Even though it was quite a temperate evening she felt a coldness spread over her and she huddled into his side.

"Christ, that's a creepy building in this light," she grumbled as they walked past the cathedral and she looked up at the two towers that passed an unnerving resemblance to fangs biting into the starlit sky.

## V—V

'Father' LeClerc stood on the cathedral steps and waited for the police to do everything they needed to. They closed off Frollo's office pending further investigation but eventually left and reopened the Place du Parvis for pedestrians to cross again. He watched them all go about their business and wondered if they were at all interested in the events that had just taken place.

A glint of light caught his attention and flickered in his eye as if someone was trying to catch his attention with an Aldis lamp. He focused on its source to see it was just the light's reflection off a man's walking stick and was about to move his attention elsewhere when something about his gait stirred a memory.

The man walked purposefully and with pride. There were probably hundreds of people all around him but, as far as he was concerned, they were no more consequential than autumn leaves underfoot.

The memory conjured an emotion and that was anger. But it was stupid. Why would he feel angry towards this man when the one he was thinking about must have been dead for over fifty years now?

The man he was watching now was about as relevant to the memory as his young, male companion was. And should he bestow an ancient, yet relative, emotion on the boy, too? Ah, but wait, not a boy but a girl. A young woman who had managed to hide her femininity but for two obvious features.

For the briefest of moments, she turned her head towards the church and the street light lit her face and then another associated emotion came forth.

LeClerc shook his head and considered that he must be developing Alzheimer's in his old age. It could only be a coincidence. The man? Fair enough, he was a reasonable doppelganger in his movement and the girl had a passing resemblance when she flashed her face briefly through a light with her head angled upwards and he was in an elevated position. But to rationally contemplate that they could be the same people was beyond insanity.

Insane or not, he had started to follow them across the precinct without realising.

The couple walked along in silence and crossed the Seine over Pont au Change where they followed the river westwards.

What was he hoping to achieve from this? Even in the unlikeliest event that they were the same people, would what that mean? Would it claim back those lost years? Would it rekindle that relationship? Would he get his own back?

Yes. He could do that. He could do that even if it was not them. He could allow this delirium to continue and allow him closure when he wreaked sweet revenge.

«Do you have a spare cigarette?» a voice called him from behind.

He turned to see a young man, not yet out of his teens.

«No, I do not smoke,» LeClerc replied and returned his attention to his targets but his way was now blocked by another two youths.

«What about money?» the boy from behind demanded.

LeClerc was more angry than scared. This predicament seemed to be more of an inconvenience than a threat to his safety.

«I have no money,» he growled and turned on the boy to display his dog collar. «Observe, I am a man of God and have not left with any money.»

The boy was obviously upset. «You must have something,» he spat and made a grab for LeClerc.

The old man suddenly realised his vulnerability and backed away, only to remember his retreat was impeded. The other two boys grabbed him whilst the first rifled his clothes.

«Shout and I will kill you,» the boy said calmly. He pulled out the silk purse and grimaced at it. «What the fuck is this? Are you one of those kind of priests?»

«It is nothing,» LeClerc said.

The boy pulled the strings and peered inside and was even more upset. «What the fuck?» he demanded.

«It is nothing,» LeClerc urged.

The boy calmed upon realising that it may have no immediate face value but it was obviously worth something to the old man.

«You will get us money and I will give this back,» the boy bargained.

«You will return the purse and I shall refrain from killing you,» another man stated from behind them.

They all turned to see Professor, still supporting Penny.

«No!» she admonished. «Threats of death don't work on these guys. That's too extreme. You have to bring it down a notch like, 'Give it back or I'll tell everyone at your school you have a small penis.'»

Professor scowled with aural pain.

"Where did you learn such French?" he demanded.

"You pick stuff up," she told him.

"'J'informerai votre école cela tu avez de petits pénis'?" he demanded. "That's not just 'picked up.'"

"Aw, that's basic," she stated. "A five-year-old could string that together."

«Hey!» the boy demanded and had now brandished a small flick-knife. «You two, money, now.»

His silent associates cast LeClerc to one side, the boy threw the dust filled purse on the floor.

Penny pushed her father to one side and staggered on the spot. She drew her fists up to her face. "Allons, alors, fils d'un putain-chien," she challenged and her father shook his head with absolute dismay.

The three boys just stared at her for a second and then began laughing.

The two rear guards suddenly stopped laughing and the boy looked around to see what had happened.

Penny, apparently had not changed her stance and was still standing - albeit somewhat unsteadily - ready to strike. His minions had folded in half and were writhing on the floor in pain, clutching their midriffs.

The boy was confused, angry and a bit scared. Although he was a good few feet away from her, he still jabbed his blade in her direction.

She just wobbled a bit and scrunched her eyes in concentration.

"Ta mere suce le penis d'animaux pour l'argent," she decided.

«Penelope!» Professor cried. «What the hell do you think you are doing?»

LeClerc's attention was drawn away from trying to retrieve his bag back to the young girl. That had to be more than just a coincidence. What he said and the way he said it.

The insult, the incessant bickering and the overall unusual circumstances had taken their toll with the boy and he took a step forward thinking she had become distracted. Unconsciousness came from out of nowhere as she delivered a spot-on roundhouse kick to the side of his head and he crumpled on top of his compatriots.

Penny wobbled on the spot as her striking foot returned to its original position.

«My apologies, Father, for my daughter's language,» Professor stuttered as he picked LeClerc up. «You try to teach your children right from wrong but, at some stage, you have to let go and hope they follow the right path.»

LeClerc was unable to answer. He was too shocked to speak. He was insane, he had to be, that was the only explanation.

But if he *was* insane then surely he would not know that he was insane. Or care.

When he had returned to the sanctuary of the Cathedral, he took the opportunity to pull out a small silver locket from under his shirts, pop it open and inspect its contents.

He did not care if he was insane or not. Events were coming full circle.

## 4 (*Maintenant*)

## Result of the Dangers

Professor had helped LeClerc to his feet while Penny tried her best to stay on hers. He asked the Priest if he wanted an ambulance.

«No, thank you. I am fine,» LeClerc replied graciously.

«The police then?»

«Heavens, no,» LeClerc laughed. «I think they may have learned a lesson more worthy than the police could ever teach them.»

Professor nodded and smiled.

«Besides, God will judge them eventually.»

«Can we help you to get to somewhere?» Professor asked.

«I think your young lady is after more attention than me,» LeClerc stated as Penny staggered towards the wall to lean over it. «I am only across the bridge at the Cathedral.»

«If you are sure,» Professor said and bowed to take his leave. He took Penny's arm and tossed it over his shoulder and they continued on their way back to the hotel.

LeClerc pondered following them some more but realised how suspicious it might look if he was to be discovered again. Instead he looked down at the three prostrate youths at his feet and picked up the silk bag.

«Yes, you will learn your lesson tonight,» he told them and pulled a handful of hair from each of them. The boys yelped from the sharp pain but just curled themselves into tighter defensive balls.

LeClerc slipped the hair into the bag and calmly wandered back to the Cathedral where he locked the main door behind him and made his way up to the pulpit. He opened the Bible that was there and turned the pages to Romains, chapter thirteen, then traced his finger down to verse eight. He placed the silk bag in the middle of the book and pulled it open; the few clumps of hair unravelled onto the page.

He placed his palms onto the Bible, either side of the bag, closed his eyes and recited,

> "Je passe l'eau sans nacelle,
> Je passe l'eau sans bateau,
> Ma mere est oiselle,
> Mon pere est oiseau."

The lips of the bag rustled and a gentle breeze picked up from behind him flustering the naked candle flames. It whistled around the room collecting dust within its maelstrom until it started to generate an almost tangible quality.

It circled the grand hall and came to rest in front of LeClerc at the pulpit. He opened his eyes and, despite this being the fourth time he had looked at the creature, he was still taken aback by the ghastliness of it.

Without the dust motes giving it a form, it also seemed composed of condensation within a heat haze. Its transparent, insubstantial mass caused the light behind it to bend, giving it the appearance of definitive mass. It was half the size of a human adult but also much bulkier; it had the volume of a human adult if not the stature.

It had facial features although they were hard to specifically identify. Its gelatinous qualities meant there was nothing to focus on. Your eyes would keep slipping through. It also meant that its shape would keep shifting.

Generally, though, it gave the appearance of extreme deformity. Its face was practically flat, its nose seemed to be lacking a bridge so its nasal cavity was exposed to the world. Its lower jaw was thrust forward so its teeth jutted up over its top lip. Its teeth were jagged and uneven. A heavyset forehead forced its eyebrows into a precipitous outcrop that would have overshadowed its eyes if it had any. A few strands of hair wafted in its own updraft and a lump of crumpled cartilage sprouted from either side of its head in some manner of ears.

The whole disfigurement was topped off by an expression of frustrated rage.

LeClerc was relieved that the spirit had delivered itself to him in this manner. It was a dichotomous being fuelled by contradictory emotions and, because of that, existed as two physical manifestations. This one was its vision of harboured animosity whereas the other - its propensity for affection - was the face of a pretty young girl. High cheek bones, wide eyes and long billowing hair.

The pair of incarnations were not mutually exclusive, though, and tended to flow through each other. This version before him was even more hideous when following the vision of innocence and beauty and more so again when the two merged. It was an insult as well as an ocular affront to think such beauty should come hand-in-hand with brutal ugliness. It wavered in front of his face, seemingly unwilling to reveal its better half to him.

«Let no debt remain outstanding,» LeClerc told it.

Just before it turned, he saw her eyes looking out from her cage of hideousness, imploring him to stop the carnage, but she was whisked away before he could even consider changing his mind. Even if he wanted to.

LeClerc returned to one of the side offices and retrieved a small leather satchel. He opened the flap and poured its contents over the desk. There were ten small, paper envelopes. He rifled through them, checking the letters that were written on each one, and, finally, chose one.

The spirit passed through the Cathedral doors leaving a dirty stain where its collected dust body got left behind.

Now it was nothing more than an isolated draft that crossed the precinct, weaving its way between the last of the late night revellers. Each person that the ghost brushed past had an involuntary shudder as its coldness crept across their skin.

It drifted over the Seine to the opposite bank where a group of youths had gathered. Two teenage girls were huddled together and laughing at the three boys who had accosted LeClerc. They were still nursing their sore bits.

«I don't know, Corky, maybe *we* should have tried to take the old man,» one of the girls screeched.

«I told you, Teri, to shut up,» the instigator, Corky, told the females but they continued their raucous cackling.

«You were beaten up by a girl,» Teri roared. «You should have seen your face after Eric and Yellow had been laid out.»

«Not that Yellow will be doing much laying again for a while,» the other girl added and they upped their volume.

One of the bigger boys actually managed to appreciate the pun and chuckled while still massaging his testicles.

«What are you fucking laughing at, Yellow?» Corky demanded.

«Hatti said a funny,» Yellow said defensively.

Corky looked like he was going to exploded but then he changed his mind. He searched the air around him for inspiration and then drew his knife. The joviality stopped.

«There's no need to be like that,» Yellow complained.

Corky lifted the knife and dragged it across his throat ensuring that the blade dug deep enough to cut through his trachea. He did not make a sound while doing it apart from a gargled hiss as his windpipe ruptured.

His hand dropped to his side and he just stood there staring back at his comrades as they stared at him. The gargling noise increased as his blood poured into his throat and began suffocating him. His legs weakened and he dropped to his knees. His eyes rolled up into their sockets and he fell forward. His blood generously filled the cracks in the pavement around him.

Was it a joke? A trick? The four youths did not know what to make of it.

Then Yellow stepped forward and drew the others' attention. He was frowning in concentration and looking around him. He focussed on the low wall that ran along the bank of the river, calmly walked up to it and then slammed his forehead against the corner. The sharp edge of the wall sunk into his skull just below his hairline and his continued downward momentum flipped the roof of his head off leaving him looking like a *Pez* dispenser.

His body slumped to the floor scraping blood and brain down the wall. His legs did not stop twitching for ten minutes.

Before Yellow had crumpled to the ground, the horror had finally settled itself into the girls' consciousnesses and they started to panic. They looked to Eric for some kind of support but he had the same expression of pained incomprehension that had crossed the other boys.

«Eric?» Teri asked, fearing of what he was likely to do next but mostly fearing that whatever it was that was happening would strike her next.

V—V

Anjo had cleaned off the whiteboard in his office. It was mounted on, and took up the entirety of, one wall. It had previously been littered with press clippings dated at least three years old, some sort of network of names and a littering of profane graffiti.

He had now listed the names of the three suicides in three different colours and started tree diagrams of friends, family and associates. Next to that, pinned in the middle of the board, was a large map of the city with the three incident scenes marked on; colour coded to match the victims. On the other side were the names of the places and a series of associated themes hoping to link any of them.

Matilda and he were staring at the board. He had his jacket off and shirtsleeves rolled up, she was sitting in a chair next to his desk. He tapped the end of a green marker against his chin.

«Nothing,» Anjo growled. «Less than nothing. These two at tourist attractions are cancelled out by the Boulevard de la Chappelle.»

«Unless Mineur had just come from Monmatre,» Matilda suggested.

«He had not,» Anjo stated. «He had just come from work from the east.»

«Two blue collar workers and a priest,» Matilda noted.

«Again, the two's connection is countered by the third.»

«They are all male,» Matilda suggested.

«So we shall keep an eye out for all men in the Paris area,» Anjo snapped and Matilda just shrugged.

«So what's next?» Matilda asked.

«Google,» Anjo stated.

His phone rang and Matilda lifted it from the receiver.

«Allo?» she looked up at Anjo. «He is. I will.» She hung up.

«Well?» he demanded before she had a chance to say anything.

«The museum curator has been murdered,» she told him.

«'Murdered'?»

«Yes, shot twice in the chest and once in the head.»

«Coincidence?» he pondered and she shrugged.

«Also,» she said. «Three more suicides.»

«Already? Witnesses?»

«Two girls.»

«Where?»

«Quai de Gesvres.»

Anjo's eyes lit up.

«Just across from Île de la Cité,» he declared. «Our man may have made his first mistake.»

He grabbed his jacket and dashed for the door while she calmly gathered her belongings together then followed him out.

«Or woman,» she shouted after him.

Anjo cursed himself for getting involved. Every quiet moment gave his brain a chance to question what the hell he was doing. Was it because he wanted to be a policeman again? Was it because of some misguided, altruistic belief that he was going to be able to make the world a better place? Or was it because of her?

He had to answer 'Yes' to all of them. She had sparked something in him, not with her pretty face or petite form but because of her enthusiasm. Everything he had tried to do to her had backfired. Instead of him quelling her fires of eagerness, she had fanned his dying embers. He had remembered what it was like to really catch a bad guy. To do the absolutely right thing in the knowledge that it would make a difference.

She had been right. This was big. This was not some unsolvable, random killing in a darkened alley for a couple of hundred Euros. This was not something that would waste hundreds of hours of manpower trying to track down some crack-whore who would probably be dead in an alley.

If they found the root of this problem then they could stop it and prevent other people from dying. The person responsible for this was a twisted psychopath who needed stopping for the good of society. And there were bigger issues behind this; connections and reasons for it happening. If there was an undercurrent that insidious in the city, then he wanted to flush it out.

He was barely aware of his surroundings as this internal debate raged. It fuelled his intent to a flaming pyre of his jaded principles and allowed his original devotion to burst forth, phoenix-like.

There was that and the hypnotic state the flashy lights on his car always put him in.

He came to attention when they reached Place du Châtelet and an abundance of flâneurs blocking their way. They pushed through the throng to the front and were allowed access to the scene after showing their badges to the officer on crowd control.

Matilda went straight to the body of Corky and looked closely at it while Anjo marched over to the incident officer.

«Well?» he demanded.

«Two girls say he slit his own throat and the other bashed his own brains out on the wall,» the officer said.

«And the third?» Matilda asked as she inspected the puddle of blood around Corky's body.

«Down there,» the officer stated and pointed over the wall onto the parallel road, Voie Georges Pompidou.

Matilda looked over to see a few more police. One was taking photographs of Eric's body just lying next to the river. «What happened to him?» she asked.

«He drowned,» the officer said.

«You pulled him out? He doesn't look very wet,» she commented.

«No, he put his face in the river and drowned himself.»

«Where are the girls?» Anjo asked.

«In the ambulance. They seem to be in shock.»

Anjo indicated to Matilda to follow him over. As they got nearer they could see Teri and Hatti were huddled next to each other in the ambulance with a thermal sheet wrapped around them. A plain clothed man was sitting with them and making notes on a large pad of paper.

«What do you think?» Anjo asked.

«Not the same as the first two but the same as the last,» she stated.

«Yes,» he said. «The same *modus operandi* but different. Different how? Different why?»

Matilda shrugged. «He has the means to get people to kill themselves but he has more than one reason to kill people.»

Anjo nodded. «Yes, two different motives from the same killer.»

They reached the open doors of the ambulance and looked in.

«Croquis,» Anjo greeted and the man looked up quizzically. He peered at them from over the top of a pair of half-rimmed glasses.

«Inspector Anjo?» he enquired. «Why are you here? This is not a murder.»

«No, but it may have something to do with a case we are working on,» Anjo explained. «What have you got?»

«The girls said that the three boys tried to mug an old man tonight but were stopped by a young woman,» Croquis reported. «This is them.»

Croquis held up his sketchpad to the inspectors and there were rough drawings of Professor and Penny.

«Girl?» Anjo asked.

«Er, yes,» Croquis replied. «This one.» He pointed to the drawing with the short hair.

«I want copies when you are finished,» Anjo demanded and Croquis nodded.

«We plaster the drawings up everywhere around here,» Anjo told Matilda. «Hopefully someone will have seen them during the evening and we can either find out where they were going or where they came from.»

«Notre Dame,» Teri said weakly. «We saw them cross the bridge from Notre Dame.»

«Croquis, give them to me now,» Anjo ordered.

«But they are not finished,» the artist complained as he handed the pad over.

«These are an odd couple,» Anjo explained. «Someone would've seen them.» He passed the pad to Matilda. «Copies, now. Get constables onto the island and ask around. Send someone to the hospital and see if the waitress recognises them.»

Matilda took the pad and marched off to the nearest group of officers to bark some orders.

«They will know we are getting closer,» Anjo said. «They will not rest easy tonight.»

# 5 (*Maintenant*)

## Little Sword in Pocket

Cunningham was nonchalantly walking along the hallway of a hospital. He smiled pleasantly at the nurses who stared at his scarred visage and they either tried to smile back or turned away quickly from being caught gawking. He did not mind, so much, he was quite used to it.

His two associates followed a few paces behind him in an attempt to not look too conspicuous. They did not want to look completely *in*conspicuous, just not too conspicuous. There is nothing that comes to the attention of people more than someone who was overtly conspicuous or someone who managed to blend into the background. It was always the latter who would come to the memory as an all important after thought.

Cunningham walked up to the ward reception desk and the nurse behind raised her head to him.

«Hello, I am here to see my sister,» he said. «Marie Témoin.»

The nurse looked down at her notes until she found an entry.

«She is down the corridor in room sixteen, on the left. She is heavily sedated at the moment, so you probably won't get much of a reaction from her.»

«That is okay, I just want to be there if she needs me,» he replied. «Thank you.»

He indicated to his companions to stay there and he progressed down the ward. He came to the room and gently opened the door.

It was dark inside apart from a solitary bed-side lamp shining a spotlight on the floor next to the bed. The waitress from the café was lying in it with her hand bandaged and an intravenous drip, feeding her a steady flow of drugs.

He stepped inside, quietly closed the door behind him and walked over to a chair beside her bed. He angled the lamp to shine into her face and her eyes clenched from the assault.

«Marie? Can you hear me?» he called softly.

Her face reacted to his voice and she inhaled deeply.

«Marie? Ah, hello, Marie. How are you feeling?»

«Hallo?» She blinked her eyes to try to focus to the brightness.

«Let me move that for you,» Cunningham offered and redirected the spotlight off her eyes.

«Thank you,» she said.

«Are you feeling rested?» he asked.

«Yes, thank you.»

«I am sorry for waking you but I need to see how you are doing and that means asking you some questions.»

Hospitals are strange places. For some reason they completely throw your senses off balance and there is an automatic process to answer some of your most intimate details to some complete stranger, presuming that s/he is a doctor. Of course this means that, with the correct tone and delivery, a real complete stranger can get questions answered without rousing too much, if any, suspicion.

«That is okay,» she said. «I don't think I was really sleeping, anyway.» She rolled her head over to look at him but could only see the glint of his eyes, his short blond hair and a warm smile.

«How is your head?» he asked.

«A little sore but okay.»

«Good,» he said. «I want you to tell me everything that happened in the café. Do you think you could do that?»

Her breathing quickened. «I don't know what happened,» she spluttered. «Really. There was lots of noise outside then the front of the café exploded and I just hid. When the noise had gone I got up and the man was on the counter. Then he made me stab him.»

«There was nothing else?» Cunningham asked. «He didn't say anything?»

«No,» she replied. «I don't think so. I don't remember.»

The warmth had slipped from his voice. «It's strange the way the brain can store things that the eyes see. All it requires is the right stimulus to release it.»

He started to pull his gun from his pocket when the door swung open. There was a gendarme with a piece of paper in his hand.

«I am sorry to disturb you, Miss Témoin,» the constable said and marched into the room after flicking the light on.

Cunningham dipped his head away from the light and pushed himself out of the policeman's way as he approached the bedside.

«Do you recognise either of these people?» the gendarme demanded and thrust the paper into her face.

She was slightly taken aback by the sudden change in mood but looked at the crude drawings of Professor and Penny.

«No,» she said.

«You are sure? They were not in the café before the accident? Or maybe you saw them pass outside?»

«No,» she said.

«May I see?» Cunningham asked and the gendarme reactively turned to give him the drawing.

Marie looked at the Swiss Guard for the first time and frowned. She had presumed he was a doctor of some sort so was very confused to see him there in jeans and, what looked like, a garish Christmas jumper.

«Who are you?» she asked Cunningham.

The constable looked from Cunningham to Marie and back again.

Cunningham clenched his jaw and pulled out his 90two.

The cinema has a lot to answer for. Its overzealous need to exaggerate life has meant that most people believe a gun shot would sound like the boom of a howitzer and, should they ever hear one for real, would not really know it. Given enough dampening, like a closed door or the ambient noise of people talking and trolleys being pushed around, a couple of gunshots could simply be mistaken for a slamming door.

Cunningham checked the corridor before stepping out of room sixteen. There was no attention being drawn his way and he received a nod of validation from his comrades. He closed the door behind him and calmly walked back past the reception where he then handed the drawings to one of the other guards.

"Call home," Cunningham ordered. "Bring in the reserves. I want them here by tomorrow morning."

# BOOK 5

## 1 (*Allors*)

## The Effect which Seven Oaths in the Open Air can Produce

Penelope looked as if she was about eight years old. She was standing in the entrance hall, waiting patiently. She was dressed according to her father's wishes: the deep purple, full-length dress with petticoats to billow the pleats. She wore a matching bonnet and shawl.

She listened carefully and heard a noise from upstairs. She took the opportunity to adjust the dress and pulled the britches from riding up her backside. She patted herself down in time for Professor to come down the stairs.

He stood in front of her and titivated with her collar until he had not changed anything about her at all.

"Are you ready?" he asked.

"Yes, sir," she replied.

"Are you prepared?" he demanded.

"Yes, sir."

"Show me," he instructed.

She shook her arms and two smoothly crafted stakes slid down into her hands.

He nodded as she inserted them back up her sleeves to click them back into their housing.

"What else?" he asked.

"The dress is loosely tied so can be shed when I pull the front bow," she told him.

"You are sure? If it snags -"

"I have tested it three times and carefully retied," she said.

"Do not interrupt me, Penelope," he chastised and she bowed her head. "I ask only out of concern. If any item does not operate as you need it to then it could mean your life. Do you understand?"

"Yes, sir," she said.

"Continue."

"I have my Damascus bowie knives on shin straps, wakizashi in my back, shuriken in my purse, retractable steel garrotte, brass knuckle lined gloves and stiletto tipped shoes."

He looked down at her elevated Mary Janes and she dutifully snapped her heels together to produce a three-inch blade from each of her shoe's toes. The well-oiled metal and locking mechanism made a noise like '*snikt.*' A repeat of the inflection caused the blades to retract with equal speed and sound.

He gave her another inspection from head to toe.

"What is the fascination with these Oriental weapons?" he enquired.

"They have history," she said.

"So does the foil," he countered. "It is elegant and discreet."

"My wakizashi lets them know I'm going to kill them, not take them out for dinner," she said tersely.

"Mind your manners, young lady," he advised but she did not avert her gaze this time.

"This is your first time out alone, Penelope. I know we have been an indomitable force together but, at some time, you will be forced to operate on your own."

"I understand that," she told him. "I am ready."

"Are you ready to kill?"

This caused her to falter.

"Penelope?"

"Yes, sir," she said positively. "If I do not kill them then I will be dead."

"Good girl," he said and smiled with pride. He had done everything he could to ensure she would be able to protect herself. First there was the camouflage; she was lucky in that vampires did not seem to concern themselves with feeding on children. Whatever the reason for that might have been did not mean they did not just indiscriminately slaughter them if they felt like it. The clothes she wore allowed her to blend into the crowd as well as the shadows and were customised to conceal any number of weapons.

The one thing that did concern him was her level of fitness. She had been trained to the absolute level that her physical limitations would allow but then a long term underlying illness had struck her down and she had been bed ridden for almost a year. He thought she was going to die. That was why he had insisted that he should not get too emotionally involved with her when she was first born. Things like that can only develop a weakness and end in heartache.

She had pulled through but had been left weakened and they had needed to start from scratch to build up her strength, stamina and reflexes.

Throughout his life in this position, and the many assistants he had taken, he had always found that the first, and largest, stumbling block was mentally preparing yourself to strike without hesitation. To kill another being without a second thought as to the consequences seemed to be something a lot of people needed time to get their head around.

He smiled at her. She wanted to jump up and down on the spot with joy. She wanted to wrap her arms around his neck and squeeze him tightly. She wanted to scream and giggle and run around and do everything that he told her was improper behaviour for a girl in her position. She did not want to draw attention to herself by acting foolishly but he actually smiled at her. He was happy with her. He was proud of her. He liked her.

She loved him and wanted to tell him but then the smile dropped.

"Off you go, then," he suggested.

Another missed opportunity but she would mention it when she delivered her report when she returned home.

If she returned home.

He opened the door for her and she stepped outside.

"Be careful," he said.

"Thank you."

He thought there should have been something else to say but he could not think of it. Then it was too late to say anything as she was already wandering down the street.

He closed the door and thought about reaching for his hat and coat but decided against it. She would know if he was following her or not. It had to happen in every parent's life, that time when you just had to let go.

She walked along the evening avenue just thinking to herself.

Would it matter if she died? What would it feel like to just stop being? Could it be any worse than the way she was feeling now?

She had just had her fortieth birthday and although she knew the relative implications of what that age should mean she could not step outside of the physical truth that she was still a child. Yes she had a lifetime's worth of experience and knowledge but she had not even started puberty yet.

She felt like she should be getting treated more like an adult but it was hard to enforce that belief when she still had not developed the inkling of breasts. She was four times her physical age *and* a late bloomer – typical!

She was frustrated with the tedium of it all. This perpetual state of adolescence could be fun if she had someone to share it with rather than her father who had about as much idea of what fun was as a Catholic priest. At least the vampires seemed to enjoy themselves.

Well, right up to the part when they got a stake through their chest, anyway.

But no, of course she was not allowed to mix with other children. Not to the extent of forging a friendship of any sorts because by this time next year they would be another year older and she would not. They would either move on or start asking awkward questions.

All she could see was how she would be living like this for the rest of her life. Not allowed to become friends with anyone because she will outlive them. So just shutting herself away from everything and everyone. She would become like him. She would still be living with him!

That thought caused a physical reaction and she reeled slightly.

She could see herself being one-hundred-and-twenty with ample bosoms, working ovaries and all the associated upholstery and still being told to brush her teeth before breakfast and be in bed before seven.

*Death before dishonour*, she decided.

In all fairness she could understand why it was necessary to isolate themselves from the surrounding society. She knew why it was important to keep a low profile from people and potential vampires alike. But none of that explained why he was so distant from her. Surely, with them both being in the same existential boat, they should turn to each other even more, not try to build more walls.

Bloody parents.

She nearly slapped her hand to her mouth for thinking that but remembered she was all by herself.

"Enfer sanglant," she muttered and smiled when there were no admonishing words.

She smiled and giggled to herself. He had let the reins loose. Maybe not let go altogether, but there was a certain amount of slack now. If she had been let out on her own this time it meant that she would be able to negotiate even more solo time in the interest of training and development.

*Damn the rules*, she thought. She could finally meet people if she wanted to.

«Damn the rules,» she said. What was he going to be able to do about it? Unless he followed her, he would never know.

«Stupid shit and fuck» she shouted and she heard someone laugh from the other side of the street.

She bowed her head with embarrassment and increased her pace. She could sense a presence getting closer.

«Hey you, little girl,» a boy shouted from behind. «Wait.»

She anxiously toyed with the stake release mechanism even though she knew he was not a vampire. The night time street of Paris held more dangers than the undead. She might have been just a girl physically but she still knew of the existence of abduction, murder and rape.

«That's not how you swear,» the boy said and she relaxed slightly.

He caught up with her and she slowed her pace. He was a teenager.

«Don't worry, I don't want to hurt you,» he said. «I just wish to educate you. If you want to survive on the streets then you need to know how to curse properly.»

«I know curse words,» she told him.

«Oh, I heard that,» he laughed. «But you don't know how to use them. You can't just shout random words. You don't even need to use curse words but need to know how to conjure a good insult.»

«Go on then,» she dared.

«Ah, you are younger than I thought,» he teased. «Perhaps I should not stain your fine reputation.»

«I thought as much,» she sniffed and picked up her pace again.

«What?» he demanded.

«You are all talk and have nothing to back it up.»

He laughed loudly. «You are not too short of the lip yourself,» he complimented. «Okay. I will tell you.»

She stopped and turned to him.

«Try this, 'Your mother sucks the penis of animals for money,'» he said and watched as her eyes widened.

He laughed again. «I knew that would be too much for your innocence to handle.» Then he noticed that her wide-eyed expression was directed over his shoulders. He turned to see a demon looming over him.

«Your mother sucks my cock for fun,» the beast screamed at him through razor sharp fangs.

The boy was mesmerised by the sight. The creature's jaw seemed to have dislocated itself to enable it to get its mouth that big and its eyes were blazing with red fury.

Then the monster's expression changed to one of perplexed discomfort. It looked down to its chest and the boy followed its gaze. Under his arm was another, at the end of the arm was a stake which had been thrust into the monster's breastplate.

The boy's vision faded to black as Penelope clamped her free hand over his eyes and spun him out of the way just as the vampire erupted into a ball of light that vanished into the sky.

The boy's strength failed him and he collapsed onto the floor.

«What?» was all he could say.

There came an unholy scream from further down the road.

«Oh shitty, blue-balled mother fuckers,» Penny commented and looked down at the boy. «There are more of them.»

«More?»

«You had better run,» she advised and he rediscovered his strength. He was lost to the darkness as the next vampire approached. She kept her face hidden from the creature, and pulled her bonnet further over her face to block as much ambient light as possible.

*Try not to reveal yourself for fear of being recognised. Let them think you are just a child. They will find no sustenance in you but they may decide you will make for good sport. Let them think that for as long as you can and you will live for longer.*

«Child,» the vampire called. It was a middle-aged woman, dressed in much the same way as she was as was the fashion then. Children were considered to be just small adults and so were clothed in such a manner.

«What happened just here?» the vampire continued while another appeared behind her; then another two.

«I am not sure, ma-ma,» Penelope said timidly. «A man was here, and then a monster and then he was gone but now I cannot see.»

They were closer but not yet close enough to get her.

*Remember, the first stumbling block is getting your mind around it. Kill without hesitation.*

Penelope pointed her right arm out at the woman and the stake jettisoned from her sleeve and embedded itself into the woman's chest. She barely managed a squeal before erupting into a ball of light.

*Without consideration of the consequences.*

The other three were startled by the attack. Even more so when the stake magically sprung back into Penelope's outstretched hand.

Her left hand dipped into her purse and she deftly let loose with four throwing stars that embedded themselves in two of her remaining foes to her right.

She allowed her arm to continue on its arc and ejected her left stake into the third vampire. He managed to move but still got it impaled in his shoulder. She activated the recoil so the thread it was attached to hauled the projectile from the punctured vampire, back to her.

Her right hand grabbed a silver ring that dangled from a bracelet on her left wrist. As she pulled, it unwound a thin chain that she wrapped around the approaching vampire's neck and pulled. The cord tightened around its throat and dug into its skin, cutting through until it reached bone.

Penelope punched it in the face, easily snapping its weakened neck.

She knew it would not stop the creature outright but it would negate its abilities to do anything until it had a chance to heal and by then she would either have neutralised the other two or be dead. Either way, it would not be a concern any more.

Another hand movement released the stake and garrotte, allowing the limp headed one to drop to the floor in pain and confusion.

The other two had recovered from their attack and resumed their advance.

Penelope raised her hands to the red bow around her neck, which caused them to pause again. That was good, it meant they were wary of her. Any weakness they showed could be used to her benefit.

She pulled at the two ends of the ribbon and her outer garments split down the middle in a flurry of velvet and lace that she lifted over her head leaving her in boys' britches and white blouse.

The vampires launched themselves at her as the deluge of cloth poured over her. She squatted and pulled her bowie knives from the sheaths strapped to her shins.

She was only little, anyway, and her comparative strength against a vampire was fairly negligible so she had been doing some research on various fighting techniques and had discovered the world of martial arts; the technique of using opponents' weight and momentum against themselves. She had not found anyone who could train her directly, after all, it was hard enough getting away from her father at the best of times and apparently it was unheard of to teach these secrets to gaijin. From what she had read, the basic principle seemed to be simple physics.

The vampires were lunging at an open space and, as they passed overhead, she thrust her knives up giving their bodies a bit of extra leverage to flip them over.

Clothes and bodies scattered to the floor and the vampires writhed around, trying to hold their insides in.

She slipped the blades back into their leather scabbards and pounced on the two disembowelled undead. She stabbed each one with her stake and they flared into the night.

She stood and walked calmly over to the last one. Its throat was just zipping closed as the skin healed itself around the wound.

The vampire's vision cleared just in time to see her swinging the half-meter Japanese sword she kept strapped to the small of her back. His head popped clean off and his hands searched the empty space until it realised it was undone. The body collapsed and detonated.

Penelope waited a second for any further assaults but none came. She tucked the sword back into its saya, strapped the errant stake back into the launch device on her left arm, wrapped the garrotte into a bracelet again and then pulled the gusset of her britches out of her backside.

She started to gather up her dresses and considered that this should qualify as a successful night out but wondered whether she really wanted her night alone to end.

Five in one evening was pretty rare so the chances of any more appearing were very slim indeed. It meant the rest of the evening was hers to do with as she wanted.

Well, as much as an eight-year-old girl was going to be allowed to do.

She dressed herself into her billows, carefully threaded them together then checked all her equipment for access and working order.

She had no specific target in mind so just walked, enjoying the peace and ability to think and, on occasion, speak freely. Although when she did open her mouth this time she ensured that there was no one lurking around to think she was mad.

Her meandering took her down to the north bank of the Seine and in the distance she could see the Eiffel Tower.

*There would be people there,* she thought and felt the need to enter into discourse with someone. Anyone. Even a drunk would prove to be pleasing company on this evening.

As she crossed Pont d'Iena, she was disappointed to discover the Champ de Mars was deserted.

Practically.

Nearing the base of the tower revealed a lone figure staring up at the monument and she had a sickening feeling that it was her father. Always one step ahead of her. But as she neared she could tell this man was much younger, much more slender and more sophisticated with his dress sense.

«Good evening, sir,» she greeted him quietly so as not to scare him.

He turned and, at first, looked straight over her head. He lowered his gaze and smiled at her. He was dressed in a lustrous dinner suit with a top hat and cane. Smart, oiled black hair glinted under the hat's rim, bright eyes sparkled behind round rimmed glasses and a thick black moustache curled above his lip to give him a permanent smile.

«It is quite late for such a young lady to be out, is it not?» he enquired amicably.

«I only live across the way,» she lied. «I like to be out here some evenings.»

He looked up at the spire poking at the stars.

«It is a magnificent sight,» he commented. «A testament to man's ingenuity.»

There was something about the man that troubled her.

«That's what it is,» he remarked. «I thought I knew you from somewhere.»

Something about him being here and no one else.

He looked at her again and frowned.

«But not actually you,» he trailed off.

*Oh, for crying out loud*, she groaned internally. *What are the odds of that? Five vampires in one evening* and *a bloody Apostle?*

«Are you *his* offspring?» the 'Apostle' asked. «No, you're more than that. You're his assistant, aren't you? A bloody child. No wonder we have not been able to pick you up. None of his others have ever lasted more than a couple of months, but you? You've become notorious. A regular talking point amongst the elders and it turns out you're nothing but a little girl.»

How could something so flattering come with something so cutting at the same time? Like it really mattered what she looked like, or what her age was, or her gender.

«Fuck off,» she growled and he reeled. «How dare you talk to me like that.»

She watched calmly as his eyes flared. «How dare *you* young lady.»

«Fuck off,» she said again. «I only take that kind of debasing abuse from my father. Not some decomposing, slur of nature like you.»

«You would do well to mind your manners, miss,» he snarled and placed his face in front of hers. «I may not be able to feed from you or turn you to my bidding but I can still flay the skin from your body and piss on your twitching flesh.»

She fluttered her eyelashes at him innocently and pouted her bottom lip.

«You can fucking try,» she said.

He grabbed at her shoulders and she just dropped her body so he was left holding the bundle of loose dresses. She slipped out under his legs and brought her feet out behind her. He was already leaning forward but the added assumption of him leaning on her had overbalanced him. Her extra shove sent him toppling over onto the ground. His hat tumbled across the floor.

She was already rolling herself to her feet but he was vampire and, although in a heap on the floor, was able to use his heightened reflexes to get up and prepare to strike.

Her hand went to her purse.

*Damn! Only two left.*

She flicked the shuriken at him but he was too quick and actually managed to catch one in mid air. He spun it back at her and it was only because she anticipated the action that let her get away with just a graze across her shoulder rather than it embedded in her neck.

She needed a distraction. *Make them watch the left hand so they do not see what the right is doing.*

She fired a stake at his head and allowed the twine to unravel. He avoided it easily but was mildly confused by the trailing tail the projectile carried. At the same time as that, she had fired her second stake up at the meshwork of iron. She hoped that this was not going to be a futile gesture. The chances of it working were very slim indeed.

He watched the wooden missile arc up to the girders and there followed a distant '*ping*' as it bounced off one and her rope began to slacken as the stake fell back to the ground.

He thought about smiling but realised he had a four-inch steel blade sticking in his thigh. He collapsed onto his other leg and Penelope used the opportunity to start running away.

She was not strong enough for him. She was not quick enough. She was not experienced enough and, despite everything she had said earlier, she was not ready to die.

«Fucking bitch!» the Duke screamed from behind her.

The vampire was not likely to give up until one of them was dead. She needed her father.

Her chest tightened as she felt the after effects of the illness start kicking in. Breathing was becoming increasingly difficult and she could not maintain her pace any longer. She stumbled to the floor and wheezed weakly.

The Apostle landed on the path a few steps away from her.

«Another trick?» he demanded but she could not respond.

He cautiously moved forward and placed his hand on her head.

«Such a shame for you to expire in this manner,» he sympathised and pulled her knife out from behind his back.

She did not react; she could not. It was as much as she could manage to keep air getting to her lungs.

«How unsatisfying,» the Apostle stated and he slumped his shoulders. «Perhaps it would be more of a punishment to keep you alive and have you looking over your shoulder every night, waiting for my return.»

Her lips had started turning blue.

«In which case, we can't have you passing away until I'm ready for it to happen,» he said and moved his hand from her face to her chest.

He rolled his eyes and tutted. «Fluid in your lungs. You mortals are so delicate and yet so unwilling to take care of yourselves. It was far too soon for you to be walking the cold, damp streets. You shall die when I am ready,» he hissed, put his lips to hers and blew.

She pushed herself away and began coughing. It felt like she was suffocating as her airways completely blocked. She managed to cough again and a mass of thick pink liquid gushed from her mouth. She got to her feet as another wave erupted from the back of her throat.

When she finally managed to control her breathing she looked around to see what direction her death might be coming from but the Apostle was nowhere to be seen. Only her knife was left in the path. She retrieved it and hurried home, trying not to look over her shoulders as she went.

This was more like she should be: a scared, little girl needing her daddy to make it all better. But that was not going to happen, was it? She would get home and blub about everything and in the end he would tell her to straighten up, quieten down and then go into where she went wrong. He would lecture her on how lucky she was to be alive and that she had compromised the degree of her involvement, not to mention their home.

She barged through the front door and called to him. Tears of frustration and fear were rolling down her muddied face. Everything was becoming tangential. She could feel her brain trying to slip away from the matter at hand and focus on inconsequential things. She wanted hot chocolate.

«Father?» she called.

She wanted to go to bed.

She stopped halfway along the hall in fear as she realised she had not taken off her shoes. She looked back to the front door to see a path of muddy footprints further damning her cause.

She stopped calling because she wanted to get this cleared up before she explained the Apostle.

See? There. She needed to prioritise. Father, Apostle, footprints, then chocolate.

She was staring at the wall while she sorted her list out and then focussed on a framed embroidery that had been mounted above an occasional table.

*Il n'y a aucun endroit comme la maison*, it told her and she thoroughly disagreed. There were about a thousand other places she would rather be right now than -

«I'm ready,» the Apostle said from behind her.

She spun around to see him standing in the doorway to the living room. They watched each other warily. She thought about calling again but realised that if he was there then he would probably be dead. If he had not been there then she could only hope that he would be back in a minute.

*A second,* she corrected herself. *Be back in a second.*

She dropped for her knives and got her hands on them just as the Apostle grabbed her forearms and pinned her back onto the table. She drew her legs up and pressed them against his stomach to push him away but he did not budge. He pressed his whole weight down on her until his feet came off the floor and he was crushing the air out of her. She could not get leverage against anything; there was no way of giving the blades any velocity to hit him and she could not move to unbalance him. All he had to do was wait for her to pass out and then he could do whatever he wanted.

*Any second now,* she hoped and looked at the front door.

«Oh, he's a long way away,» the Apostle told her.

She desperately searched for something, anything that could create a diversion or be used or be a nice image to be the last one she ever gazed upon. Certainly not the embroidery.

The brain can make connections between the most tenuous of associations and, as could be seen from Penelope's distressed state, her mind could flitter around as seemingly randomly as a butterfly.

*Embroidery,* her brain said, *Chocolate, footprints. Shoes.*

«There's no place like home,» she growled and clicked here heels together.

*Snikt.*

The Apostle flinched as the pair of three-inch blades shot out from the toes of her shoes and sank into his stomach.

She clicked her heels again and the serrated edges cut further into his flesh as they retracted.

«You -» he growled.

«There's no place like home!» she spat into his face.

*Snikt. Snikt.*

Again the knives dug deeper and he realised that his position of power had now become his undoing. He had pinned her with the full force of his mass to the extent that if he was to adjust it to the slightest degree she might be able to completely unbalance him. He could not move his hands because of her grip on her knives, he could not get back on his feet because of the tension within her legs trying to push him away and he could not lean any further forward. He bellowed in pain, anger and frustration.

«There's no place like home!» she shouted, trying to drown out the noise of his wails.

*Snikt. Snikt.*

He was falling forward, though, as the holes in his stomach became bigger and her feet slowly slipped inside his body.

«There's no place like home! There's no place like home!» she screamed maniacally, wanting to distract her mind from the sensation running through her feet as they sunk into his intestines.

*Snikt. Snikt. Snikt. Snikt. Snikt. Snikt.*

She tried wriggling her feet a bit and, at last, found some space to move.

*Snikt.*

There was a clink of one of the blades against the bone of his spine. Instead of pulling the steel back in she dug around with her toe until the obstruction gave and she had cut through the vertebra.

Another almighty scream from both of them charged her with the strength to push with her cramping legs and rip his trunk in two. His hips and legs dropped to the floor and his torso toppled onto the table next to her. She wrestled her hands free from the writhing half-dead.

His legs spasmed of their own accord and she kicked them across the floor so he would not be able to reattach himself easily.

She panted to regain her breath and could feel her will slipping. Best not to stop. Do not allow your adrenaline to turn stale in your body, for that is when shock can set in.

«Bastard!» she screamed at the Apostle and stabbed him in the arm with a bowie, pinning the limb to the table.

«Fucking bastard!» she roared and immobilised his other flailing hand with the other knife.

He wriggled helplessly then finally came to rest and stared at her.

«What now, bitch?» he demanded tenaciously.

She drew her sword from her back and pointed it at his face.

«I'm going to make you eat both your own buttocks,» she told him and his expression changed to concern, crossed with confusion.

Professor returned to their house thirty minutes later to discover the Apostle's legs had degraded to nothing more than dried husks whilst his body still remained crucified to his hall table. He noted that there were only his legs and (for some reason he did not want to know why) his rear and crotch were missing.

Penny was systematically force-feeding the vampire his own innards. Every time it looked like he was starting to heal a bit of himself she would carve another slice of him off, stuff it in his mouth and ram it down his throat with the sword hilt.

As soon as she knew that her father had seen what was going on and it had completely registered, she picked up a stake and thrust it into the Apostle's chest.

His muffled howl seemed to be more out of relief than anything else.

They silently went to their respective rooms, packed their belongings and moved out.

He never broached the subject of the situation to her, ever. He could only pray that she would also keep the finer details to herself.

## 2 (*Maintenant*)

## A Tear for a Drop of Water

Professor lifted his head from the sofa and yawned. The morning sun was trying to peak through the blinds that covered the skylights around him. He could not remember the last time he had slept so soundly. It was, quite possibly, the best night's sleep he had ever had in his life.

He took in his surroundings and his eyes fell on the half-empty bottle of Macallan whiskey on the desk.

He could have cried.

Penny awoke after having the worst night's sleep in her life. She did not want to move. Every instinct in her body told her that if she did then she would either throw up or her head would explode.

What the fuck had happened last night? There was the meal and red wine that went down her throat like it was blackcurrant cordial. And then ..?

There had been a fight and the booze started getting to her. Her father had to help her get back to their room and then ... What? She had passed out? He had put her bed? HE HAD UNDRESSED HER AND PUT HER TO BED? She was not ready for that level of familiarity.

Ulp! She was not ready for that sort of exertion. No matter that it had only happened in her head it still had repercussions deep into her digestive system.

God, she desperately needed a drink of water.

Okay, so she had a couple of bottles of wine last night and had got a bit tipsy but that was no excuse for the way she felt now. She had evenings back in university that comprised of pints of snake-bite with tequila chasers until four in the morning and then been in class to give a presentation at nine that day. She had not felt this bad then.

Perhaps the wine had not been as pure as she had presumed. Had she been poisoned? She knew that sometimes a hangover could make you feel like you wanted to die but all of a sudden she had this feeling that, yes, she really was going to die.

She wanted to call out for help but could not muster the strength. She had no choice but to get up but did she do it slowly and carefully - which would eke out the suffering - or just get on with it and jump out of bed and suffer the consequences?

She judged the distance between her and the bathroom and weighed up her chances of making it there without making a mess all over the expensive carpet. Her estimations were 'too far' and 'as near enough to nil as damn-it-all' respectively.

She eased her legs over the edge of the bed and swivelled her body around.

So far so good.

She pressed her feet on the floor and levered her body to a sitting position.

Uh-oh. Her head began to spin and a hot flush rose up the back of her neck and around her face. She concentrated on her breathing until the wave dissipated.

She pressed her feet down and lifted herself up. She hobbled across to the bedroom door, grabbed the dressing gown off the hook and wrapped it around her. She opened the door and scrunched her face in disgust at the brightness beyond.

"Good morning," Professor hailed. He was sitting at the table next to the kitchen, drinking a cup of tea.

"No, not really," she grumbled. "What time is it?"

"A little after eight," he told her.

She checked that the optical assault was natural. "In the morning?"

"Of course," he sighed.

"No wonder I feel so rough," she commented. "I should still be asleep."

"Oh, it's due to lack of sleep, is it?" he asked. "Nothing to do with this, then?" He dangled the bottle of whiskey in his hand.

Ah, that was why she was feeling so bad. They had got back. There had been a reprimanding for her behaviour and to prove that she was no longer a little girl, she had taken his precious bottle of whiskey and started drinking it neat, straight from the bottle. There had been words. She was not sure what words they had been and, in fact, at the time he had not known what most of them were either, but you could not mistake the tone of the words. There had been words and finger pointing, then she had said something definitive and staggered to bed.

She was momentarily mesmerised by the sloshing brown liquid in the bottle and then she could taste it in her mouth. Then she could feel it in her stomach, rejecting her body and wanting to be liberated.

She dashed back into her bedroom and actually made it to the bath before the first mouthful had erupted from her guts. Then the taste was fully realised and the smell and the look of it in the bath and the exertion to get there and everything that made her body want to turn itself inside out.

She stayed there for half an hour with the last ten minutes just reactively retching.

Luckily, it was practically all liquid so it just poured down the plughole with a quick rinse. The more solid bits, which she presumed were likely to be lumps of her rather than the meal, she scooped out with toilet roll and flushed down the toilet.

She then spent the next thirty minutes in the shower trying to wash away the rest of her nausea and embarrassment. She managed to achieve fifty per cent of her objectives and re-emerged from her room feeling awake although quite humbled.

"I'm sorry about last night," she said sincerely. "I don't remember what I said but I'm sure it wasn't very nice."

"I am also very sorry," he responded, which surprised her. "It was my fault that made you act in that manner. I should stop trying to pick up where we left off. I must remember that you are not the young girl that you used to be."

She smiled at him and thought about telling him that she had not been a little girl then either. "Thank you. Have you had breakfast?"

"How on earth can you think of food after all that?" he demanded and indicated 'all that' with a wave of his hand at her bedroom door.

"You heard?"

"Dear girl, half of Paris heard."

She shrugged her shoulders at him. "I need sustenance," she explained.

"Well, no, I haven't eaten as I did not want to disturb you," he told her.

She marched into the kitchen and checked the cupboards again.

"Cereal? Toast?" she asked.

"What are you having?" he asked.

"Fried egg sandwich," she replied without turning round. She could sense his grimace of distaste.

"Just toast, please," he said.

She made their breakfast and did not look at him as she bit into the sandwich and sucked back the yolk that dribbled down her chin.

"What would you like to do today?" he asked with as much disinterest as he could muster.

"I don't know," she muttered when her mouth was clear. "A few sights? A couple of museums? What do you fancy?"

"Yes, that suits me," he responded enthusiastically. "Notre Dame?"

"The Louvre?" she countered.

"Monmatre," he said.

"Why are you choosing all the places with so many steps?"

"I am 'suggesting' places that I would like to visit," he replied. "I am not demanding we go to these places or mentioning them because of their stairs. You don't have to come, you know?"

"Well, that would kind of defeat the object of us being here, wouldn't it?"

"So would all this petty bickering," he said and she shut up.

"Point taken," she muttered.

"Do you want to go back to bed for a couple more hours?" he asked. "Our stay here is indefinite. There's no rush to do everything."

"No, thanks. I think some fresh air might do me good."

"Right," he declared and got to his feet. "While you finish your repast, I shall freshen up and be ready in a short while."

He turned, marched into her bedroom and closed the door.

It was all too easy to turn on the automatic objection response with him. He either always took umbrage with the things she did or she inferred negativity in everything he said. She wished she could remember what she said last night. Most of it had probably been absolute bollocks but she bet some of it had probably been right from the heart.

The Macallan called to her seductively.

So did the fried egg that was resting uneasily in her stomach.

## 3 (*Maintenant*)

## Deaf

Anjo must have slept because he could not account for three hours of that night. After they had forced a newsagents to open and requisitioned their photocopier, they had their men wandering around asking everyone if they had seen the mystery couple. However, it was late, witnesses had already dispersed, people wanted to go home and Anjo's initial feelings of optimism lapsed into realism that it was not going to happen.

The bodies were cleared up and everyone left apart from Matilda and him. He had ordered her to get some rest to be ready in the morning but she had insisted that if he was to continue brainstorming then she would help. She had lasted a couple of hours and then the relative comfort of the couch in his office beckoned her weary body. He had draped his jacket over her and then sat behind his desk to start free association writing. It was one of the best ways to discover tenuous relationships; at that point when the conscious was switching off and the unconscious was not hindered by logic or relevance to start scrawling whatever it was thinking off.

As he cleared the sleep from his eyes, he looked down at his pad and was rather disappointed and disturbed to see he had just written, 'Matilda,' over and over again.

She stirred and rolled on to her side with her back to him. He could not help but follow the line of her waist, over her hips and down her legs.

He ripped the page out, screwed it into a ball and threw it at her head.

«Oh, I'm sorry,» she grumbled. «Did I fall asleep?»

She sat upright and then shivered.

«Me too,» he admitted and more writing caught his attention in front of him. Another page of, 'Matilda,' which he hurriedly ripped out and threw in the bin. He quickly checked the other pages but they were empty.

«Did anything come to mind?» she asked and yawned.

«No,» he growled and pushed himself onto his feet. «Coffee?»

«Yes, please,» she replied and stared at the various networks on the whiteboard.

He staggered out of the office to the coffee machine around the corner.

«Are you okay?» she called.

«My leg has fallen asleep,» he replied and poured two cups.

«So we are just waiting for his next move?» she asked as he handed her a cup.

«No, we still have not *Googled* their names,» he told her.

«Does that really work?» she asked and sipped the steaming black liquid. She grimaced at its bitterness but went back for another try.

«Sometimes,» he said.

His phone rang and he picked it up. «Anjo,» he said. «What? When? Fuck!» He slammed the phone down again.

«The waitress was murdered late last night along with an officer,» he reported. «He had gone to show her the drawing. We should get over there.»

Matilda jumped up and tried to straighten her crumpled suit as best she could. She handed Anjo his jacket as he marched to the door.

«Do you want to go home first?» he asked but she shook her head and encouraged him onward.

Matilda was forced to jog through the precinct offices to keep up with her partner's long striding pace.

«Anjo!» a woman screamed from the other side of the open-plan office.

He was so close to the exit that he considered pretending to ignore it but remembered how hard his life had been for an entire month after the last time.

Matilda thought he was going to make a break for it so ran into his wall-like back when he came to an abrupt halt.

«Yes commissioner,» he grumbled.

«My office, please,» the woman hailed from behind him. He turned with his head hung low as if just caught by his headmistress attempting to bunk off school.

Matilda watched in awe at his sudden change in humility. He sullenly wandered past her, refusing to give her eye contact as if in doing so he would see his fall from grace reflected in her eyes.

«Bring your girl with you,» the woman instructed and then he allowed his dour gaze to connect with hers to let her see that she was implicit in his downfall.

By the time they had crossed the open space again, the woman had entered her office and was sat behind her desk. She was in her late forties, smartly dressed in a dark blue trouser suit and burgundy blouse. Her hair was turning to a whiter shade of red that she had tied back tightly behind her head. She wore large, round, brown-framed glasses that would intensify any expression given. Mostly they were scowls and glares.

«Inspector Anjo,» she said flatly.

«Commissioner,» Anjo greeted her.

«Shut the door, child,» she told Matilda, which she did without a second thought of protestation.

«There is something very satisfying about seeing you stride through the precinct with purpose again,» the Commissioner continued.

Anjo raised his head slightly, thinking that this meeting might be a commendation rather than condemnation.

«What is this?» she asked and pushed a case report across her desk to him. Anjo flipped a couple of the pages over and read the reports.

«It is from the museum death,» he said.

«You *were* there, then,» she stated.

«Yes,» he replied certainly. «I - I mean we - were called in because of the nature of the death.»

«But you did not take on the case?»

«No, it was a suicide,» he replied and that feeling of doom returned as he realised where the conversation was heading.

«I see,» she said. «And you are happy with that verdict?»

«All the evidence suggested so.»

The Commissioner tapped her pen thoughtfully on another file in front of her.

«And I see your name on this report too,» she stated and flipped the paper across the desk.

«Yes, the car crash,» Anjo concurred. «It was coincidental that I was one of the first on the scene.»

«And highly irregular,» the Commissioner muttered.

«I was only there to help out,» he explained. «I was not on duty, as such.»

«Are you sure?»

«It was a road accident,» Anjo declared.

«Oh, *I* know what it was, Anjo,» she responded. «I'd like to know what you *think* it was.»

«There are things -» Matilda blurted from the back of the office but was quietened by a raised hand from Anjo. The Commissioner just glared at her.

«It is nothing,» Anjo stated. «I just wanted to make sure.»

The Commissioner leaned back in her chair and sighed.

«Sit down, Anjo,» she instructed and he did so, obediently. «What *are* you doing?»

He just stared at her and shrugged his shoulders.

«Seriously, Anjo,» she re-emphasised. «What is it that you are doing?»

He still did not reply and made sure that when he returned her admonishing gaze then it denoted absolute incomprehension.

«How long have you got?» she demanded. «Two years?»

«Eighteen months,» he growled.

«And you thought you might go out in a blaze of glory?»

«Nothing like that.»

«Perhaps you are trying to impress someone,» she suggested and blatantly redirected her eyes to Matilda.

«No,» he replied absolutely without diverting his gaze.

She sighed again.

«I don't know what to say, Anjo. You were, once, our top officer, up until The Confectioner. You lived the job. God knows you sacrificed enough of your personal life for it.»

That caused him to look away.

«Have you spoken to her?» the Commissioner asked and he shook his head.

«Then you regressed. Caved in on yourself. Came in, did your hours and then went home again. Sure, your cases were being closed one after the other but they were no longer being accompanied by any arrest sheets.

«We all understand why you lost your edge, Anjo. Everyone knows why you stopped caring but do you know what? Nobody cared because you were still a good man and a good police officer. But now, something has happened to you and you are heading down a path of self destruction. You seem to be making up your own case based on your own objectives. You are making a fool of yourself and destroying any credibility you once had!

«What were you thinking distributing the sketches of two people based on the ramblings of two hysterical hookers?»

«They weren't -» Matilda started but was silenced again.

«You are using up valuable manpower chasing ghosts and ultimately making a fool out of this department and that's where I draw the line, Anjo. Do you understand?»

«Yes,» he said.

«Find something more constructive to do if you really want to educate your protégé. Don't go around making up conspiracies in the hope of piecing together some tenuous puzzle.»

«Yes, of course,» he said.

«They were just coincidental suicides, Anjo. Nothing more,» she stated.

«A man crucified himself!» Matilda roared. «How is that 'just' a suicide?»

«Matilda, be quiet,» Anjo ordered.

«Young lady, I have looked at the reports for all of these cases -»

«And what about the clues?» Matilda demanded.

«Matilda! Be quiet,» Anjo instructed more adamantly.

«You have been reading too much Nancy Drew,» the commissioner stated. «Real police work isn't aided by codes and riddles. It comes from science, logic and a whole lot of luck.»

«And you say he stopped being a policeman,» Matilda accused. «At least he has an excuse. What is yours?»

«Matilda!» Anjo bellowed and hauled himself to his feet. «You will learn to mind your place! Go wait outside.»

Anjo was unsure whether Matilda was going to scream at him, hit him or start crying. The expression of confusion that swept across her face nearly had him apologising to her but in the end she just nodded and walked out. He composed himself then turned to face his boss.

«You are correct,» he admitted. «I have been allowing her enthusiasm to get the better of me.»

The Commissioner nodded. «I can understand why. She reminds me of you when you first joined us.»

«I will talk to her,» Anjo said and she indicated that he could leave.

He joined Matilda outside the office and closed the door behind him.

«Never let the Commissioner in on the case until it is too late for her to take you off it,» he advised and began to cross the office again.

«I do not understand,» Matilda complained.

«You were right,» he told her. «She stopped being police many decades ago when she became a politician. You cannot trust politicians, not in our job. They are too concerned about image, budgets and their careers before they start to think about justice or are willing to take chances on hunches.»

They started back across the office space.

«So we are not stopping?» Matilda asked.

«Absolutely not,» Anjo replied. «When the Commissioner gets involved it usually means you are heading in the right direction.»

«You think she knows something about it?»

«She knows nothing but what is put down in front of her.»

«Then how -?»

Anjo stopped abruptly and Matilda had to jump to one side to stop herself from bouncing into him again.

«It is just something you learn, Matilda,» Anjo explained. «When a higher ranking officer tells you to back off then it is encouragement to continue.»

«Who says?»

«Everyone says,» he stated. «It is a well-known fact. What did you do when I said the museum crucifixion was just a suicide and should be left that that?»

She looked guiltily away. «I carried on investigating,» she confessed.

«Exactly,» Anjo praised and continued his progression.

«But if everyone knows it then doesn't that mean she knows it?» Matilda demanded.

«Yes. I suppose.»

«Then is she giving us unauthorised consent to continue the investigation?»

«No. She is telling us to stop.»

«But if she knows that by telling us to stop it will only encourage us to carry on, isn't she just telling us to carry on?»

«No!» Anjo cried. «How else can she tell us to back off without telling us to back off?»

«Then how do you know when to back off and when to carry on after being told to back off?»

«You just know, Matilda,» Anjo snapped as they entered the car park. «If she doesn't tell you to leave it then it means you are doing something right or it is not worth her while to stop you. You need to know when you are on a real case or are just 'chasing ghosts.'»

He pressed the button on a set of keys he produced from his pocket. A black Citroën DS beeped its horn at them and they veered towards it.

«But how?» she asked pathetically as she slipped into the passenger seat of his car.

He slammed his door shut and fired up the engine. «You knew at the museum,» he reminded her, «and I know now. You *just* know.»

They spent the rest of the journey to the hospital in stoic silence until they reached the ward and Anjo approached the scene officer. «What happened?» he demanded.

Matilda walked straight past and into the room.

«The night shift said her brother came to visit,» the officer reported. «She went off shift shortly after and nobody else saw anyone come or go.»

«Not even the dead officer?»

«No. Her medical report said she was to be left resting until the morning rounds when they were both discovered.»

Matilda stepped out again. «No drawing,» she stated.

«Get to the woman who saw this 'brother' and find out if it was this man,» Anjo demanded and thrust the picture of Professor into the officer's face.

«It was not,» the officer said. «She said it could have been the boy. The short hair looked the same but he had a scar and -»

«What boy?» Anjo asked.

«The other picture.»

«It's a girl,» Anjo told him.

«Really?» the officer asked incredulously.

«Matilda, come,» Anjo ordered.

«One shot each,» she said, «straight in the forehead.»

«The same M.O. as the curator?»

«Until we get a ballistics report -»

«Was it the same?»

«I believe so,» she said.

«That's good enough for me. Could this girl disguise herself as a 'brother'?»

«Maybe she is really a he?» Matilda suggested. «It would be easier to apply these than hide them.» She cupped her breasts in case he had not known what she was referring to.

«And the scar?»

«Easy enough to apply a fake one.»

«So is he clearing up his path or anticipating our moves?» Anjo wondered. «From now on, we have to keep any more progress between ourselves and only a select number of officers we really trust.»

«You suspect internal interference?» she asked.

«Anything is possible in this case, I fear.»

His mobile phone started ringing and he answered it.

«Hey, no phones allowed,» a nurse told him but Matilda shut her up with a flash of her police badge.

«Yes? They did? You are sure? Excellent. Run a check from the credit card. What? Cash?» He hung up and turned to Matilda. Although his face displayed an element of frustration, his eyes were bright with excitement.

«They were at a restaurant next to the Cathedral, last night. The time of the order states it was just after the priest killed himself,» he told her. «Coincidence? I think not.»

«So what now?» she asked as they got back to his car.

«From the Cathedral to Pont Notre-Dame; they were heading west, on foot, implies they are staying somewhere local,» he deduced.

«What restaurant?» she asked.

«Vieux Bistro? I do not know it,» he confessed.

«Not on your income,» she laughed.

«So, expensive tastes, eh? Although, they paid by cash so the lead ends there but this is the break we needed, Matilda.»

They almost jogged back to the car and she smiled at his enthusiasm. This was how she imagined it would be like working alongside the great Inspector Anjo: racing from scene to scene, putting the pieces together, methodically deducing a motive and revealing the perpetrator. She was so excited she wanted to squeal.

«Pardon me?» he asked.

She had not, had she?

«Hm?» she enquired innocently and hoped she was not blushing.

«I thought you said something,» he explained and started the engine.

«No, just thinking.»

Anjo drove back to the crime scene of the night before and parked.

«There must be fifty hotels within walking distance of here,» Matilda suggested despondently.

«This is the nature of true police work, Matilda,» he chided. «Laborious, boring, tiring.»

He pulled his phone out and dialled a number.

«Julia? Anjo. You have the drawings there? Fax them and your number to every hotel in districts one to four. Call me when you get something.» He hung up then looked smugly at Matilda. «Breakfast?»

## 4 (*Maintenant*)

## The Danger of Confiding One's Secret to a Goat

Brandon was woken by his phone ringing. He had, at first, objected to carrying a mobile because he thought they were inappropriate for the church but, when he had been forced to take one, he discovered it did have some uses. However, he also discovered how acutely annoying they were when everyone had exactly the same ring tone and so he had figured he was being incredibly clever by 'downloading' a unique tone; namely the sound of a real phone. He was now discovering that it was to be his mobile's everlasting curse to cause confusion when it rang as he lunged for the bedside phone and placed the receiver to his ear.

"Hello?" he mumbled and took a couple of seconds to realise that the ringing had not stopped.

"Hello?" he said again and then realised the real source of the noise. He rolled out of bed – tangling his arm in the landline's cord and his leg in the bed sheets – and grabbed his jacket. He got to his phone before the answer service could kick in.

"Hello?" he bellowed.

"Ja? Eminence?" a gruff voice asked.

"No. What? Henry? Yes. No. Er, what?"

The other end remained silent.

"Hello?" Brandon asked cautiously.

"Allo?"

"Henry?"

"Ja?"

"You are in Paris?"

"Ja?"

"You have found the relic?"

"Nein."

"Oh."

"But we do ask around. We have contacts. I just check in."

"That is fine, Henry," Brandon sighed, trying to hide his disappointment but failing miserably. "Call me again when you have something."

"Ja."

The line went dead and, for a moment, Brandon considered going back to bed and burying his head under his pillow. Then he thought that, as long as he was in Paris, that he might as well do a bit of sightseeing.

V—V

Geoffrey stepped resolutely through customs, flashing his Extra Fast Track pass at any officious looking official who approached them. He was followed by Jacques and then Hugh who was carrying two shoulder bags and a suitcase.

"I am *not* your lackey," Hugh complained.

"But I do recall you stating quite categorically that you *are* the strongest," Geoffrey teased.

"This was not what I was talking about," Hugh growled.

Jacques, although bagless, was keeping out of the fight and studying his Blackberry, scrolling through a list of emails.

Hugh dropped the suitcase and indicated to a porter to approach.

"Anything?" Geoffrey asked.

"Yes. One of our boys in blue says there's an investigation going on that might be of interest," Jacques annotated. "There's a picture." He tapped the screen and tilted it slightly for Geoffrey to watch from over his shoulder as the image downloaded. It was the sketch of Penny and Professor.

"What is it?" Hugh demanded and Jacques showed him. "Who are they?"

"Suspects," Jacques said.

Geoffrey watched his compatriots carefully as thoughts processed.

"Why are the police involved?" Hugh asked. "Do they know about the artefact?"

"It doesn't seem so," Jacques said as he re-read the email. "It seems they are wanted in connection to a number of bizarre deaths. Apparent suicides."

"Then how do we know they have anything to do with anything?"

"Because, dear boy," Geoffrey sighed, "bizarre is what artefacts are about. It's too much of a coincidence."

Hugh pursed his lips and squinted his eyes defiantly. "Don't patronise me."

"Don't give me reason to," Geoffrey replied.

The porter loaded the three bags and directed the men towards the taxi rank outside.

"It's my place to question everything," Hugh stated testily. "Does anyone know what the purse can do?"

"It's a religious relic," Jacques said. "*It* doesn't 'do' anything but what it represents can make men do anything."

Outside the airport, they were greeted by a black limousine and a chauffeur holding a card with a horizontal oval drawn on it.

Jacques strolled over to the driver. "The Knights are drawing closer," he recited.

"Oui," the driver replied, "the nights are long but my bed is warm."

Geoff unashamedly sniggered in the background causing Jacques to roll his eyes with disdain. The chauffeur looked between the men with confusion.

"Those are our bags," Jacques said and the driver approached the porter, barking orders in French.

Jacques turned on Geoff but was mildly taken aback to see Hugh with a wry smirk across his face.

"It is all rather archaic," Hugh stated in his defence.

"It's traditional," Jacques argued.

"So is burning Sodomites," Geoff muttered as he bundled into the back of the limousine. "Ooh, truffles."

"And Bank Holiday *Carry On..* films," Hugh added.

The men spread themselves comfortably in the back of the car: Geoff, with his back to the driver, masticated heavily on a chocolate ball while pouring himself a generous glass of champagne; Hugh took the long, perpendicular sofa and rifled through the selection of newspapers next to him; Jacques dropped onto the back seat and adjusted his suit jacket to avoid it getting crumpled. "I realise we are out of practise," he said, "but I would appreciate a degree of professionalism, gentlemen. We are ambassadors of our Holy Order and representatives of all those who have come before us."

Geoff and Hugh had both stopped everything that they had been doing. Even the champagne seemed to stop effervescing. From the front of the car, they heard the chauffeur get into his seat.

"Sorry, Jacques," Hugh said.

"M' forry, Shack," Geoff spluttered.

The limo's engine fired to life.

"It's time to put our game faces on, gentlemen."

They gently pulled off and Jacques opened his briefcase and turned on his laptop within. Geoff leaned across to Hugh.

"Did he say, 'to put our gay faces on'?"

Hugh rolled his eyes and buried his face into his newspaper.

After a few subdued minutes, Jacques drew his attention away from his computer. "There's more on these unusual suicides: seven in total have been reported in and around Paris over the last couple of days, one managed to crucify himself."

"That can't be a coincidence, can it?" Hugh asked rhetorically.

"And if that wasn't enough validation for being here, it also looks like we have interest from a few competitors too. A number sweep has pulled up a series of communications between Vatican numbers here in Paris to the Priory of Sion and Gottesfreunde."

"It was a good call to bring the hardware, Geoff," Hugh commended and received a bow of acknowledgement from his younger companion.

"Let's not be too hasty to brandish the steel, gentlemen," Jacques warned. "Ah, here's a better scan of our primary suspects." He swung the laptop around to show his partners the larger, better defined sketch.

"He looks familiar," Hugh suggested.

"Which 'he'?" Geoff demanded.

"The young one is a she, Geoffrey," Hugh chided.

"How can you tell?"

"Well, isn't it?" Hugh leaned in for a closer inspection.

"It seems that the majority of the action has taken place at Notre Dame," Jacques commented. "Get the driver to take us there as our starting point."

## V—V

Christophe had had trouble sleeping that night. He had dreamt he was working in God's call centre and was trying to put a call - from himself - through to another department – him again - but it only ever kept coming back to him.

He repeatedly apologised to himself, explaining that he had no idea why his call would not go through to him, but he was getting angry on the other end of the phone.

Eventually he put on a silly voice and pretended to be the department he wanted. When that happened, he forgot why he was calling, apologised and hung up.

Christophe had woken in a mood and did not want to be in Paris any more.

Although he could not quite remember the details of the dream, he felt his annoyance rise even more as he picked up his mobile and selected the last number dialled in his call history.

The line rang and he was preparing to deal with the female auto-operator when a man's voice came on.

«Hold on,» he stated flatly, «your call is being redirected.»

The line rang again and when it was answered this time, Christophe could hear an incredible amount of background noise.

«Hallo?» the same gruff voice answered.

«This is Christophe.»

There was a moment of silence; Christophe was unsure whether the person on the other end of the call was trying to remember who was calling or wondering whether he should disavow all understanding.

«Yes,» he finally replied but still did not allow the Cardinal the courtesy of too much information.

«You do remember me, yes?»

«Yes,» the man replied succinctly.

«I was worried I might get your answering machine again,» Christophe chuckled.

«Why?» the man demanded.

Christophe took the phone away from his ear and silently cursed himself in Latin for not letting them get on with it. He put the phone back to his ear and smiled - he had heard somewhere that it would be conveyed in his speech.

«No reason,» he growled with unfettered irritation. «You know why I am calling?»

«Yes and -»

«I do not need to know any details,» Christophe interrupted, eager to get this over with quickly. «I am just checking in. You are in Paris?»

Again, there was an uncertain pause until the man inhaled deeply and replied, «No.»

Christophe was about to erupt into an apoplectic rage until he remembered to whom he was talking. Or perhaps, to whom he was not talking. He smiled with genuine pleasure this time, content that he was finally getting to grips with all this clandestine, double-bluffing bullshit.

«Oh, I see,» he sang. «You're *not* in Paris, then?»

«That is what I said,» the man replied abruptly.

«So you're *not* on the case yet?»

«Correct.»

«And you have absolutely no idea where the artefact is.»

«What artefact?»

Ooh, they nearly got him. Christophe's rising bile receded again.

«Excellent,» he sighed and took the phone away from his ear. He pressed the disconnect button and cut the man off mid sentence. That made him feel even better; knowing that he was in absolute control of the conversation.

«No, really. We -» was all the man managed to get out before the call died.

Christophe eased back into his seat and decided to switch his phone off for the morning. He deserved some time off.

Meanwhile, at a petrol station in Dover, a man sat in the passenger seat of a car and looked at his mobile with confusion. It looked as though he was trying to calculate some complicated trigonometry in his head as the driver got in.

«What is the matter?» the driver demanded.

The passenger winced in mental anguish as he looked up. «I think I double booked us,» he confessed.

## V—V

He had been living a monastic lifestyle for more decades than he was allowed to keep count of. Keeping a count of how many years he had been serving could be misconstrued as being boastful which, of course, is a symptom of pride which is one of the seven deadly sins and so one's term of service should never be recorded or compared. One of the hardest things in the world is trying to deliberately lose track of something so simple as counting years and, therefore, is one of the first things that the clergy look at on an applicant's CV. As long as every previous position was held for a period of 'don't know' then you should get through to the interview stage.

On top of the devout Catholic decree of abstinence was also a sideline in the Oriental philosophies and practices of Ninjitsu. It sounded like a lot to take on – or, perhaps, a lot to surrender – and an almost conflicting set of ideals, but really once you had already given up everything for one belief system then there was not really much to sacrifice for the other. It was just a case of praying during periods of 'meditation', 'rigorous exercise', 'shadow stalking practice', 'hyper-efficient death-dealing sparring' and 'being upside down for long periods of time'.

Other members of his monastic orders were incredibly jealous of his ultra-extreme self-denial which meant they were probably going to go to Hell, which upset them even more.

The Black Monk's room was as uncomfortable as he could have made it to befit his intense temperament. He was very high in the Vatican ranks (if there was such a thing for a monk, which there is not because to have a hierarchy would be to encourage desire and ambition) so he was not the kind of man to live in squalor with bugs and dirt and no air conditioning. So the adequate hotel room had to be stripped of its excesses: the king-size bed had been upturned and wedged against one wall to cover the TV, PS3 and minibar; the carpet had been pulled up at one corner to bare the wooden floorboards beneath and his hassock was spread out as a mattress or, perhaps, blanket; the curtains had been taken down to ensure the Lord's glorifying sunlight could not be hindered entrance and the digital alarm clock had been covered so he could not be upset by the ridiculous hour the Lord's glorifying sunlight woke him.

The Monk was going about his morning ablutions in the ensuite: purging his bowels, baptising his teeth and absolving his hair – what was left of it. He pulled the Fila hood back over his shorn scalp, adjusted it to ensure complete shadowy coverage of all his features then wandered back to his sleeping area. He kneeled on the floorboards, next to a weathered brown suitcase, and placed his hands palm to palm for a moment's silent prayer. Only he knew whether it was a prayer for assistance, forgiveness or strength.

He then turned his attention to the suitcase and flipped its top open. Inside were a number of black items of clothing and a bright green pair of three-quarter swimming shorts. He idly rifled through the top few contents then, as it became more apparent that he could not find what he was looking for, his rummaging became more insistent and frantic. After he had thoroughly overturned everything, he quickly scanned the whole room then returned his attention to the bag, indiscriminately tossing each item out to the side until the case was completely emptied. Then he picked the suitcase up and checked underneath it, whipped his hassock out of the way and finally rooted through all of the clothes he had strewn across the floor.

With a resigned exclamation of, "Ugh," he slumped his shoulders and stared at the ceiling – another silent prayer?

He forced himself to his feet, slouched over to the upturned bed and picked up a plump pillow. Holding it by one corner, and with his head hanging in embarrassed shame, he flipped it over his shoulder to hit himself on his back.

"Ow," he said with no conviction whatsoever.

He pulled the pillow back and repeated the action over his other shoulder.

"Ow," he said and sighed heavily. "Leccacazzi!"

V—V

Hatti had not slept well that night; she had woken often from the visions of her friends doing those things to themselves. The doctors had given her Diazepam, which was meant to help her sleep but it had only made her dreams slightly more trippy and more disturbing.

It was almost a relief that she was finally being woken by something external and that it was sunlight slipping through the gap in her curtains. Sometimes it is not the nightmares that are the scary part, but the waking in darkness and the mind not being able to distinguish between conscious and unconscious.

Although she was awake, she kept her eyes comfortably closed, enjoying the moment and psychological warmth the light projected.

Then it flickered away. Perhaps a breeze had fluttered the curtain, although she did not remember having left her window open, nor could she feel it against her skin.

It flashed against her eyelid again, causing her to scrunch her eyes from the brightness and confusion.

Perhaps it was her mother walking around her room, bringing her a cup of tea. She had not heard the door open or footsteps on the floor, nor could she smell any indication of breakfast.

The light danced annoyingly across her lids so she finally opened her eyes to identify its cause. It was sunlight, but it was being reflected off a metallic surface from the foot of her bed. She blinked, trying to adjust her eyes to the light and focus on its source. It slipped away again and she could make out the silhouette of someone sitting in a seat with the reflective material in his (or her) lap.

«Hallo?»

«Good morning, Hatti,» Cunningham greeted her warmly. «I'm sorry, did I wake you?»

Confusion started to give way to concern.

«Who are you?»

«I wanted to ask you some questions about these two people you saw the other night,» he told her and lifted the sketch into her sightline.

«I don't -»

«I tried speaking to Teri, but she wasn't very helpful. I hope you will be considerably more so. She was practically hysterical.»

«Mum?» she called loudly.

Cunningham leaned forward in his seat to allow his face to be illuminated by the shaft of sunlight; it glinted off his pink eyes and made his scar look almost moist. «She is downstairs, Hatti, seeing to breakfast. Now, which way did these two go after they had finished with your friends?»

Hatti's mother had put on a fine spread for breakfast, obviously anticipating the appetites of Cunningham's co-workers who sat at opposite sides of the round table, liberally tucking into warmed croissants, hot chocolate and pastries.

"Pillow?" one suggested and flicked the crumbs from his striped jumper.

"Of course," the other said as he dunked his bread in his cup then popped it into his mouth.

"To smother or silence?"

There followed the slightest scuffle on the floorboards and a whimper from upstairs then a perfunctory pop that elicited absolute silence. Footsteps calmly descended the stairs and Cunningham entered the kitchen. He stepped over the woman's body that was blocking the doorway and took the empty seat between the two guards.

"She said they headed west along the bank," he reported. "We are getting closer but we are running out of time. We will have to stop being so discreet."

The three men looked at each other's attire, build and physical appearance.

"In our enquiries, I mean," Cunningham amended.

"Oh. Brioche?"

## 5 (*Maintenant*)

## The Rat Hole

They found a small café and had just sat down with their coffee and pastries when Anjo's phone rang again.

«That was quick,» Matilda praised.

«That is why it will not be Julia,» he sneered and answered the call. He listened intently then said, «Okay. We will be there shortly,» then hung up.

He rubbed at his forehead and sighed.

«There has been another suicide last night,» he stated.

«Where?»

«Montrouge,» he said.

«All the way out there?»

«Yes, I know. He is changing again,» Anjo groaned.

«Are they sure it's the same?»

«They said he was discovered an hour ago by downstairs neighbours. He was found hanging from a ceiling beam.»

Matilda lightened. «That is good, no? Just hung himself?»

«By his own intestines,» Anjo added and watched as Matilda's jaw threatened to fall on the table. «The neighbours were complaining about a constant tapping on their ceiling all night and found him there.»

«We should go see?» she asked.

«You want to?»

«Not really but I am intrigued.»

«Very well,» he sighed. «Get these to go,» he indicated the coffees, «and I shall get the car.»

The level of enthusiasm had flipped to its polar side of melancholy. As they drove across the city, Anjo kept running the elements of the case through his mind to find that every time a common connection arose, it was cancelled by something else.

There were at least two parties involved. Someone was causing these people to kill themselves. Not by popping pills or jumping off buildings - apart from the one that jumped off the building. These were not pre-meditated suicides where the victim ponders his or her life and then does the deed. No, these people were coming to the decision to end their being on the spur of the moment and so did it in the first way that came to hand. They continued to do it no matter how painful it was until the job was done. Not a call for help, these people were absolutely certain that they wanted to die.

What kind of person could have that sort of a hold over someone? And what could that hold be?

«Matilda,» he said and made her flinch - she had been dropping off to sleep. «Get someone to check the victims for mobile phones. See if their actions were triggered by a text message or something.»

That would explain their motives. Something like a hypnotic trigger.

There were two different sets of deaths. One lot were just killing themselves and the other were trying to pass on a message. Were they trying to say who was making them do it or why they were doing it?

Then there were these new, blatant, executions of witnesses. Certainly not the same person but obviously to do with it.

Now his 'Odd Couple' were also causing conflicting thoughts. A girl who dressed like a boy - or vice versa - and an old man. Would they really be so brazen as to be seen casually wandering across the scenes of their evil doing? Or was that a double bluff?

It felt like the answer was there but he could not see it. He was too busy looking at the finer details to be able to see the whole picture. Or it was more like he was one of the finer details and could not step outside the picture to see what it all was about.

Hm. Something about pictures. Something about paintings.

«This is the place,» Matilda told him as they pulled around a corner to a street of terraced apartments.

The scene was as messy as they had expected but not nearly as horrific as they had imagined. For some reason they had independently assumed that this one would escalate in the 'meaning' department, that another element might be added to their list of things to try to connect these people. Maybe there would be pentacles smeared across all the walls in effluence or a strange text etched into the ceiling by a loose tooth. Perhaps a secret stash of child pornography or home videoed snuff films. At least a cowl and some black, dribbly, aromatic candles.

No. It was just some bloke's apartment. He had cleared all the furniture to the outer edges of his living room apart from a dining room chair that he needed to hang himself from.

There he was, dangling from a ceiling beam by, what looked like, some sort of spongy, moist tubing. Well, that was what it looked like if you did not already know what it was.

«How can it be possible?» Matilda gasped as she stared fixedly at the body.

Two of the man's shirt buttons had been undone at his belly from where the tube emerged. His shirt had, at one stage, been white but was now completely drenched in blood. He had pulled his innards out, wrapped them around his neck to anchor them and tossed them over the beam. This must have taken a few efforts, as there were a few snake-like splats dotted around the ceiling light.

Upon completion of the task, he had then tied the offal back around his neck to finish the job.

«What? You want to analyse the tensile strength of the duodenum?» Anjo demanded as he barged passed her.

«It's incredible,» she said.

«We are not sure whether death came from strangulation of blood loss,» a plain-clothes officer stated. «The softness of his intestines would not have restricted the airflow that quickly.»

«Semantics,» Anjo growled and studied the expansive stain of blood through the carpet.

The officer turned his attention to Matilda. «See how his feet are only a couple of inches from the floor? We estimate that his intestines must have been slipping about a centimetre an hour.»

This sparked Anjo's interest. «How many hours?»

«Stretching?»

«Since he began the task,» Anjo demanded.

«Impossible to tell,» the officer told him. «We can calculate a time of death from an autopsy, even estimate how long he was hanging there but there is no real way of knowing how long he had been building the courage to do this to himself.»

«No!» Anjo bellowed. «This was not premeditated. Look at this. No one would want to die like this or would go to the effort to die like this. A decision was made to end his life and he just did it. How shall I do it? Ah, the ceiling beam; I shall hang myself. What can I use? The television cable?» Anjo marched over to the corner of the room where the TV had been tipped over and revealed a torn flex that had been yanked from the wall. From there he also discovered an analogue clock that must have been sitting on top of the television. He lifted it up to see that its face had been smashed and its hands had stopped at ten-past-three.

«Oh, please,» the officer begged.

«Sometimes life really is like the movies,» Anjo stated.

Matilda did some mental arithmetic. «But no one could have got from the city to here in that time.»

«Which confirms we are either dealing with two people or my text theory,» Anjo said.

«What people?» the officer demanded. «This is suicide. They have all been suicides, Anjo.»

«*Inspector* Anjo,» Anjo reminded him. «Matilda, find me something.»

Matilda slowly spun on the spot and studied the blood patterns on the ceiling

«There is no suicide note,» the officer told them.

«Tell us what you do have,» Anjo barked.

The officer rifled through his note pad and began reading.

«Not much,» he said. «His name is Andrew Mainsvers-LeHaut.»

«Posh name,» Anjo sniffed.

«He was thirty-two and single. He was a waiter and has parents in Boulogne.»

She looked at the spread of blood across the floor from all angles and then followed his point of view to look at the walls around him.

«I see nothing,» she confessed.

«So this belongs to the second set?»

«I'm not sure,» she pondered and continued gazing around the room.

«Tell me what you are thinking,» Anjo urged.

«It feels more like the first,» she said.

«Perhaps it is a contest,» Anjo suggested. «They are taking it in turns to see who can outdo the other?»

«Perhaps,» she said softly and her inspection stopped at a large bookshelf that covered the wall behind the man.

«He enjoyed reading,» she stated and walked over to the shelves. The books were very orderly filed alphabetically by author and then in descending size. She traced her index finger along the tightly packed spines, noting each name and title as she went along.

Adams, Asimov, Austen, Banks, Barker, Baudelaire. Bronte and

Bryson wobbled in their spaces as she passed across them.

«There is a book missing,» she said. «Is there one around?»

«We have not seen one,» the officer said.

«You did not see the clock,» Anjo stated and the officer huffed.

All the officers present started shifting furniture around, searching for the elusive tome.

«I have one,» a gendarme called, «but it is only an address book.»

«It will do for now,» Anjo said and took it. «Any idea what the missing title could be?»

Matilda shrugged her shoulders. «It could be anything. Another title by an author of either side or one with a same name or something by somebody with a surname starting with B. R. O. O., B.R.O.T., B. R. O. U. or B. R. U.»

«That's it?» Anjo asked. «It is something to get someone on to.»

«There are probably more combinations and millions of titles,» she replied. «It would be impossible to go through all of them.»

«Something might show up,» Anjo argued, «but only if we look for it. Get someone on it, Matilda.»

She nodded to him as he started to flip through the dead man's address book.

«We shall also cross reference addresses and telephone numbers of the other victims,» Anjo muttered.

Matilda's mobile phone started ringing and she answered it quickly.

«Yes? Yes, he is here. I will.» She hung up and raised her eyebrows at him.

«Another one?»

«No,» she said quickly. «Two more. Both happened during the night, too. One in Neuilly and the other in Pantlin.»

Anjo looked at all the elements they had discovered with this one so far. As per usual, the manner of the death did not seem to matter, despite its bizarrety, but more the things that the victim did prior to or during his demise.

*His*. Again, another male. Could that really be an issue?

«What were their genders, Matilda?» he demanded.

She was ready for the question. «One was female.»

Anjo felt a wave of relief. At least that indicated a level of consistency in its inconsistency. There was no way he was going to be able to convince the commissioner that these suicides were anything more than just that, at the moment. He certainly was not going to be able to get her to issue a city-wide warning alerting all males that they might be next.

«Matilda, stay here and see what you can find then head back to the cathedral»

«Where are you going?»

«I need to go back to the museum. I think there is something I missed.»

«I put everything in my notes.»

«I know you did but I did not really look at the scene,» he confessed.

«I was not concentrating. I need to see it all in context.»

Anjo headed for the door.

«You are taking your car?» Matilda demanded.

«Of course,» he replied.

«How will I get around?»

«Take his car.» Anjo pointed at the officer.

«Wha?»

Anjo nodded at him insistently and he resigned himself to the fact that there was no point in protesting. He dipped his hands in his pockets, pulled out a set of keys and threw them to Matilda. She caught them deftly and smiled sweetly at him. «Thank you, Jean.»

Anjo gave the room one last cursory inspection in the hope something else might present itself then marched out of the room.

Matilda took her time reviewing all the elements before heading to the door. She could not help but notice the officer, Jean, flashing her the occasional glance.

«Er, Matilda?» he called nervously before she escaped the scene.

She stopped and swivelled round on the spot. «Yes?»

«If you wouldn't mind waiting for a couple more minutes, I should be finished and I could drive you back into the city?»

«Only if it would not be taking you out of your way,» she suggested.

«Oh no, not at all,» he replied too eagerly and closed his notebook so quickly it rapped his knuckles, making him drop it on the floor.

Matilda used the moment of him flustering his composure to giggle to herself then regain her straight face when he returned his attention to her.

«Right you lot,» he declared to the other officers still busying themselves with their duties, «carry on and call me if anything else turns up.» He marched to the front door and held it open for Matilda. «I'm taking Ma- er - Inspector Autout back to the city.»

No one paid him the slightest bit of attention and he did not seem to notice. Matilda slipped the car keys back into his hand as she passed him; he was sure her fingernails caressed his palm as she did so.

# 6 (*Maintenant*)

## The Two Men Clothed in Black

Anjo's journey back to the city centre passed without any conscious effort from himself. Instead of thinking about driving, his thoughts were purely focussed on the eclectic elements of the case and that their inability to find a link between them was the one thing that bound them together and convinced him that there was something more insidious afoot. Something, at some stage, was going to crop up and direct his attention to some high-standing official which would jeopardise his life and shake the very foundations of society.

He pondered about calling in some favours from a few 'associates'. Get them to snoop around the corridors of power in the hope of tracing a connection backwards. Parliament? The police? The church? A church. His free-association thinking had brought him back to Notre Dame and he pondered its potential significance for a fraction of a second before casting it aside. Notre Dame was but one incident scene of many. Why not the museum? Why not the hospital? Why not the letting agency?

«The church gets blamed for everything these days,» he sympathised.

He parked his car in an illegal space and deftly flashed his badge to the duty gendarme who was bearing down on him.

«Ah, Inspector. I was not aware that you were returning,» the gendarme explained. «In fact -»

«You were told I should not be allowed back?» Anjo demanded.

«Not quite,» the officer stuttered. «The rumour was that you wouldn't be back because you would be closing this quite quickly.»

«That was the rumour, hm?»

«Because of the way you left, that's all.»

Anjo considered allowing the boy the knowledge of everything that was happening. He seemed trustworthy and god knows he needed as many good officers on his side as he could muster, but there was still too much going on without anything definitive to hook a young initiate. At one time his name and reputation would have been enough to enrol almost any officer onto whatever taskforce he was forming. Now, his name and reputation had officers sniggering behind his back. That was, at least something; he had not deteriorated so much to have them laugh in his face.

«I forgot something,» Anjo said. «Watch my car.»

«Yes sir,» the gendarme barked and snapped to attention.

Anjo marched to the museum entrance, invigorated further by the boy's attitude. He *was* regaining his reputation and some respect. He would keep an eye out on that boy for when this was over. Badge 1138.

He surprised himself. He had not even looked for the officer's number, but there it was. An insignificant detail etched into his memory. Another sign that his game was returning to form.

Was that a good thing?

Yes! Absolutely! He had stopped fighting it. He was no longer in denial. Inspector Rene 'The Bloodhound' Anjo was back and heaven help those he was tracking down.

V—V

Neither of them could come to a decision over where to go. They were both on the defensive and felt obliged to acquiesce to the other's choices. In the end, Penny suggested that they spent the day going their own ways to reconnect to the city and then they might have better luck tomorrow.

His argument, however, was that he had not gone there to reconnect with the city and believed that if they fell at this stumbling block then all obstacles that got in their way would not be overcome.

Penny had pressed her point further and he gave in.

She then told him she was going the visit the Louvre and he declared that it was an amazing coincidence but that was exactly where he was planning on visiting first.

He had got her and there was nothing she could do about it. She wanted to complain, to say that he was not allowed to go there because it was her private place, that he was never interested in museums but that would only make her look petty. She supposed that it did mean he was trying to make an effort, even if it was in such a sneaky, underhanded, manipulative way.

They left the hotel and walked to the museum, idly commenting on the clement weather and whether Penny could give him plenty of warning if she was going to throw up in the middle of the street.

She took on an air of indignation and told him that she was feeling fine. She hoped that her abrasive tone covered her outrageous lie and that her hands rammed deeply in her jacket pockets would disguise her rising DTs.

"I never understood why you came to this place so much," Professor stated as they strolled across the pedestrianised area toward the glass pyramid. "These places strike me as being elaborate mausoleums. But without the corpses."

"Nice," Penny sneered. "I have two main reasons why I spent so much time here. Firstly because I regard the place as a commemoration of lives past, and secondly because you never liked coming here."

"That makes sense," he mused. "I never did allow any time to yourself apart from your training." His voice trailed off and he looked incredibly uncomfortable. Whatever subject the natural progression of his conversation was going to uncover was not sure it wanted to come out. Was this to be his first proper apology?

"My first Apostle?" she asked and he reeled like the words had just shoved their bum in his face and farted.

"Yes, yes, whatever," he blustered, wafting away at the words and resurfacing memories. It was one of those strange experiences when he would like to think his imagination had embellished the details over the years. He actually presumed that his mind had managed to scar over some of the more graphic moments and it was actually worse than he could remember.

Her jaw tightened into a sadistic smirk and her eyes twinkled as the memory of her baptism returned. Her first solo outing and the day she discovered her rock of a father could be shaken.

"You needed somewhere," he continued as nonchalantly as he could.

"Somewhere to reflect. Somewhere you could believe where you were away from it all."

"Did you have somewhere like that, then?" Penny enquired. "What *did* you do while I was in there?"

"For a long time, I didn't need anywhere to go because I had your mother. When she left, no matter where I went, there was no peace to be found. If I got solitude then I would think about the wrong things anyway."

"I do wish we talked more," she said.

"It wasn't the done thing, then. Talking. I was your father and therefore a rock of discipline. 'Relating' to you then in the manner that has become systemic today would have shown some sort of weakness which could have proven fatal on our line of work."

"So showing that you cared could've got us killed?" Penny asked.

"It would have certainly drawn an unstable element to our relationship," he explained. "Less objective."

"Wow," she gasped. "That's cold."

"I felt it was necessary at the time," he said. "Considering the years that followed, I may have made a mistake. But we are both alive and we are both here. I much prefer this outcome than wishing to go back, change things and potentially lose you."

"I suppose," she muttered.

"You disagree?"

"It just sounds like an easy way to get out of accepting you were a bit of an arse."

"Wow," he mimicked. "*That's* cold."

They had taken the escalator down into the lobby, paid their entrance and were wandering around the galleries more engrossed in their conversation than the exhibits.

Despite the renovations since her last visit, Penny was on automatic, her body was being drawn to her reflective spot. Only to be stopped by some yellow police tape.

"What the fuck?" she demanded as she was brought back to reality.

"Penelope!" her father admonished. "That was entirely unnecessary."

"Why didn't they tell us that this wing was closed to public viewing?" she complained rhetorically.

She paced the line of tape like a caged tiger, hoping to see someone on the other side get too close for her to physically lash out at and sate her wrathful ire.

"Excuse me," Professor called calmly and she spun on her heels ready to snap at him but she discovered he had his back to her and was directing his attention to a passing security guard.

"Si?" the guard replied. He was young, tall and stocky, looking more like a bouncer than the usual near-retired wardens.

«Oh, pardon me,» Professor apologised, presuming the guard had thought he was Italian. «We were just wondering why this particular wing had been closed to the public? Is there cleaning going on? I can smell quite a powerful aroma of bleach.»

«Yes. Cleaning,» the guard replied with difficulty. «Someone killed. Much blood.»

«Thank you,» Professor said and turned back to his daughter with a quizzical expression on his face. He silently took her arm in hers and directed her towards the exit.

When they were clear of the building - and it had become obvious that he wanted her to deliver the feed line - she unlocked herself from him and demanded, "What was it?"

"What was what?"

"That look you gave me."

"I found it rather odd that a French museum would hire a man who couldn't speak the language."

Penny looked decidedly unhappy. "I thought you might have discovered something suspicious," she grumbled.

"We're retired now, remember?"

"Yeah," she mumbled.

"You're disappointed that I didn't suspect some sort of necromantic conspiracy?"

"Well, I have to say that our attempts at bonding through nostalgia don't seem to be working too well," she commented.

Professor stopped in his tracks and looked absolutely crestfallen. "Really? I thought we were making quite good progress."

"After last night?"

"We're still talking now aren't we?" he asked. "We haven't left it another fifty years."

She wanted to go off on one but was finally coming around to the idea that her rants just were not helping the situation. She had to make a conscious effort to listen to the things he was saying and, in this case, he was sort of right. Indiscretions were starting to be inconsequential.

She sighed then pursed her lips at him. "Can we at least go back to the hotel before we do all those steps? I need to change my shoes."

He gave her Dr Martens a cursory glance. "You need something more hard-wearing?"

"Shut up."

V—V

Anjo strode purposefully through the museum's corridors and did not get lost once. He did not know the building at all and had been blindly led to the scene that first day but, now his instincts were returning, the route was as clear to him as if he had travelled there every day for a year. Twice at weekends.

He came to the yellow tape and deftly ducked beneath it. He looked around the room which had been thoroughly hosed down. Aside from the few holes in the wooden crossbeam, there was no real indication that anything had happened here.

He tried to remember the scene and place all the elements before him. There was Matilda measuring the surface area of the blood pool on the floor. There was the body, pinned to the ceiling, smiling and pointing at the wall. Really? Was it that simple? A clue about the painting?

If that was the case then why had he not made it more obvious? If he had killed himself then setting all this up must have taken some time no matter how spontaneous it was. If he had wanted to leave a clue and it was about the painting then he should have made it clearer.

Perhaps there was a clue within the painting? As he was dying he looked over and noticed something? The man's smile. It was not one of satisfaction that he had accomplished something, that he had found peace; more like it was a smile of amusement. Something had caught his fancy within the painting. But what?

An irony of some sort. Had he just had his last –

«Excuse me,» a troubled voice called from behind Anjo and he whirled on the spot to see a large security guard. «You not be in there,» the guard said.

Anjo frowned at the man. «You are not French,» he accused.

«Italian,» the guard confessed.

«When equal opportunities go too far,» Anjo sighed and fished his badge from his jacket pocket. The guard studied it for a second and then nodded his understanding.

«How long have you been here?» Anjo asked suspiciously.

«I join on-»

«No, just today. How long?»

«Since opening.»

Anjo rooted in his pockets again, pulled out his sketch and showed it to the guard. «Have you seen these two?»
The guard looked at the crude drawing and shrugged.

«I believe they are connected to this crime in some way,» Anjo said and forced the paper into the guard's hand. He then went back to his pocket and pulled out a creased business card. «I believe they might come back. Call me if you see them.»

The guard nodded enthusiastically and watched as Anjo looked around the room once more. There *was* something about the painting. He ducked under the tape again and marched out of the wing – he needed to get to his computer.

When Anjo finally disappeared around a corner, Cunningham stepped from a shadow.

"Show me the picture," he instructed and the guard handed the drawing over.

"They were here," the guard said. "As soon as the museum opened. They came here, looked, asked if it had all been cleaned up and then left again. She was very angry."

Cunningham looked up quickly. "Who is 'she'?"

The guard leaned over the drawing and tapped at the sketch of Penny.

"A girl?" Cunningham demanded and the guard nodded. "How could you tell?"

The guard stared at the assassin in confusion. "She had boobies."

## 7 (*Maintenant*)

## More about Claude Frollo

Their drive back into the city was taken up by Jean stuttering polite conversation at Matilda while she dutifully and politely responded at the appropriate times but was not really paying attention to the subject matter.

She was lost in her private world of assumptions and possibilities. Her mind was trying to combine elements from all the incidents scenes in the hope that even just two pieces of this ridiculous puzzle might show some kind of uniformity. Even if they would not fit together then they could at least be the same colour. Or maybe be two corner pieces, to get her started. Hell, even two straight edges would be better than the random collection of varying sizes, patterns and material.

She had it in her mind that the first death was the one that held the clues. She wished she had gone with the Inspector to the museum. He and she were a good team and were able to bounce theories off each other no matter how sublime or inane they might seem. After all, they had formed this case together from out of nothing.

She could still see the man - Brian - smiling at the painting. It was serene, as if he was resolving something with his death. A moral victory? Had it proved a point of some sort? Won an argument?

'See? It *is* possible to commit suicide by crucifixion. Erm, can somebody help me down now? Hello? Bugger.'

Perhaps he had a sense of humour and the smile was of the ironic tragedy of proving a rhetorical point.

An ironic smile ...

«- Anjo?» Jean asked and ruptured Matilda's train of thought like a burst appendix.

«Pardon me?» she blurted, slightly embarrassed that she had been blatantly ignoring the man and incredibly embarrassed by the trigger that had woken her up.

«Are you all right?»

«I was lost in a train of thought,» she confessed. «I am sorry.»

«That's okay,» Jean chuckled. «You sort of answered my question anyway.»

«Which was?»

«How you were finding it working alongside Anjo?»

She thought about her answer before giving it. She knew that Jean was asking a loaded question; most officers' opinions of Rene Anjo went along the lines of, 'broken man,' or, 'ghost of his former self'. They were the respectful descriptions used by colleagues who knew of his history and past abilities. The younger officers tended to call him things like, 'embarrassment' or 'wash out'. She had even heard someone call him, 'a liability'.

«He is a great detective,» she eventually replied.

«Oh? How so?» Jean asked.

«He sees everything and can store the slightest detail to recall at the necessary time,» she divined. «But he has allowed himself to be haunted by, what he considers to be, his failures.»

She looked across to Jean to see how he might take her outlook and noticed a genuine expression of consideration.

«That is very interesting,» Jean pondered. «I can see him being haunted as much by his successes as his failures too.»

Matilda scrutinised him in the hope of witnessing the slightest inflection of derision but he stared, emotionless, at the road ahead.

«You know Anjo?» she asked.

«He has always been there,» Jean replied. «Although I have never really worked with him, I have watched him. I was just a gendarme when he was working on the *M&M* case but I saw how much that changed him. It is good to see him doing the job properly again.»

Matilda continued to watch Jean, still expecting to see the corner of his mouth turn up and reveal a deeply embedded sarcasm. All she saw was him thinking about something.

«But?» she asked and jogged him out of his concentration.

«'But'? Oh, I am just concerned about the case itself and whether it is the right one for him.»

«In what way?»

«This is his, er,» Jean sustained this final phoneme for quite some time before the words he wanted fell into place, «rebirth, if you like. Yes, ha! His renaissance.»

She wanted to debate how any case could be wrong if it was having a positive effect but something about that word jarred in her memory as if having broken a dream.

«He is making more of something as simple as suicide,» Jean went on, oblivious that he was really only talking to himself again. «He is searching for a conspiracy where there is not one. It can only end in tragedy. Failing to find the answer he wants will either set his confidence back again or he will try to build a conclusion that would suit his theories.»

She wondered how deeply she wanted to get herself involved in this debate. To offer her truthful opinion would probably end up as an outright argument and, of course, she expected Jean would not take 'Little Matilda's' point of view to be anything other than adolescent hero worship.

«I do not think he would do that,» she answered simply and kept her focus straight ahead.

«Perhaps,» Jean commented without any conviction at all.

Needless to say the rest of their journey went without any more conversation between them. Jean would sometimes rhetorically comment on the driving abilities of his fellow motorists. Well, they may or may not have been deliberately rhetorical but they certainly became as such when Matilda refused to dignify them with a response.

Instead, she allowed herself to immerse into the conundrum of the case again only, this time, an element of doubt had worked itself into the puzzle. What if her judgment had become clouded because of her emotional attachment? Not 'emotional' like that, but her sheer exuberance at working on a case like the M&Ms directly with Inspector Anjo rather than the previous cases of watching him enter, comment, then wander off again.

Those cases where she was just about to start investigating only to find the case had been closed. And any time she dared confront him, he would bawl her out.

She was desperate to get into a real investigation, had she now put her objectivity (along with her career) on the line because she needed a bit of job satisfaction?

Was she taking Anjo on a carousel ride of her enthusiasm or had he strapped her onto a rollercoaster that had not been completed yet?

«We are here,» Jean announced as he drew the car to a halt. He turned the engine off and turned to her. «I did not mean to upset you, Matilda,» he apologised. «I respect you and Anjo as officers very much. You have shown a degree of investigative ability that I could only dream of having, and he ...»

His inability to complete his sentence grabbed her attention more than his words did.

Jean was staring out of the windscreen at the parked car in front of them as he pondered whether to continue with his statement.

«I can see that Anjo likes you a lot,» Jean blurted, «and it makes me very jealous.»

Matilda placed a consolatory hand on his arm. «You are a good police officer, Jean, but, more importantly, you are a very good man. There is nothing to be jealous of. This 'case' that we're on may be just a ghost chase but I cannot help but ask questions and, for as long as I do not get a satisfying answer, I will continue to search for one. Whether that is Anjo's motivation, I cannot tell you, but know that I am not being led astray by him or my emotions.»

Jean turned to her again and smiled. «I am glad - well not glad that you are probably ruining any chance of a career by chasing this ghost - but glad you are in control of what you are doing.»

She returned his smile. «Thank you for your concern,» she said. «And thank you for the lift.»

«You're welcome. I had to come back into the city anyway. Would you like me to come with you?»

«Not at all,» she told him. «You have gone out of your way enough for me already.»

«It would not be a problem and I would enjoy watching you at work.»

«Even if it means associating yourself with a career suicide?»

«Who knows? You might even be able to use me as defence during your inquiry.»

«Not if I have taken you down with me,» she warned with a coquettish grin then she got out of the car.

They walked over to the Cathedral, Jean deliberately remaining a pace behind Matilda, and as they neared the main doors they noticed a large crowd gathered on the steps. Matilda delicately tried to push her way through the throng but the bodies refused to budge: either because of her lack of insistence or because they were too tightly packed in.

«Pardon me,» she urged. «Police business.»

One man emerged from the crowd before her. «There is no business here today,» he grumbled. «They say the church is closed *because* of the police.»

«The suicide?» Jean asked.

«No,» Matilda said. «We concluded our investigation last night.»

«Clear the way!» Jean ordered and managed to grab a bit more attention. The back rows parted and, as soon as the innards of the congregation realised something was afoot, a subliminal order osmosised through to the extremities until everyone became aware and affected by the officers' presence.

Matilda could not help but shrink into herself as the crowd parted for their passage. So many people on the brink of revolt could quite easily have overpowered them and broken down the cathedral doors. It was only the unconsciously ingrained ideologies of the institutes of church and law that stopped the mob from taking just what they wanted.

Jean reached the door then turned on the crowd. Matilda had been following so closely that she found herself almost resting her head on his chest. He raised his badge over the heads of the throng and waved it from side to side.

«Go about your business,» he instructed. «There is nothing to see here.»

The crowd stared at him with disbelief and he shrugged his shoulders at Matilda who stared up at him with her wide eyes even wider in the belief that they were on the cusp of creating a riot.

«I always wanted to say that,» Jean confessed.

Matilda raised herself two more steps so her eye line was just above the heads of the restless. «Ladies and gentlemen,» she called but could barely be heard beyond the eighth row of people. «This is no way to behave on the steps of a house of God! Yes, this building is a national landmark and social institution but it is also a sacred place and deserves to be treated with respect. Please, distil your anger and disperse from this place before this situation escalates beyond your control or intentions.»

The front lines stopped jostling and were deeply moved by her words or were affected by her deer-in-the-headlights expression. They slowly turned and began weaving their way through the outer ranks, spreading the message and their calmed intent as they went.

«That's what I said,» Jean muttered sulkily as he watched the remaining protesters disperse.

Matilda released her pent-up anxiety with a loud sigh. «That was scary,» she noted. «You could feel that they were on the edge of revolt.»

«It's a good job there weren't many students, otherwise it would have all kicked off,» Jean stated as he walked past her and approached the door.

«Are they really that passionate about their beliefs and rights?»

«They are really that drunk with nothing better to do.»

Jean banged on the door. «Police! Open up!»

«You have already tried that one,» a voice replied from the other side. «Go away, we are closed.»

«No really, we really are the police this time,» Jean argued with an edge of disappointment in his voice.

«Piss off,» the gruff voice instructed.

«That wasn't very Christianly,» Jean grumbled.

«Catholic,» Matilda corrected and Jean raised his eyebrows in understanding.

Jean returned his attention to the door as if willing it open with his mind. Then he grabbed the handle and rattled it furiously. The door clicked and edged open.

The officers stared at each other.

«Gah!» the voice from inside exclaimed. «I told you to stay out!»

Jean slipped his foot into the gap before the door could be slammed closed again and pulled his badge from his pocket.

«"In their hands they will keep you up,"» the voice preached, «"so that your foot may be crushed against my door."»

«Look!» Jean screamed. He flapped his badge around wildly as his tarsals ground painfully together under the weight of the door.

The pressure ceased and Jean's badge was taken from his hand. Matilda gave the door a gentle shove and stepped through the widening gap. Jean limped after her.

Inside, they were confronted by the crooked form of LeClerc who subserviently returned Jean's identification.

«Assaulting an officer of the law,» Jean growled.

«I was simply protecting myself and the Cathedral,» LeClerc explained.

«Why are you closed?» Matilda asked.

«I was told, this morning, that police needed access to the scene and I couldn't have members of the public wandering around.»

«What police?» Jean demanded.

«You?»

«We did not call.»

«No? But you are here.»

«So who called?»

LeClerc just shrugged his shoulders. «Police,» he replied.

«Father,» Matilda interrupted calmly. «We have come to ask more questions about the death of Father Frollo.»

Again, LeClerc just shrugged his shoulders unapologetically. «I do not know what more I can add.»

«How about you pretend this is the first time you have said what you do know and tell us,» Jean instructed testily.

As LeClerc shot a glance at Jean, his expression flickered from one of resignation to something more malicious. It was for the briefest of seconds and was lost in the shadows of his brows to the over-towering officer but Matilda, who stood at LeClerc's eye level, clearly saw the spiteful glare.

«I was attending to the vestibule after Frollo had locked up when I heard a commotion outside. When I came to see what the noise was, I discovered the priest in a mess.»

«That's it?»

LeClerc shrugged.

«Had anything happened during the day that might have caused him to take his own life?»

«Nothing out of the ordinary. Frollo was a quiet man who kept his business to himself.»

«What business?»

«I do not know. He kept it to himself.»

«How long have you been appointed here, Father?» Matilda asked.

«'How long?' What has that got to do with anything?» LeClerc demanded.

«The longer you have been here would allow you more insight into Frollo's life and perhaps the people who might have wanted him dead,» she explained carefully and was pleased to watch his expression change from belligerence to fear.

«It was suicide,» LeClerc stated.

«Was it?» she asked rhetorically.

They stared at each other for a long malevolent moment.

«I was told he jumped,» LeClerc muttered.

«Does the name Brian Gagnant mean anything to you?»

He was getting better but still winced slightly at the mention of the name.

«No. Should it?»

«Perhaps.»

«What do you know about the deaths that occurred last night across the bridge?» Jean demanded with hostility.

«A priest,» Matilda gasped to herself and saw a look of fear spread across LeClerc's face.

«What are you hiding?» Jean demanded.

«I ... I ...» LeClerc's eyes darted around the Cathedral then finally settled on Matilda, wide and alarmed.

«I know nothing,» he declared but then stepped in so close to her that his cheek caused her earring to tinkle. «They are listening,» he whispered. «Follow me.»

LeClerc turned and began to lumber to the front of the cathedral before either law enforcer could offer any protestation. Jean flashed a glance of concern at Matilda but she was already following the old man towards the pulpit.

He had taken his place behind the podium and placed his hands reverently on the large Bible thereon. As Matilda stepped up next to LeClerc she saw a small cloth pouch on the book.

«Inside,» LeClerc whispered and watched her face crumple with incomprehension.

She eyed the purse with suspicion and intrigue, then tentatively reached out and picked it up. She handled it delicately, massaging the old material, feeling for a clue as to the contents.

LeClerc had stopped watching her and had closed his eyes.

She loosened the drawstrings and widened the opening. She dipped her fingers inside just as LeClerc began to speak again. «I cross the water without a barque, I cross the water without a boat. My mother is a bird, my father is a bird.»

«I do not understand what you are tying to tell me,» she told him.

LeClerc opened his eyes calmly at her. «I am afraid you understand too much,» he muttered as a light draft bristled his hair from behind.

The breeze wafted against her face and with it came a foetid stench of stale mausoleums. Yes, her experience had allowed her to know what stale mausoleums smelled like.

«What is it?» Jean demanded from behind her.

She tried to speak but her voice had become dry and hoarse as if breathing in the air had sucked the moisture from her throat. Her pulse and breathing had quickened although she was not entirely sure why. Over the past week, she had been witness to more extreme brutality than in her entire career and none of it had caused her heart to skip a beat so why was this old man and his little cloth sack causing her -?

He was still staring at her as things went click in her head. Not all the pieces came together but at least she was shown the puzzle box cover and could finally see what picture the pieces were supposed to make.

She cleared the blockage from her throat. «It is him,» she stuttered.

«It is too late,» LeClerc whispered with sincere sympathy.

The breeze trailed around the church; when it was not wafting the candles it was unsettling the dust that sparkled in the red spotlights from the stained glass windows. It began as a general flurry of disturbance that swirled around the grand hall, carefully licking at the delicate flames, glistening motes and tails of the officers' coats. Then condensing, ensnaring the particles within a tighter form and holding a concentric orbit centred on Matilda.

It whipped around, trailing dust, leaves and litter into a rising maelstrom of blatant, intentional harm.

«What is it?» Matilda screamed above the whistling menace.

«Love, hate, death, life,» LeClerc replied without taking his eyes of her. «An embodiment of dichotomy given life by the hand of God, himself.»

LeClerc felt a point of hard metal press against the back of his head.

«Stop it,» Jean ordered.

«I cannot.»

«Stop. It,» Jean said with a gentle press of the gun barrel with each word.

«It cannot be stopped after it has been given its decree.»

«I will kill you,» Jean stated.

«To try to stop it would be to defy the word of our Lord and incur a far more serious repercussion than mere death.»

«I fucking hate you religious zealots,» Jean growled and holstered his gun.

The vaporous mass came to rest before Matilda and condensed further, forming translucent features amidst the water-like body. She saw pained, forlorn eyes form from the globule and, for a moment, all sense of fear waned and she felt genuine sympathy for the thing. The eyes became misaligned and receded into a heavy set forehead. A mouth, deformed by a cleft pallet, decayed teeth and wilted bottom lip, attempted to speak to her; urging, instructing, imploring.

The earnest expression of its malformed features caused her fear to return but it was not until its features warped to a fresh, young, high cheekboned girl with eyes ablaze with hatred and lips drawn back over clenched teeth in feral rage that she decided somewhere else would be a better place to be right now.

Matilda turned and ran, not daring to look back to see if that vengeful spirit was following; not needing to because she was sure she could feel the tempest teasingly flicking the back of her hair.

There were the main doors mere meters away from her and the delusional potential of freedom beyond.

A sharp pain in her back caused her feet to stumble over themselves and she fell, winded and shocked, to the cold stone floor.

She rolled onto her back, expecting to see that sinister spectre looming over her. Instead, she discovered Jean, on all fours at her feet, his head hung low and his back undulating with deep breathing.

Matilda searched around them, desperately seeking for some sign of the horror but the cathedral was at rest again.

«It is so angry,» Jean muttered, «and yet loves so unconditionally.»

«Jean?»

Jean lifted his head but did not look at her directly; his eyes flickered from side to side as if trying to resolve some inner debate.

«It's in me,» he said and then looked at her, «but it wants you. Run.»

Jean's internal dilemma finally resolved itself and he sat back with a calm expression. He reached into his holster for his pistol and pulled it out.

Matilda scrabbled backwards in concern for her safety until Jean turned the gun against himself.

«I can't live like this,» he said dreamily and pressed the barrel to the bridge of his nose. «No one can.»

The top of Jean's head erupted in a shower of hair, skull and blood yet the force of the bullet and the blast caused no more of a reaction than a slight nod. But as the man's essence rained down, fragments and droplets began to gather in the reforming poltergeist and it stared at Matilda with unashamed detesting.

*... spontaneous suicide ...*

*... chasing a ghost ...*

More pieces, more picture, but no one to show.

# BOOK 6

## 1 (*Allors*)

## An Awkward Friend

Penelope Helsine had made a very important but necessary decision: today was the day that things would change everything for good. Primarily, it would change her outlook on her life which was in desperate need of a surge of positivity right now.

The whole vampire wars had become too much. Too many people were dying too frequently: mortals and undead alike. Not that she really cared about snuffing out the candles of evil but its increasing necessity did get her thinking profoundly about their, and her, existences and the general reason for 'it all'. Was this her lot in life? Was her ultimate purpose simply to be a minister of elimination? To not find rest until she had caused the extinction of a species of creature? What gave her the right? Who had given her the task? Her father always professed that they were conducting the work of the Lord, trying to equate the balance between good and evil but where did he get that from? She knew that vampires must have been around for centuries before her or her father had got involved with this crusade but knew of no other Hunters: present or past.

Was that her destiny then, to perform this religious mission (without actually being called to do it), protect those who do not know of the threat, ask for help nor seem to appreciate the act? Then, when that time came when she was to make that fatal mistake, fall to overwhelming odds or (glass half-empty girl!) finally succeed, was she supposed to slip into the shadows of anonymity? Unrecognised for her deeds, not remembered for her life, not mourned for as a loved one?

Well, fuck that, quite frankly.

Her father might be quite resigned to that little scenario, accepting of the duties befallen to him, gaining some perverse enjoyment from his martyrdom but he volunteered for the job. Perhaps, because he actually got the calling, he understood the rules, reasons and objectives better than she did. She prided herself on having a bit more brain to question the things set before her. For example, if vampires had been around since the dawn of time, then did that not imply that they were just one of God's creations? Not necessarily creatures of evil but of necessity like sharks, lions or mosquitoes. So, on that basis, was it not possible that she was actually acting against the word of God on some level? Thou shalt not kill. Simple as that. Do not kill, or you'll go to Hell. The Ten Commandments did not include a footnote for each entry that listed circumstances that stood as exceptions to the rules like some legal document.

*Thou shalt not worship false idols[1].*
*Thou shalt not create graven images[2].*
*Thou shalt not take the Lord's name in vain[3].*
*Thou shalt not work on the Sabbath[4].*
*Honour thy mother and father[5].*
*Thou shalt not kill[6].*
*Thou shalt not covet they neighbour's ass[7].*
*Thou shalt not steal[8].*
*Thou shalt not bear false witness[9].*
*Thou shalt not commit adultery[10].*

What was it about humans' nature that made them think they were more important than any of God's other creatures which, in turn, allowed them to bend the rules as they wanted?

She did some mental arithmetic and worked out that she must have crossed off at least six of the Rules during her line of work and could not work out how she was going to explain to St Peter that she thought it was okay to do so because it seemed like the right thing to do at the time. Was there an ignorance caveat written on one of the tablets by Moses' lawyer (a representative of the entire human race) that made some allowance for objective thinkers who might question the validity of three millennia old doctrines that had been translated and edited by kings, fundamentalists and sexual deviants (not

---

[1] *Unless thy idol be really cute, a good singer and dancer.*
[2] *Unless they be totally bling, innit!*
[3] *Unless it doth make for a very funny punchline.*
[4] *Which is Sunday, Monday or Saturday: which ever doth be most convenient to thy trading days.*
[5] *Unless thy mother or father know less than thou or are being totally embarrassing in front of thy friends.*
[6] *Unless thou doth kill in the name of God; or the person in question doth be particularly naughty and deservest it under condition Leviticus 24:20 'An eye for an eye'; or thou art **really** hungry.*
[7] *Unless thy neighbour hath a particularly sweet ass.*
[8] *Or rather, Thou shalt not get caught stealing.*
[9] *Unless bearing true witness may be used in evidence against thou.*
[10] *Unless thy neighbour hath a particularly sweet ass.*

mutually exclusive to each other) who, by some freakish chance, all happened to be men!

Espousing her suffragettisms at the Pearly Gates and calling St Peter a patriarchal, oppressive misogynist probably would not be the best way to get into the man's Good Book. She wondered if she could get some Pearly Chains to take with her, for just in case.

The levels of contradictions made her head spin. How could she defy the word of God doing God's work? How could she be a conscientious objector when she wanted to believe so fervently? How could she be objective about her religion when she knew that the very act of questioning it was an act of defiance in itself?

Was it because of her desire to try to be neutral which was causing her such confusion? When was it that she felt at peace, completely assured in what she was doing was right? When she was fighting for her life and when she was fighting with her father. The two seemed to be increasing in occurrence in relation to each other.

Yes, she had been killing and, recently, dishonouring her father more and more. It was the final proof that indicated she was treading a clearly signposted path to damnation. So, this morning she had made a decision that had been playing on her mind for a very long time as the action that could sway the balance of her morality in either direction; from part-time saint to fully-fledged sinner. Of course, because she had successfully persuaded herself that she was damned anyway, then a few extra crosses on The List probably would not make any difference.

It was 1948 and she was closer her hundredth birthday than her seventieth. The two recent wars had caused the father and daughter team to travel east, across Asia, in an attempt to avoid the mortal conflicts until there was nowhere that was either not involved, or their presence was an overt oddity and brought an unwanted amount of attention. By the time they had reached 'home' again, the Allies had succeeded in overthrowing the Axis and the whole of Europe was celebrating their liberation. They had left Paris nearly fifty years ago when everyone was nihilistic as to any future. Now, upon their return, the mixture of emotion was quite overpowering: so much joy over the victory intertwined with incredible sadness over the losses had complete strangers falling into each others arms crying, laughing and comforting.

Professor was uncomfortable by the slightest display of emotion at the best of times and so this extended period of celebration had him trapped in their apartment almost twenty-four-seven, which allowed Penelope the freedom to experience the thrills of the fragile, transient human condition albeit vicariously.

Paris was a great place to be right now; the end of war, the release of civil liberties, a dawning era of female rights, a change in fashions and her personal freedom. All of these things added together finally meant she could walk around in public looking like the young woman she was (finally) growing into.

As was her father's standard mode of operation, she had been forced to blend into their adoptive cultures across the Eastern continents. Cowls, gowns, cloaks, hoods and scarves had all played their part in hiding their ethnicity and sexuality from the eyes of others as well as herself. Her acclimatisation to Parisian culture had, at first, left her blushing with the almost indecency of how tight the clothes were and how much flesh she was exposing. There was absolutely nowhere to hide a three inch flick knife, let alone her foot long Bowie.

Her vulnerability would have been two-fold had it not been for her devious diversionary tactics that forced her father's exodus across Asia to spend some quality time (for her) in China where she was able to further her melee and weaponry expertise. Now she had killing implements so sheer and svelte that the adhesive she used to glue them to her body left more of an impression through her clothing than the blades themselves.

Since returning, she had taken quite an interest in the expressionistic jazz movement that had been fuelled by the revolutionary ethics against the war, capitalism and harsh American Rock 'n' Roll. She had seen this 'Beatnik' movement as an opportunity to dress in a manner that would send her father into apoplectic shock (if she ever allowed him the opportunity to witness the skin tight three-quarter length leggings, fitted t-shirt and cardigan). At least, she would reconcile with herself, they were black and conducive to hiding in the shadows of the underground bars she was able to infiltrate. The other good thing about them was that they were so tight that they were easily concealed beneath her larger, more acceptable modes of dress. She was lucky that her father had stopped 'frisking' her many decades ago after the incident of 'discovering' her long awaited development of breasts.

She found herself mixing among so many different walks of life; artists, office employees, soldiers, musicians and even clerical. It was one of the only cultures that she had experienced first hand that was so accepting and non-judgemental of its participants. In those darkened corners of the rooms, anonymity was guaranteed, if you wanted it, and your level of interaction was entirely up to you. Some people would randomly and, supposedly, spontaneously get up to perform and, whether it was awful or not, at least the effort of self-expression was genuinely appreciated.

Obviously she was one of the anonymous non-participants. But there was something within her that desperately urged her to get up into the spotlight and do … something. But that was the problem. She had been raised and trained to be a killer, not a creator. She had been taught to be reserved and distrustful of others, not open and expressive. The only time when improvisation and imagination had ever been encouraged was when she was required to create killing implements from the most innocent and banal of objects. She did not think a public display of fashioning of the club's cutlery into makeshift shuriken would receive the same hearty applause of validation as a poem entitled, 'Wibble,' or suchlike. Even less likely to be appreciated when she displayed their effectiveness during an expressionistic dance routine influenced by Oriental combat movements which climaxed with the utter evisceration of the entire audience.

Instead, she used these times to mingle and, after so many years of isolation and alienation, she honed her skills in socialisation and finally got to know other people. She developed friendships, learned more about the mortal human condition and made real connections.

Especially the connection she made with *him*.

She usually allowed other people to make the first move to communicate with her, ensuring, of course, that she never came across as being aloof and scaring people away, but she had decided to approach him. She had seen him at a couple of other clubs, although probably would not have noticed him had he not been sitting in the prime places she wanted to; the deepest recessed tables, furthest away from any chance of being interacted with.

He appeared to be the same age she appeared to be; old enough to look like a young adult but probably too young to actually be allowed in the bar. He was quiet and unassuming and when she came up to his table, he actually reeled as if being physically assaulted. Shy; she liked that.

Penelope talked, practicing her newly acquired communication skills: starting with references to the superficial décor of the current establishment; perhaps the weather; even being so bold as to compare this place to some of the other bars she had seen him in. He sat and, for want of a better expression, listened. Listened in the sense that he would flick his eyes towards her until she caught his gaze and he would instantly look away again. Eventually he actually started acknowledging her comments and observations with a subtle nod of his head or a half-hearted, embarrassed chuckle. Then, he actually spoke to her.

At first, she managed to completely disregard the comment due to the momentum of her banal ramble on her observations about the inherent sexism of the egg on top of a *croque-monsieur* making a *madame* and the gender discrimination it subliminally reinforced in society.

«Sorry, what?»

He gave her another sideways glance. «I said, 'I have to go now.'»

«Oh.»

«Will you be here tomorrow evening?»

«I can be.»

«Perhaps you can talk at me some more then.» And he left.

She was in shock. They had had a conversation and, within those few exchanges, she was not sure whether he had been incredibly rude or asked her out on a date.

It turned out, it was neither; simply the inarticulate ramblings of a socially inept teenage boy.

But, as is the way with these things, repeated exposure over time led to desensitisation, familiarity and affection.

Penelope had a boyfriend.

## 2 (*Maintenant*)

## Good Souls

Anjo decided that this place would win no Michelin stars. In fact, he was surprised that the place was even allowed to be open at all: for all manner of health, hygiene and safety infractions. The floors were covered with mud, there was a dog in the corner of the room and he was sure he had seen a rat scamper under his table earlier.

The room had a distinct Mediterranean feel to it with its terracotta walls and crockery. Short, fat homemade candles in the centre of the table sputtered their imminent demise, implying it was either close to the end of the evening or the hosts were a bit tight with their electrics.

It must have been a party he was at. A number of tables had been connected to allow for about thirty people to sit round, although seating had only been set down one length.

Seating. That was a laugh. He adjusted his position on the hard wooden stool and felt the numbness of his buttocks transcend with a warm, prickly sensation.

The twelve other guests were engrossed in some heated debates. Or debate. He could not tell if there were lots of different arguments or lots of people involved in the one argument. Anjo was about to eavesdrop when the man he sat next to, who was not engaged in any of the discussions, gave him a nudge and pointed to the breadbasket. Anjo grabbed it and passed it to the man.

«What is going on?» Anjo asked. «Why are they so upset?»

"I am leaving," the man said as he broke a bread roll into small pieces onto his plate.

Ah, an office leaving party. That made sense. Work colleagues always got rowing on social events.

He looked along the table again and wondered why there were no women present. And why was everyone just wearing their dressing gowns? He looked down at his own garb and was rather concerned to discover that he, too, was similarly attired and, not only did he himself contradict his theory about the female presence, he was actually going to be a mother soon.

A hand rested itself upon his arm and he looked up at the man again. There was something oddly familiar about him. Something about the way the candle flames illuminated an aura around his body. There was something distinctly calming about him and, more specifically, his touch.

"Why can't we all just get along, huh?" he asked wearily. "Why have things got to always be so difficult?"

It was all too much and Anjo found it impossible to reply.

The man nodded sympathetically at him. "You had better go now," he said. "Look after her."

«The baby?» Anjo asked with surprise and was taken more aback when the man just laughed at him.

"How can you be pregnant, Rene? You're a man," he chuckled. "No, it's Matilda who needs your attention."

Anjo lifted his head so quickly from his desk that his neck made an audible crack.

«Matilda,» he gasped as if it was his first breath and he had been drowning in his dream.

He scrabbled around in his pockets, although he was not entirely sure what it was he was looking for. At one point he even stroked at his middle-age spread expecting a small kick of returned acknowledgment.

He had just found his mobile phone when his office door crashed open and a general furore of noise barged into the room followed by a sixty-year old desk sergeant.

«Where is she?» Anjo demanded before the man could make a sound.

«Hospital Hôtel-Dieu. She is critical.»

Anjo grabbed him by his elbow and twirled him out of the room. «Tell me the details on the way.»

«Witnesses say she was running from the cathedral in quite a state but there is some question as to why,» the sergeant panted.

«I'm sure there is,» Anjo grunted.

«Some have the impression that she was being chased, others think she was late for something.»

«Skip the finer details.»

«She dropped her phone, put her head down and ran into a wall.»

Anjo nearly stopped in his tracks. The sensation was incredibly disconcerting; it had been a very long time since he had allowed something to startle him. «She did it on purpose?»

«Definitely. All the witnesses say she changed direction to hit the wall.»

Why? Why had she tried to kill herself? Why had they all tried to kill themselves?

This time he stopped dead and it took the sergeant a few inertial steps to realise. He turned in anticipation of the inspector's next question.

«No,» Anjo declared. «They did not 'try', they succeeded. Why did she *not* kill herself? Why did she only incapacitate herself?»

«She did not want to kill herself?» the sergeant suggested.

Anjo looked up so quickly that it made the sergeant flinch. «Yes. To stop herself from killing herself.»

«It does not make any sense.»

Matilda's actions made perfect sense. Finally, he had an inkling of a motive to link the deaths. Something. Something was making them want to kill themselves. They did not want to until the something made them and when it did make them, they had to do it immediately. Matilda had found a way to stop that something from making her do it.

Now, what was that something? Hypnosis? Subliminal suggestion? Virus, poison, coercion? Whatever it was, it suggested the actions of a third party and, because of Matilda's involvement, indicated that the deaths were not random.

This long overdue epiphany had brought Anjo completely out of his sleepy haze and reminded him of his prior attention. What he had been doing before he had woken. He spun on his heels and retraced his steps to his office.

«What about Inspector Autout?» the desk sergeant called.

«Tell me the moment she is conscious,» Anjo replied from over his shoulder before slamming his door behind him.

He threw himself into his seat and waggled his mouse to wake his computer from hibernation. A *Google* page lit up the screen with streams of results for search parameters of all the victims' names. It had, so far, been a fruitless endeavour; every combination and variation of their names had come up with thousands of potential links; most of which were either personal sites, family trees or something to do with people with similar names.

What had it been about that painting that had amused Brian so much during the throes of his demise? Had the painting just been the inspiration to his ironic dénouement or was it the catalyst to his understanding of the root of his demise?

Anjo pulled up an image of the work of art on his screen; it instantly caused his dream to resurface. People coming together, socialising, talking, arguing, laughing, celebrating.

He had been doing this wrong. His search parameters had been too formal. He knew these people were not work colleagues: past or present. They had to know each other socially and if they did then they would refer to each other by first names only. The inclusion of their surnames had only widened the result possibilities.

He deleted the surnames in the search bar and jabbed return. Still, thousands of potential pages popped up and nothing obvious on the first page satisfied his curiosity.

What was it? There was one thing preventing this case from coming together. One thing that enable him to take it all to the Commissioner and shove it in her face. One thing that Matilda would probably be able to suggest.

The thought of her name made him search for his mobile again. He patted his pockets for the familiar mass, located it and pulled it out from his inside pocket. It was off for some reason so he pressed the 'on' button. The screen lit up for long enough to show him the battery was flat and that there was a voice message waiting for him.

Pulling his USB cable out of his drawer and plugging it into his hard drive, his eyes focused on the painting on his screen - party, special occasion, memories. The other end of the cable would not slot into his phone so he flipped the gadget over and his vision settled on the camera lens.

Was it that simple?

He tentatively hovered his cursor over the 'Images' link on the *Google* page. These moments were precious - he had learned that a long time ago - and they needed to be respected. These were Schrodinger moments when the very opening of the box was the dependent factor in what lay waiting inside and, by that nature, the very manner in which you broke the seal, the way you read the address and how you accepted it from the postman all played a part in what was actually inside.

Anjo exhaled and clicked.

The thumbnails that illuminated the screen in ascending order of relevance were too small to divine any immaculate detail, and the captions beneath them seemed to be varied reiterations of his site search results. One picture, however, caught his attention for its framing and subject structuring. It looked, from this limited perspective, like a group of people sitting around a large table and, in its caption, every first name from each of the victims was in bold.

Anjo clicked and bowed his head in reverence of the act.

A personal blog opened called *Hey, Suze!* Anjo had to scroll through a number of entries - the latest being dated yesterday - and noted the banal commentaries of a woman who had little purpose going on in her life other than updating a blog which very few people would be interested in.

There were accounts of shopping trips, reviews of TV programmes and the occasional film, but mostly it was simply ruminations on the inconsistencies and eccentricities of her life.

And then there was the photograph; a momentary snapshot of a dinner party at a restaurant. Thirteen people having a mixed yet heated debate about something. It was quite low quality resolution but Anjo could recognise Barry Gagnant as the figure on the far left, then there was the car crash victim, James Mineur, and next to him, Andrew Mainsvers-LeHaut. The others could have been anyone and Anjo only had first names to relate to them: Peter (was leaning across the table), Robert (a peanut shaped head of a man), Mary (looked drunk from the way she was leaning on Peter's arm), Suzette (the only one seemingly aware of the photographer; the blog's author?), Tom (pointing at the ceiling quite indignantly), James (holding back Thomas), Philip (looking like he was having a heart attack), and Matthew, Thad and Simon (all having their own private debate on the subject).

Anjo rifled through the identification photos of the other victims and tried to match them on his screen. The rough pixilation aside, he could not convince himself that the priest, Frollo, or the three street punks were present. However, that could not dissuade him that his theory finally had some reinforcement. And now, he also had a list of names for other potential victims and potential murderer or -ers.

He copied the web page onto his hard drive, then printed the image and text. Well, he eventually printed the image and text after printing thirty pages of the entire blog, then adjusting the preview to get rid of the adverts and finally having to reformat the entire layout in Word because the photograph kept printing across two pages.

Then he emailed the jpeg, its url source location and list of names to the forensics department, asking for "enhanced resolution for identification purposes, a physical address connected to the blogger's IP address and cross-referenced searches on the subjects' Christian names." He pondered about cc'ing the Commissioner on the circulation list but decided that she was probably intercepting and monitoring all his communications anyway.

He sat motionless for a moment, backtracking his thoughts to what it was he was supposed to be about to do and what else he needed to do. After all this time reacting to the events going on around him, he finally had something to act proactively to, but there was almost too much to deal with. He needed to cross-reference all the names to the victims' address books, he needed Matilda to bounce ideas off of.

Names.

Matilda.

Phone.

His PC alerted him to an incoming email and he discovered there were two: one from forensics and one from HR.

Forensics read:

**Anjo. Tracing IP now. Will call. Re photo - you been watching too much CSI: would be like trying to enhance child's scribble - just end up with exactly the same scribble but in high resolution.**

The HR email wanted Anjo to send a receipt of him having read the message before it would allow him to actually read it. He contemplated leaving it alone and that way he had evidence of his ignorance to whatever trouble he might be in now. However, past experience had taught him that, by ignoring the message, he would be forcing one of them to actually come down and visit. And they never brought biscuits. Unless you were getting your pay docked.

He sighed, clicked and read:

**Rene,**

**In accordance with staff policy handbook section 53(vii) - Inclusion, Acceptance, Tolerance and Understanding of the Diversity of Ethnic, Cultural and Religious Ideologies, we need to bring it to your attention about the inappropriate use of the phrase 'Christian names' recently flagged in one of your departmental communications. It is, of course, a common misconception as to the root meaning, the colloquial use**

**of and possible offence caused by such a phrase but this does not mean it is acceptable -**

Anjo clicked delete before the current urge to tear gas their offices turned into an obligatory duty.

Doing something. What the hell was it?

He Alt-Tabbed back to the blog to read the commentary attached to the photograph.

*Saturday - Illottonatti!*
*It was strange meeting everyone for the first time; face to face. Stranger putting voices to words rather than faces to names. After a few heated discussions, everything was agreed upon by everyone, and the papers were signed.*
*Now, we pray and wait.*

That was the end of the entry and Anjo furiously scrolled through multiple pages trying to find any kind of reference to this covert group but there was nothing more.

The woman kept records of her life with no contextual references anywhere; in or outside of her blog. These were just private musings kept as a reminder for herself.

«She could have been dead for months and nobody would know,» Anjo muttered to himself.

He entered 'Illottonatti' into *Google*, knowing that it would be a futile gesture, only to have *Google* ask him if he was sure about his spelling.

He remembered he had been doing something with his phone and searched his pockets for it while a name nagged at his conscience, then his computer *binged* the arrival of a new message.

He Alt-Tabbed between windows, expecting another berating from HR about his inappropriate use of the word 'Thursday' because of its potentially offensive implications to non-Norsemen.

It was from Forensics. They had a name. They had an address.

Anjo was out of the room before the bold black summary title in Outlook had changed to 'read'.

Anjo's phone remained face down on his desk, obscured by the blurred printed photo of the Illottonatti and patiently filling up with power.

V—V

Crowds were amassing at the steps of Notre Dame Cathedral.

After Matilda had run out, LeClerc had shut and bolted the doors closed again for obvious reasons but telling the disgruntled crowd that it was still because of police authorisation. The people stopped hammering at the doors but did not disperse.

As he watched the gathering congregation, it dawned upon him that perhaps his plans needed to be accelerated. He dashed along the aisle, being careful not to step and slip in Jean's spillage, took out the silken pouch and placed it on the open Bible.

He then produced about half-a-dozen little envelopes from his trouser pockets and carelessly tossed them onto the pages. Each envelope had a set of initials written on – *PP, JM, MI* …– and while he was searching his pockets to ensure he had them all, one – *SA* – slipped from the altar without him noticing. He ripped the envelopes open and emptied their contents – strands of hair, nail clippings, a scab – at the opening of the pouch.

Without the same dramatic flourish, he rattled off the spell – "Je passe l'eau sans nacelle, Je passe l'eau sans bateau, Ma mere est oiselle, Mon pere est oiseau." - whereupon his spirit servant presented itself again.

«Sorry,» he told it. «There is so much to do and so little time to do it. Let no debt remain outstanding.»

And, before it even had time to fully form, it whisked off on its way.

# 3 (*Allors*)

## A Bridal Night

The air was heavy with heat and moisture. Overhead, the sky was laden with oppressive dark clouds that refused any sense of respite through either a cleansing downpour or circulatory breeze. The prelude to this summer had seen copious amounts of flash rain followed by intense warmth which almost immediately evaporated the excess water. Increased industrial output over the past decade had created a sponge-like net across the stratosphere which prevented any of the vapours from escaping and accumulated them, hanging over the city like Damocles' swimming pool.

Paris could do nothing but wait in eager anticipation for the inevitable. As the days passed, and the inevitable showed few signs of coming, the eagerness turned to dread of its arrival.

Robert was waiting. Under normal circumstances, it would have been something that he was very comfortable with; he was an exceptional waiter. He had, for the most part of his life, been waiting. What for, he did not know but he knew that something monumental was coming his way. Right now, however, he was nervous, impatient and very, very excited.

Orphaned when he was seven, Robert was adopted by the church and raised in modest quarters in Notre Dame to do daily chores, serve in the choir and take education from the resident priest. Everything in his life had been mapped out for him; the church dictated every move he needed to make. Had he not done everything he was instructed to then there was always the threat of being sent back to the home or, more simply, he might be taken to with a birch stick. Unfortunately for him, he had been getting closer to having to make an important decision about where the rest of his life was going to take him; his sixteenth birthday was only a week away and he was being forced to choose between continuing his Holy path of discipline and abstinence or being released into the World on his own. With no-one. With nothing.

What a choice.

Recently, that choice was being made easier and swayed towards a certain direction in terms of 'with no-one'. So easy, in fact, that he had decided that very morning what he was going to do. She had changed everything for him - his confidence, his happiness, his experience - and he was now willing to risk everything he knew and trusted to be with her forever. He was going to profess his love, symbolised by his sacrifice of everything.

Naturally, Father Musnier was incredibly displeased with this choice, not only considering it to be a personal slight on his parental abilities but also that he was falling from the sacred path of enlightenment. So displeased, Musnier had immediately cast him out of his life and church.

Robert eagerly awaited her arrival to tell her everything about his planned potential future with her.

Despite his banishment, he had managed to keep a key to one of the back storage rooms where he arranged to meet her and, as punctual as ever, she arrived.

She was magical. The way she moved was so sleek and elegant: as silent as a soft breath, as gently as a caress. The way she talked was uninhibited and invigorating: as rapid as butterfly wings; as dulcet as angel song. The way she looked was as if sculpted by a Renaissance master: skin as smooth as alabaster; her face, symmetrically perfect; her hair, strands of golden icing; her bright red Alice Band, the cherry on top.

«What is the matter?» Penelope demanded upon seeing his expression. «Are you hurt?»

Robert snapped out of his reverie. «No, I was just appreciating you.»

«Stop it,» she ordered and hid her face in embarrassment.

«I have something to tell you," he said but she stepped forward and pressed a finger to his lips.

«Don't talk,» she ordered. «Not yet. I have come to an important and necessary decision; things need to change. There is something I must do.»

«I was -» She pressed her finger harder against his lips to make him stop then replaced it with her own lips and kissed him passionately.

She pulled away and whispered, «I don't have much time. Father is suspicious and I might lose my nerve.»

«What?»

She took one careful step away from him. The sun broke through the clouds for that moment and cast her in silhouette but, despite being swathed in shadow, he could quite clearly see she was removing her outer garments.

«Penelope?» he questioned nervously, his voice breaking on the third syllable.

«Shh,» she replied as she removed her underwear. «Take off your clothes.»

«Why?»

«It would be very hard to make love with them still on.»

«No, I mean, why do you want to do this now? What about waiting for marriage? Or a better time?»

«There is no better time, Robert,» she told him and walked forward again. She had suddenly realised she was the only naked person in this not-entirely private room and knew if she was closer to him, there would be less of her to be seen by him and, at least, someone to hide behind should they be discovered.

He mistook her tactical advance as predatory confidence rather than shyness and stumbled backwards, tripping over some storage boxes and landing on a pile of burlap sacks.

Her plan had backfired and instead of minimising his view, he now saw her in her full glory.

«Oh god, I'm sorry Robert,» she blurted, «I just thought this might be something ...» She ran back to her clothes and clumsily scrabbled with them, trying to find appropriate limb holes to put herself in.

And Robert saw her again for the fragile, vulnerable and beautiful creature he knew she was. As he had been willing to sacrifice everything he could for her love, he now realised this was her willing to sacrifice her most precious possession to him.

«No, Penelope, it is I who should apologise,» he said, pulled himself to his feet and dashed to her side. He pulled her up right and stared deep into her eyes until she composed herself to look back. «I am sorry. I did not understand. I would very much like to make love to you.»

She smiled demurely at him and began to unbutton his shirt until he could slip it from his shoulders. Then she unbuckled his belt and he shuddered as the back of her hand brushed against his yearning erection.

«Sorry,» she giggled but did not stop with his disrobement until he was as naked as she was.

They embraced, locked lips, pressed themselves together to feel each other and get beyond the bizarreties of biology. His stiffness pressed into her stomach, her pubes tickled his thighs, their sweat collected in rivulets and dribbled down their bodies.

They stopped kissing and inhaled sharply, then walked hand-in-hand back to the sacks and lied down together; him awkwardly on top of her to one side, trying to support his weight on his elbow. She pulled at his shoulder to roll him fully on her and spread her legs to make him more comfortable. He licked his lips with nervous expectation and shuffled his knees forward until the tip of his penis touched the inside of her thigh and he reflexively withdrew.

She jumped from his reaction and they both laughed.

«It's okay,» she assured him.

«I don't know where ...»

«Shall I ...?» She reached down, grabbed his shaft (from which contact he nearly jumped out of the room) and guided it into her.

His head stuck at her entrance and he tried to thrust forward but she pushed her hands against him and grimaced with the pain of the friction stretching her vaginal wall.

«Wait,» she gasped. «Not wet enough.»

«What do I do?»

«Move slowly, don't try to enter, massage me with your fingers.»

He dutifully did as he was told, if not somewhat awkwardly, supporting his weight on one arm, gently pushing his hips so his penis just moved up and down slightly while exploring with his free hand.

«Here,» she said and guided his fumbling to her focus on her clitoris, sending little shock waves through her body every time he, unintentionally, hit her target.

What limited foreplay there was, eventually had its desired affect and her increased moistness allowed him more movement and he tentatively pushed forward.

The pain was still there though and she was very close to telling him to stop, that something had to be wrong. None of the literature she had studied had told her about this aspect. Not that a bit of pain had troubled her before, god knows the number of battles she had been in over the century or so had resulted in her being hit over every inch of her body at one time or another, but this was supposed to be 'right' and at the moment it did not feel that way.

«Do you want me to stop?» he asked softly. The tremble in his voice showed he was trying to control himself so much: physically trying to maintain his position and lustfully trying to maintain his delicate movements.

*Aw, bless him*, she thought, wrapped her legs around his and pulled him fully in.

They both grunted from the exertion: her from the sudden sharp stab of agony; him from the overwhelming pleasure of warmth and tightness.

«Don't move,» she instructed between breaths. «I need a moment.» She inhaled deeply, flexing her pelvic muscles, working the pain away and, when she was ready, she thrust her hips up to absorb him totally. She moved away again to explore the sensation of his movement inside of her; his fullness rubbing against every nerve within her; the end of him giving that extra forceful touch as deep as it could; his body forcing down on her clitoris when he was fully immersed. She could see why people did this so much. Given more practise and familiarity, she could imagine that it could be amazingly pleasurable.

It could be better now if it was not for the coarse, itchy sacks she was being ground into.

Something changed in his movements and she looked into his face: sweat was pouring from his brow, his cheeks were bright red, it looked like he had stopped breathing. She had read about this moment.

«Robert!» she shouted. «Not yet!»

«I ...»

She reached up and maliciously tweaked his nipple in an attempt to distract him from his pinnacle.

«Ow!» he screamed. «Why -?»

He did not have any more time to question her because she had pushed him off her, flipped him round in one swift movement and mounted him.

*Let him have the distraction of the rough sacks,* she thought as she reinserted him.

«This does not feel right, Penelope,» he spluttered but she ignored him, not bothering to tell him how 'right' it really did feel.

She raised her body perpendicular to his, staring deeply into his eyes, moistening her lips and breathing heavily. She ran her hands through her hair, removed her final restriction and held the Alice Band in front of her, enjoying the symbolism. She leaned forward and slipped it over Robert's head, giggled coquettishly then thrust her pelvis forwards and backwards very slightly; not wanting to over stimulate him but absolutely wanting to enjoy the pivoting motion of his hardness inside her. After a while, her thighs began to cramp so she fell forward and began to drive up and down in long, deliberate strokes. She looked into his eyes and could see his moment creeping up on him.

*Goddamnit, if he comes now I will fucking kill him.* «What is happening to me?»

«Oh, Penelope,» Robert groaned.

«Yes, say my name,» she ordered.

«Oh, Penelope, I-»

«Yes, call my name.»

«Penelope, I-»

«Shout my name.»

«PENELOPE!»

That was not Robert's voice. That was ☐–

«WHAT THE HELL DO YOU THINK YOU ARE DOING, YOU LITTLE SLUT?»

Professor stormed into the room, grabbed her by the hair at the back of her head and threw her towards her clothes. She scrambled madly around for balance, to ward off any more attacks and to find coverage of any kind. He stepped purposefully closer to Robert who tried to bury himself in the sacks around him.

«If you ever come near my daughter again, I will kill you,» Professor said too calmly for comfort. «Do you understand?»

«But I love her,» Robert managed to exhort.

«If that were true, then you would not have defiled her in such a manner.»

He turned his back on Robert and marched back to Penelope, screaming at her to put her clothes on faster.

Everything changed for Robert that day. It was the day that he lost everything.

## 4 (*Maintenant*)

## The Beautiful Creature Clad in White

"Penelope!" Professor roared and his daughter poked her head around the corner from the kitchen.

"What?" she demanded with irritation.

"Explain this," he told her and flapped a bouquet of paper in her direction.

She approached with a mixture of indignation and curiosity and stared at a couple of crude drawings he held up at her on one of the sheets. There was something familiar about the portraits, as if bits of the features belonged to people she knew but the overall image was unfamiliar. After a second, clarity hit her. "Is that supposed to be me? I look like a boy!"

He nearly said something but managed to stop himself. However, his face had already registered his response and she caught his expression.

"I do NOT!" she told him forthrightly.

"I was simply going to suggest that, from a distance -"

"You do not want to continue this topic," she warned.

"Anyway," he backtracked but realised he had raised her hackles.

"Yes, and 'anyway'. What do you mean, 'explain this'? Why do you presume this has anything to do with me?"

"Because it does not have anything to do with me, Penelope," he reasoned and raised his eyebrows accusingly at her.

"Well, unless it's something to do with the plumbing in here, I don't see what I could have done to warrant such an unflattering sketch."

"Apparently it is from the police," he told her. "Luckily it went straight through to the manager's office and she brought it directly to me."

"Why would they be looking for us?" she queried and took the moment to study her features in the wall mirror to her side.

"Well, since I haven't been doing anything to draw the authority's attention recently -"

"Like 'recent' has anything to do with you and the law's attention," she muttered as she angled her head to inspect her face from the left. "Remember Hungary?"

He glared at her.

"I haven't been doing anything naughty recently either," she eventually stated.

They simply stared at each other for a long contemplative moment. Their respective thoughts hinging on the possible impact on their continued rapport rebuilding this interruption could cause. The potential return to their old style of running from city to city could mark the return of old behaviours, beliefs and attitudes. This unprecedented turn of events could have unquantifiable effects on their futures together. These butterfly sketches today creating a hurricane in their mañanas. Who could possibly predict the long term implications this might have on their relationship.

On the other hand, it would mean they could take a break from 'getting to know each other' and have some 'proper' fun together.

"Strike fast. Strike first," they said in unison, looked at each another and smiled.

"It says we were last seen at Île de la Cité," Professor stated as he read from the accompanying cover sheer.

"That fucking church," Penny sighed.

"It's more than -"

"I just don't understand what you see in the place; it gives me the creeps."

"It might not have anything to do with the *Cathedral*," he overstated.

"Whatever."

"It probably has more to do with your state of insobriety last night."

"Mm-hm. Yep. Thought so."

"However, I don't see the harm in revisiting the priest we rescued."

"Pfft. 'We'?"

"We should disguise ourselves. I would imagine this has been circulated to the majority of hotels in the area."

That renewed her enthusiasm. "I like disguises." She spun on her heels and began to trot to her room.

"Put a dress on, then no-one -"

She stopped abruptly and turned her head. "You put a dress on," she instructed.

"I was simply suggesting -"

The back of her raised hand cut him off and she resumed her journey. Her steps were less enthusiastic; a little bit heavier perhaps; almost stomping, then she ensured the bedroom door was closed with more effort than was absolutely necessary.

She inspected the fully stocked walk-in wardrobe for ... what? What look was she going for? Comfort? Fashion? Gender obscurity? Then she inspected herself. What look *was* she going for?

Once upon a time she kept an eager, envious eye on the latest vogues; always yearning but never being allowed to express herself. Then, when she had fully embraced independence, there was something about being unobtrusive that must have either become ingrained or simply made sense. Keeping herself off the vampire radar was a transferable skill to that of boys and girls too. By dressing in such an androgynous manner kept any potential unwanted amorous advances and most bitchy criticisms at bay. She was neither a target nor a competitor.

She was still a girl though, wasn't she.

Wasn't she?

Could she honestly say that she knew what it was supposed to feel like to feel like a woman so she could say that she did not feel like one? Or did. She felt like ... What?

There was only the fantasy of a bygone icon that reminded her she was a heterosexual female but, otherwise, there was no emotional indicators to suggest any form of gender or sex. When was the last time she had seen a guy she fancied let alone allow to touch her; to hold her? Was it a conscious decision to deliberately distance herself from all boys? Was it that this guise had become so effective in its pretence of androgyny that she had come to unconsciously believe she was sexless?

She was staring at a white cotton dress: the top half was sleeveless, fitted with a plunging neckline; the waist was fitted with a thick embroidered sash; the bottom half was a billowing spray of iridescent and incandescent gossamer. It would certainly make her look less non-feminine; it could not help but reveal a variety of gender specific aspects of her body; with a slight breeze, if she was not careful, it would probably end up revealing the very specific gender aspect of her body.

Dare she?

She was so used to the all encompassing feeling of trousers that the simple thought of wearing a dress made her blush. It would be like she was walking around a public place in secret with just her underwear on. There was something naughty about the idea of being naked under her clothes. There was something embarrassingly stupid about it as well; she knew everyone was naked under their clothes but -

She shuddered when the image of her naked father uncontrollably popped up into her mind.

- but with a dress there was easier access to seeing her decorum (or lack thereof).

She was wearing it, swaying from side to side, admiring the pleats as they gently splayed out around her as if watching the echoing concentric ripples of wading, hip-deep, through still, clear waters.

Catching eye contact with her reflection, she started when she realised she was looking at herself. The shimmering white of the dress was not a colour she would normally associate with her body but, mainly, it was the dreamy, whimsical expression on her face that had made her unrecognisable to herself. It was a look that she had only ever seen on Dismal Princess films; that moment when insipid Belladerina first catches sight of the self-aggrandising and vain Prince Gloriole and falls in sooooo much love, what active brain cells she did have, instantly turn to sugar-coated, pink vicodin.

Penny was smiling with such an inane, euphoric grin across her face; a blissful, serene and, ultimately, vacuous expression that indicated a cessation of all earthly concerns and utter wondrous fulfilment derived from delicate, lacy fabric.

She did not know whether she should cry or giggle.

"What's happening to me?"

Watching her reflection with suspicion, she half expected the mirror to voice some sort of opinion on the matter or, at least, invoke some singing mice to come skipping into the room with a pink bow to finish the look. Instead, her reflection just stared back and deliberately flaunted her slim ankles, softly curved hips and waist, humble yet distinct cleavage, and her boyish haircut.

"I hate you," her reflection told her.

"A hat?" she suggested and reached for the array of pastel cardboard boxes on the top shelf.

The lids of each were liberally tossed across the room and, gradually, she gave up trying to suppress each, 'Ooh,' and, 'Ah,' of appreciation that forced itself from her mouth.

Comparatively, Professor's 'disguise' consisted of replacing every black item of clothing with a brown counterpart. Aside from looking like someone had simply tea-stained these pages, it also made it look like he had just travelled back sixty years.

He was just unnecessarily dusting off his lapels for the seventh time when the scream pierced his daughter's bedroom door and jolted his predatory instincts awake. He was through the door, rolling across the floor and brandishing the blade from his cane before she had finished, "-kin' hell!"

Blood sucking degenerates, soul starved demons, mindless ministers of doom, harbingers of the afterlife; any of these things, and their subclasses, were already on his hit list of potential threats. At no point, in any kind of lethal scenario - literal or hypothetical - was he expecting to see his daughter being smothered and overpowered by, what looked like, a cloud. As legs and arms flailed, breaks in the cover revealed aspects of his daughter he was not sure she would want him privy to.

*Cumulus humilis*, he thought and averted his eyes. "Er ... Are you quite all right?" It was, by no means, the best line he had ever come up with and, although he never really was one to quip with or verbally antagonise his targets, even he was embarrassed when the question had been fully formed.

"Fucking heels," she blurted from beneath the building congestus.

"You look -"

"Get the fuck out!"

His survival instincts were even more reflexive than his predatory. He found himself back in front of the mirror, dusting at his lapel wondering if it had even happened.

"This is exactly why, you stupid fucking bitch!" she screamed from behind the closed door. Her footsteps stomped louder and closer. The door swung open and she presented herself in all her radiant glory: a white, wide brimmed, circular summer hat; the dress; her black Dr Martens; and a face reddened with thunderous fury and stormy embarrassment. "Don't you say a fucking word."

*Cumulonimbus!*

The storm cloud followed them along the streets of Paris with every hob-nailed stomp resonating like thunder against the surrounding brickwork. However, their circumventing walk to Pont d'Arcole went unhindered, which implied either their 'disguises' were working or they had flattered themselves concerning the urgency of the APB.

They were unhindered by not unobserved; a burly fair haired man in a jumper knitted for more temperate conditions and, perhaps, designed by Mondrian, watched their movement and cautiously followed.

The clear skies had become littered with heavy clouds, forewarning a potential storm. They trapped the heat and moisture in the air around the city and made movement and rest equally as uncomfortable. People were agitated and irritable, eager to try to release some of this pent up energy through confrontation: they sniped at each other in passing, openly rowed in the streets, horns blared more earnestly.

There was more movement around Place du Parvis than usual. It was normally a very busy area but it usually carried an air of serenity about it, a sense of calm. There were large groups of people gathered around the island and small pockets of incited ire could be seen darting backwards and forwards, fanning unrest.

Penny and Professor wandered between these conflagrations, trying to not be drawn into their issues, focussing on their own but, ultimately, unable to completely extricate themselves from the snippets of conversations they picked up on.

«… closed Notre Dame! …»
«… tried to kill herself …»
«… it's the people's cathedral …»
«… something should be done …»
«… police looking for someone …»

"The shit's about to kick off here," Penny observed

"Just keep walking," Professor advised, ignoring his daughter's colloquialism for fear that any kind of additional antagonism would be the catalytic spark.

"Just a few torches and pitchforks and then I'd be sure they were after you."

As they approached the bottom steps, their intention became overtly apparent to some members of the masses.

«Hey! You cannot go up there. It has been closed to the public.»

"Keep walking." Professor urged.

"But what if –"

"Keep walking."

«Hey! Do you hear me? Hey!»

They could hear the shuffle of feet get louder; either getting closer or amassing even further.

Over the din of the calling voices and marching feet behind, Penny could just hear her father repeating some sort of mantra to himself.

"- is illegal. Public hanging is illegal. Public hanging -"

«They must be more police! Hey! Tell us what is happening! Why have you closed the cathedral? HEY!»

They were only a few steps away from the main doors and possibly less from the ensuing mob. She saw a pair of eyes peer out from a side window. The face disappeared, the door opened and a gnarled hand urgently bid them entrance.

Only now did the Helsines pick up their pace and dart into the safety of the church. LeClerc quickly shut the door behind them and locked it. Insistent hammering and shouting from the other side only lasted a few minutes.

«Thank Chri- you for that,» Penny puffed. «I thought we were done for.»

«You are more than welcome, Penelope,» LeClerc replied and turned to face her; the small locket around his neck made a delicate tinkling sound.

"I wouldn't completely dismiss that notion, if I were you," Professor suggested and indicated that she look further down the aisle.

There, still sitting in his position of prayer, was half-headed Jean, surrounded by a pool of dark, viscous, lustrous liquid.

"Ah, shitty fuck," Penny commented.

"Quite."

«Don't concern yourself with him, my love,» LeClerc instructed, «he is at peace.»

"I hope he's talking to you," she muttered under her breath.

«Father,» Professor started but was silenced abruptly.

«Do not dare to mock me!»

«I can assure you-»

«Every word that comes from your mouth is like a searing dagger through my chest! You will shut your mouth or I will do it for you. Permanently.»

"Ooooookay. Just psychotic or dangerously psychotic?"

"I should just run him through and be done with it," Professor growled through gritted teeth.

«You could not understand how many years I have lived with that voice, that tone, that menace haunting my nights. How long my heart has ached for you to return to me and yet, now, all my plans have come together at last. I have been rewarded for my Holy quest.»

The locket twinkled in a shaft of light and glinted in Penny's eye. She gave it more attention and noticed the concentric hearts to its centre and outer oyster pattern. She then turned her attention to the old man and looked beyond the shrivelled outer features to the inner gleam of his eyes. She inhaled sharply. «Robert? It can't be.»

"Who?"

«It is I,» he acknowledged warmly, «LeClerc.» He pulled out a very old, tatty and faded (but undeniably red) Alice Band and placed it on his head.

"Who?"

Penny did that thing with her face when she tried to find the best words. "The vestry boy. My, er ... you know."

"Oh. Him."

## 5 (*Maintenant*)

## Immanis Pecoris Custos, Immanior Ipse

The crowd was still gathered outside the doors of the church and a few of the rabble had taken it upon themselves to be the authoritative voices on behalf of everyone.

«They cannot do this to a public building! We have the right to know what is going on! This is a place of worship and if that has been defiled then we should be allowed to sanctify it! This is our building, not theirs! They will try to cover up these misdeeds just like they did at the Louvre!»

«What happened at the Louvre?»

«Shh!»

«For too long have we lived under the oppressive might of the law and the church! Isn't it time we regained control of our lives and those things that belong to us?»

«Are we still talking about the Louvre?»

«I am talking about everything about this city! It used to belong to the people and should once again! Let the reclamation of Notre Dame be the symbol of our revolution!»

«The Louvre might be easier; it's open.»

From the opposite end of Place du Parvis came the police cars. At first, a couple had been called in to assist with Matilda's mysterious self assault. The already affronted crowd saw this as reinforcements to attempt to quieten them and rallied more potential insurgents; mainly from the ready-for-anything student body. The law enforcers then became aware of the building disgruntlement and called in further back-up including a couple of large black vans containing fully armed and armoured riot officers for 'juste dans le cas'. They arrived at the exact moment the people's party were trying to gain entrance to Notre Dame to continue the police work they had forgotten about.

With riot shields linked and batons bared, a steady line approached the rear of the mob. When the intrigued observers of the revolt saw their approach and noticed the lack of escape options, they hastened the movement towards their objective.

Unfortunately for the police, it was at this time that the students arrived from their quarter. Seeing the police advance on the cathedral in such a manner immediately confirmed the escalated rumours that they were out to bring the entire church to the ground. Having come prepared for a skirmish, they quickly set upon the unprotected backs of the riot police (and any others in their path) breaking up their defensive barrier.

On the very outskirts, Parisians came from their shops, offices and domiciles to see their police force being swarmed by the ungrateful, layabout, outsider students of the university. Obviously the police were trying to defend Notre Dame and the tourists behind them from the students attempting another over the top prank. They had gone too far this time and it was up to the people to join the fight against the educated elitists.

A police alert went out to call for everyone.

Brandon Wuh stood on the south side of Pont au Double with his mouth and eyes agape at the carnage taking place before him. He was so shocked by what he saw that he did not notice when the top of his ice-cream slopped onto his sandals. When his phone rang, there was no confusion but an automatic response to locate his phone and answer it.

"Eminence?"
"Si?"
"We are at Notre Dame."
"Si?"
"We believe we are close."
"Si?"
"Do not have worries for us; we came prepared for this quest."
"Si."

The line went dead.
"What? Prepared? What?"

From where he stood, Brandon was pretty sure he could see a glint of light from long blades of sharpened metal.

"Dear God, what have I done?"

The Templars' limousine had been stopped in a traffic jam half a mile from the island and, funnily enough, no amount of horn honking was clearing the way ahead. After a few minutes of waiting, it became apparent that drivers were abandoning their cars and continuing their journey by foot.

Jacques pressed the button next to his arm which lowered the glass partition between them and the driver. «What's happening?»

The driver turned his radio down and craned his neck to them. «Apparently, there is a student riot outside Notre Dame,» the driver informed. «It's a big one.»

Hugh leaned forward. «Are they saying what it's about?»

The driver shrugged his shoulders. «Students. Who can say? Perhaps their bar raised the prices of beer.»

"Is this just a coincidence?" Jacques asked.

"Despite that," Geoffrey replied, "we're not going anywhere like this so we might as well investigate."

"I'll grab the case," Hugh volunteered enthusiastically and leapt out his door.

"I don't think –" Jacques called but was restrained by Geoffrey's hand on his arm.

"Look at the ingredients: riot, Notre Dame, crusade. I think the case might be a reasonable precaution."

Hugh slammed the boot shut and poked his head through the open door. "Come on!"

"And besides," Geoffrey continued, "look how excited the dear boy is. When was the last time you saw him with that expression on his face?"

Jacques had an answer but modesty and decorum prevented him from giving it.

### V—V

Mother Furca had the perfect view of the island from her balcony. She adjusted her wimple to place her binoculars more comfortably to her face. She could easily identify each departmental member of the police force as he, or she, struggled to arrest someone with the minimal amount of force. But they were completely outnumbered by other factions, of which she could not specify allegiances. It looked like the entire city had come out for this event: office workers, tourists, tradesmen, youths – sects of every social variety seemed to be represented. And at its centre was the majestic cathedral, overseeing all. She was in no doubt that it was connected to the quest, but where were her people?

A flash of colour caught her attention and she focussed her sights on a few large men in blazing pullovers – the colours of the Vatican's Swiss Guard (Special) Corps. That would mean that murderous sociopath, Cunningham, would be up to his neck in it somewhere. Getting closer by the second.

One of the guards was beheaded by a thick broadsword which raised her spirits somewhat only to discover the blade was being wielded by a middle-aged, portly, hirsute man. Definitely NOT one of her men; they would wax.

Perhaps one of Christophe's? The Priory? She was not sure she would recognise one of them if she ever saw one.

Who might the Monk have been able to contact? She imagined him doing charades in front of Opus Dei and how well that would go down.

She scanned the crowd; there were quite a few swords being wielded by equally well-fed men and women but no sign of her Knights.

She was about to go back into her room to get on the phone when she saw Brandon standing on the bridge with ice-cream on his shoes and a look of absolute horror on his face. He simply was not cut out for the real life of religious expectations.

Just as a degree of pity for him was building, three impeccably dressed gentlemen pushed past him to enter the island; one was carrying a briefcase that was as long as he was tall. They stopped at the north side of the bridge, conferred and then sprung the latches open on the case. They each pulled out a gleaming four-foot blade and marched into the fray, the front man liberally hacking and slashing, making a path to the Cathedral steps.

She smiled and lowered her binoculars to survey the entire scene. There was something touchingly Biblical about the whole thing. Old Testament, of course.

«Mistress?» a male voice called from behind her. «May I be excused? Or do you require more Hieros Gamos?»

She turned around, her sagging buttocks catching a shaft of light that managed to penetrate the clouds.

«Why not?» she mused. «Eighteen is my lucky number.»

Christophe was torn between either trusting his instincts or reaching for the telephone.

He had found a very pleasant café that served a delightfully delicate Amaretto. Everyone had vacated the premises to either watch or join the fray across the river and so he helped himself to the bottle.

He wanted to phone his contact to ensure that they were getting involved in this but his experience and developed instincts told him that because he did not think they were anywhere nearby, then that meant they surely must be at the heart of it all.

He sipped at his drink again and allowed his instincts to lead his actions.

Anjo was desperately trying to ignore his radio's pleas for every officer to attend the scene; it was just one of those things sent to try to pull him off course which meant he must be on the correct course. His sirens wailed as he cut a swathe through the traffic in both directions and, if that was not enough encouragement for other motorists to avoid him, he pressed down hard on his horn, gave little bumper shoves to the more hesitant and played *Born To Be Wild* really loud with his windows down.

He double-parked the car outside of his intended address, leapt out without turning the engine off and ran up to the front door. He considered just kicking it in until he saw the mass of it and estimated that he would lose a kneecap before he managed to budge any of those deadlocks.

He rang the door bell.

When nothing happened for longer than he was willing to wait (approximately ten seconds), he hammered on the door with the butt of his gun. The next step was to shoot the damn thing off its hinges.

He heard locks being turned, chains being rattled and the latch being released. The door opened a fraction and was held in place by a security chain. A middle-aged woman looked through the gap.

«Hallo?»

«Suzette Agneau?» Anjo demanded.

«Yes?»

«I am Detective Inspector Anjo of Prefecture of Police,» he recited and passed his identification through the gap which she stared at through thick, round glasses. The badge was then replaced with the print out of the party. «This is you in the middle?»

«Yes, but I-»

«Who are these other people?»

«I do not know,» she spluttered.

«I do not have time to play games with you woman!» Anjo reared back and raised his leg. Luckily, Suzette was so fearful that she instinctively backed away from the door so it did not smash her face in when the full force of Anjo came crashing down on it. The chain ripped itself from the doorframe, he marched into the hallway and stopped upon seeing her lying on the floor before him.

The photograph had not done her credit: the poor resolution, the shadows in the restaurant, the black clothes she had been wearing; combined, managed to give no outstanding impression of her at all but now, as she lay floundering on the floor, he saw that she was at least one hundred and twenty kilograms.

«Please don't hurt me,» she begged as she attempted to gain her stability.

«Suzette, I am sorry for that,» he said softly and knelt down beside her to support her upright. He put the photograph in front of her face again. «These people you are with: this one, this one and this one, are all dead. Others might be dead too or may be soon. Now, because you are alive this makes me think either you are killing them, or will be killed next. Do you understand my urgency?»

She panted heavily: partially from the shock, partially from having the wind knocked from her but mostly from the physical exertion of trying to upright herself.

«They were murdered? Why?» she panted.

«I am hoping you might be able to shed some light on that. Just what is this covert organisation of yours? What is your purpose? What are your secrets? Why are the Illottonatti?»

«It is just a name,» Suzette spluttered. «We all met online and only ever communicated through email. We each had a system – a code – but each was incomplete and we discovered that together …»

«Someone wants the whole code for themselves,» Anjo deduced.

«There is no whole code. Each person only submits a result and we have been trialling combinations with varying degrees of success.»

«We must find the others quickly, before it is too late. Come with me, tell me their addresses.»

«No, no, no,» she protested. «There are no addresses, only emails. No surnames, only first names. No details, only speculation.»

«Then get me a list of their email addresses; I can work from them but you must hurry!»

Now she hauled herself to her feet and marched purposefully into a side office. There, she deftly tapped at a couple of buttons on her keyboard whereupon her printer rattled to life, expurgating a sheet of paper with a neat list of a dozen addresses.

She was passing it to Anjo when he grabbed her wrist and hauled her out of the house.

«What are you -?»

«You are still alive and I plan to keep you that way. That means I do not let you out of my sight.»

He bundled her into his car, jumped in beside her and tore off back into the direction of the station.

*«Anjo! Anjo! Where the hell are you?»* his radio screamed at him.

He lifted the mic with irritation and bellowed back, «I am working! What the hell do you want?»

*«You're needed at Place du Parvis immediately. All officers must -»*

«So why are you bothering me and not there yourself? Go tell the Commissioner -»

*«You are already talking to her so why don't you tell her yourself.»*

Merde.

He calmly switched the radio off and reached for his phone and discovered its absence. *Illottonatti, Hey Suze!, recharge, message, Matilda.*

«God damn it!» he shouted and made Suzette jump so much that the car lurched across the central line.

It was all unravelling, everything that had taken so long to come together was rapidly falling apart before his eyes.

«Suzette, the people, your members, tell me as much about them as you can.»

«There isn't much to tell,» she squealed as she resisted the forces of his sharp turn that tried to push her into his lap. «One of the rules was not divulging too much personal information that revealed -»

«I get it! Secret. Clandestine. A mystery wrapped up in an enigma that never existed. What *can* you tell me, Suzette? Anything.»

She inspected her list. «Well, Brian, I think, was some sort of artist -»

«He was certainly creative.»

«- whereas James was some sort of business man. I got the impression that Andrew was perhaps a librarian?»

«You aren't terribly far off each, but what about the non-dead?»

«Well, there is another James; he talked about numbers and statistics a lot so I presumed he was an accountant or something.»

*Not twenty miles away, at the UPMC, Professor James Major was delivering his renowned lecture on his theory of Absolute Probability Predictions.*

« ... *whereby, as long as there is even the remotest chance of an event occurring, then, with enough time, it must have a one hundred per cent chance of occurring at some time. It therefore becomes easier not to calculate the probability of that event occurring at a specific time, but actually calculate the time that it will absolutely occur.*»

*A hand went up from his class.*

«*Yes?*»

«*Are you suggesting that you do not need eternity and an infinite number of monkeys to write the complete works of Shakespeare?*»

*A majority of the members of the auditorium laughed.*

«*An interesting proposition. Surely with eternity at your command, you should only need one monkey? And during that time, hasn't he, more than likely, written the complete works of everyone and a couple of original novels of his (or her) own?*»

*More people laughed.*

«*But consider this: the writing of Shakespeare's works can only take a finite amount of time to complete, correct?*»

*The student acquiesced with a shrug and a nod.*

«*Thereby, I am absolutely suggesting that it is possible to calculate the likelihood of when that finite time will occur rather than ...*»

*His students were literally on the edge of their seats and, it was partially for that reason, why the front row got quite as covered in his arterial spray as they did. Of course, the hollow-barrelled Biro that he rammed into his jugular assisted in the soaking; acting as a sort of water cannon.*

«Try not to refer to them in the past tense,» Anjo advised.

«Thad *is* only a young man and seemed the odd one out in the group. He was very handsome, bright blue eyes, tanned skin, beautifully straight, white smile and long blond hair. I got the impression he worked – works – in cold environments; perhaps a ski instructor or something like that.»

*Thad had not turned up for work for a few days, which was not entirely unlike him; he was well known for needing the occasional day off to nurse a heavy hangover but he would always call in and he would always coincide them away from a busy day. Today was a busy day and his colleagues rushed around throwing thermal jackets and trousers on while loud voices shouted instructions to and fro.*

*One man grabbed a long silver handle and yanked it hard, sliding the attached large door open on its rails. A six-foot square opening revealed an imperceptible darkness beyond until the man flicked on a light switch. Inside were wall-to-wall cage trolleys, stacked up with boxes of frozen produce.*

*«Come on! Move this old stock out so we can get the new delivery in!» the man screamed at everybody. «Damn you, Thad! You picked the wrong week to skip off.»*

*With the efficiency of a well rehearsed gang-bang, trolleys' positions were shifted around the small space for better access, swapped between partners when they were satisfied with their task and contents withdrawn from some to be inserted in others. Empty, spent trolleys were stacked and discarded into the warehouse to make room for the buxomly stacked, newcomers.*

*One worker was just finishing off his load when he discovered an unusually shaped container at the bottom. He leaned through his trolley, reached down, grabbed at its rounded sides and pulled. The spherical object did not shift, although some of its wrapping came away in his hands: it was a coarse, loosely matted, yellow hessian-like gauze. He presumed that whatever it was, must have fallen from a trolley and become frozen to the wall – it happened sometimes – so he gave the empty platform of his trolley a firm kick in an attempt to dislodge it. After the fifth attempt, with a satisfying crack of the adhering ice, the object rolled onto the platform where he got a much clearer view of bright blue eyes, tanned skin and a beautifully straight, white smile.*

«He doesn't stand a chance,» Anjo commented. «The beautiful ones never do.»

«I did not get much from Matt,» Suzette continued unperturbed, «apart from working for the government in some form. He was very quiet and careful with his money.»

*Matthew Impôt was taking a late lunch break from L'Administration Fiscale and had decided to take the Metro into the city to witness the commotion at Notre Dame for himself. He had heard on the radio that the riot was getting so bad that people were being killed and the army were being mobilised. There were already water cannons on the scene and armed police with rubber bullets and those bean bag guns. That sounded awesome.*

*He was on the platform awaiting the next train when an announcement requested everyone step away from the platform's edge because the next train passing through was not going to be stopping there. Dutifully, everyone did so, albeit only a shuffle backwards in some cases for fear of losing a prime waiting position.*

*Matthew, however, stood still and seemed to ponder the message. Then, as the train became audibly closer, he actually took a step forward and stretched his left hand out as if hailing a taxi.*

*The train, travelling in excess of one hundred miles an hour, naturally ripped his hand from the wrist and spun Matthew around like a top. His right arm flailed outwards and was clipped by the speeding train, reduced to a bloody stump and added to his twirling momentum. Arm after arm was whittled down to shoulder, then the finer extremities of his head and, all the while, he maintained his pirouette with balletic precision and the train had gone.*

*He managed to stand upright, although, because of his lack of profiling features, it was difficult to tell which way he was facing. Everyone along the platform got the distinct impression he was staring right at them. Which of course was stupid because he was completely dead, had lost his eyeballs early on and they needed to only look at where the toes of his unscuffed shoes were pointing to determine his direction.*

*He folded neatly, slumped onto the track and someone screamed.*

«Ah, now I quite liked Mary,» Suzette cooed, «despite his obvious preferences. She – er, he – was very funny.»
«'Mary'? 'His'?»

*There was a dampness spreading across the carpet. It had a very wide diameter and was expanding slowly, indicating that either the source of the flood was slow yet steady, or had happened a while ago.*

*There was no sound of dripping, just a steady hum coming from the corner of the room where a dining room chair had been placed next to a large tropical aquarium. The humming was from the tank's filter system protesting that it had become clogged with something.*

*There was a plethora of colourful fish, of varying sizes, darting around in the excitable way that fish do when something foreign is introduced to their delicate microcosm, and they were taking it in turns to explore and nibble at parts of Mary/John's face as it rested on the gravel at the bottom of the tank. One feisty pleco had attached itself to her eyeball and was chewing away, a shrimp emerged from a cleanup inspection of her open mouth.*

*She had managed to get her torso fully wedged in the tank so only from her waist down was not submerged. Her weight and fidgeting death throes had enabled the glass rim to cut inch deep lacerations into her thighs where blood poured steadily down both sides of the wall, attracting more attention from the inhabitants. Despite all of this, she had a smile on her face because, as she watched her fish from the inside of the tank, she was reminded of a silly joke and, now, she too could quite confidently claim that she was not sure how to drive this thing.*

«I have no idea what Peter does,» Suzette mused. «He seemed to be a bit of a waster, always talking about things he had seen on YouTube and the like.»

*Peter Poignard had seen this fantastic experiment on YouTube where a packet of mints got dropped into a bottle of fizzy drink and it created a huge explosive fountain. He took his camcorder and all the necessary ingredients to the Place du Carrousel and was about to set up when something occurred to him.*

*He ripped open his packets of mints and proceeded to devour them all.*

*His large frame, loose fitting purple shorts and bright yellow t-shirt had already attracted the attention of a number of casual passers but these actions were those of a performance artist. A mime, if they were really lucky.*

*Before the last mints had a chance to rest in his stomach, Peter had started glugging down the two-litre bottles of Cola Light like he had not had a drink for months.*

*Within seconds of the first bottle being finished, the closest members of the gathering audience had already noticed a physical change in the man as his shirt became less loose fitting around his stomach. His gut was swelling before their eyes and many decided this was not the kind of show they were too interested in seeing. Man walks against invisible wind? Yes. Man fills up with wind? No.*

*The last bottle had been consumed just as the first wave of carbon dioxide looked for an escape, erupting from his mouth and nose as a long liquidy burp that would cause him to suffocate if it did not stop. At this, more of his audience turned away in disgust.*

*The expulsion did stop though, when his trachea snapped forward reflexively and clamped his oesophagus closed tight. Now the building internal pressure sought any other weak points from which to release itself and his stomach skin had stretched taught. It discovered an opening further south.*

*Peter's colon prolapsed in much the same manner of an uncontrolled, high pressure hosepipe, expelling frothy excrement all around as it unravelled itself across the pristine pavement; twisting, convulsing and extending across the glass pyramid, thirty foot of fizzy shit spraying intestines with a hint of minty freshness.*

«Simon is definitely a chef,» Suzette declared.

*Simon Canan was lying face down on his barbecue and, although the flames had died down some time ago, he was still hot enough to cook off.*

«Tom is a very fastidious man. Very clean and very careful how much he drank.»

*Thomas Doigting was sitting in his kitchen. His lower jaw was hanging on by the threads of its masseter muscles where the skin and flesh around it had corroded away. His throat was in a similar state of unnatural openness and all around him was a puddle of dark brown liquid. Next to him was a collection of empty detergent bottles.*

Suzette's eyes lit up. «Phillip, on the other hand …»

*… was making toast while taking a bath.*

«And then there's Robert. He's an odd sort. I get the impression that he was a very religious man but is very cynical now. He is too old to be so jaded.»

«Religious? Old? Show me, which is he?» Anjo demanded and thrust the picture at her. He pulled the car over to an abrupt stop while she studied the people.

«This one,» she puffed and pointed at the fifth person from the left; a peanut shaped man, stooped and fragile.

«The priest!» Anjo snapped.

For all this time Notre Dame had been calling to him like a beacon but he had been so tied up in the depths of conspiracy theories that he had shirked it off as too obvious.

He slammed on the clutch and rammed the lever into first gear, pulled out without checking and sideswiped a passing car causing him to rebound into the parked cars on Suzette's side. She squealed from the tumultuous impacts. Anjo said nothing but violently steered his car back on course and accelerated even more.

He had to get to Notre Dame.

V—V

There is probably no worse a feeling for a father than to have to accept that his little girl has all grown up to become a woman; to have to look into the eyes of the boy/man who is probably shoving his penis in her vagina at every given opportunity. No worse a feeling apart from being a father who has totally not accepted that his little girl is a woman and walks in to see her naked backside going like a jackhammer, riding some spotty juvenile's stiff cock like she was competing in the one hundred meter Olympic Space Hopper finals.

Professor tried desperately to repress the surfacing memories, images and bile but was failing on all accounts.

«Robert, this is so …» Penny diplomacised.

«'Predestined'?» LeClerc suggested.

«Yeeees, although I was going more along the lines of 'coincidental'.»

«I was told that great things would come to me; your return is just one of them.»

«Yeah, about that ...»

«Truly a miracle that He would return you in the same form as you were taken from me.» With this last remark, he shot a look of pure hatred at Professor. «A second chance to renew our love and a chance for revenge.»

"Isn't there anybody in this world who you haven't upset?" Penny sighed.

"Not everyone I meet –" he tried to protest but was interrupted by a voice from the shadows that crept around the hallowed halls like the hiss of Satan himself.

"It is interesting to see you again, Professor."

"Oh, come on!"

"Interesting, yet not entirely surprising." Cunningham emerged from one of the dark recesses and stepped boldly into a stained glass spotlight that beamed down from the high walls. It almost disguised the pattern on his jumper.

"Ricardo," Professor returned, "it is interesting to see you alive."

"Did you really think this –" Cunningham rested his index finger upon his scar, "- would be the end of me?"

"I hoped."

Cunningham stepped from the light into the aisle and began to circle Professor who, in turn, pivoted on the spot to prevent the assassin from blind-siding him.

Professor gave Penny a surreptitious wave with his hand to indicate she should remove herself from the scene. She faltered before doing so, automatically getting defensive that he should dismiss her capabilities of self-preservation but remembered how he used to treat her before. He would always allow her to get into harm's way to a certain extent, ready to lend assistance should she need it. The only time he ever told her to back down was when he knew for a fact she was out of her depth.

She took a precautionary step backwards to test the garishly garbed albino's field of attention and noticed his eye flick towards her. LeClerc was not in the mood to test anything so grabbed her by the arm and pulled her into the pews, ensuring that his aged body fell on top of her.

Cunningham's 90twos were in his hands seemingly without him even drawing them. Professor's epee was unsheathed from his walking stick with equal speed – slightly faster, if truth be told, for he was able to lunge forward and deflect the pistols from shooting at their intended targets. Within the microseconds that it took Cunningham to turn and stabilise himself, Professor had dived into the opposite row of pews and disappeared.

"Have you got faster, old man?" Cunningham growled.

"No," Professor's voice echoed around the hall. "You have become overconfident in your lazy weapons. I'm disappointed."

"You think I need these?" Cunningham roared.

"I think you are dependent upon them," Professor replied from behind him and slid his blade gently under the young man's chin. "You have some explaining to do."

"I will not –"

"Don't embarrass me, please," Professor sighed. "And don't demean yourself. We both know you'll talk."

LeClerc had coerced Penny to the back of the cathedral and the outer chambers. He raised his head carefully to check they had not been followed and knocked into a set of keys that dangled from lock.

«And we both know what rooms are out here, don't we?» he rhetoricked and waggled his eyebrows suggestively.

Penny pulled her arm out of his grip violently. «That was a long time ago, Robert. A different time when we were different people.»

«No! I haven't changed since then. I have been waiting for you, all these years and you haven't changed at all.»

She shook her head at him gravely. «In more ways than you could possibly imagine, Robert. I *did* love you then but it would never have lasted: not with him, not with … things as they were, and not with me being this way.»

«He is an obstacle that can be overcome, things that were are no longer the same, and it is a miracle that you have become young again.»

«No, it's a medical condition that I have had to endure for all my life. I don't age very fast. I never have.»

«You were like this when we were together?»

«*All* my life.»

LeClerc's eyes shifted around as he mentally attempted to fit these pieces of new information into his grand scheme. «Well, we -»

«There is no 'we', Robert,» Penny interrupted. «We were a moment in time and that time cannot be reclaimed. I have to go back.»

His expression changed from desperate confusion to confused anger. «To him? This is your chance to finally be free of that overbearing monster. And you would go back? After everything he did to you? To us?»

*Bugger, bugger, bugger. Was this what I was like dealing with exes?* She could claim to have had one boyfriend in one hundred years and she was ready to swear off them for the rest of her near-immortal life.

«Please try to understand. We were young and impetuous and, despite his actions being incredibly severe, he is my father and only acted in a manner that he thought was best for me.»

«I lost everything because of him.»

«Because of us, Robert. It was our decisions that led us down these paths. It was my decision to do the things we did and I'm sorry if that had a negative impact on your life. I did love you, in a way, but I suppose I was also using you to get back at him too. If you want revenge on anyone, then it should be me.»

His eyes searched for a solution again, this time in the features of her smooth, perfect face. Had she been an angel? Or was she really a temptress? He had not wanted to have sex but she had forced him to – like Delilah – and very much like that succubus of old, had betrayed him, stolen his strength and now he had no choice but to bring the house down around their Godless ears.

«My revenge?» he said softly and calmly. «An eye for an eye. A hair for my hair,» he chuckled as he rubbed a withered hand over his smooth forehead.

*Not good.* She had been in these situations too many times to know that a complete change in an antagonist's persona usually implied that s/he had snapped; had gone beyond a point of no return; had made an important and necessary decision. One that was going to be incredibly detrimental to the protagonist.

LeClerc reached forward and swiftly yanked a hair from her short fringe. «You used to have such beautiful long hair, Penelope,» he pondered as he rolled the genetic fibre around in his fingers. «Why did you decide to become so ugly?» He stood and wandered back into the main hall.

She reeled. She had heard how words could sting and thought she understood that imagery but until now, she realised, had never experienced the feeling first hand. That word had physically hit her harder than any real blow she had been a victim of. She was wobbling in her crouched position, unable to move; she was having trouble catching her breath; she was about to cry.

*Ugly?* Call her a boy, call her masculine, tell her she was not lady-like enough and she would just shrug her shoulders, flick you a couple of vees and tell you that she did not give a shit about your opinion (although, maybe catch a glimpse of her reflection later to make sure she did not give a shit). But was she actually ugly? To a man who had professed his undying love for her, too. Was he talking about her face or was it something deeper than that? That the revelation of her actions made her out to be a hideous creature on the inside. Were her actions really *that* bad? Should she still be judged now based on the things she did when she was a different person?

*No.* "Fuck it!" He was just pissed off that she would not give him another shag. It was that old macho-bullshit ploy they used in the union bar; 'If you won't fuck me then you must be a lesbian, bitch!' And it actually worked sometimes, made her question herself but ultimately, like now, made her remember that she was woman and you would fucking regret it if you incurred her mother-fucking wrath.

She jumped to her feet and, with clenched jaw, sashayed forthrightly after her target. She found him leaning over the altar, seemingly reading aloud from the Bible but with, what looked like, a small tatty, green, silk bag laid open on the top pages. A couple of extra precautionary steps forward and she could just see a green jewel stitched onto the material.

In the distance, she was relieved to hear her father's continued expositional diatribe so knew she could focus all of her attention on her misogynistic ex-boyfriend.

«Let no debt remain outstanding,» he said quietly.

She was on the brink of letting loose with every French offensive word and phrase she could think of, including the one about 'your mother and a wheelie bin' when the sun was completely blotted out, a great darkness filled the church and a deathly silence enveloped all. It was as if the right hand of God Himself had descended and was laying peace upon his land and people when in actual fact some really big clouds had gathered overhead and indicated it was probably about to rain.

Whatever its cause, it was very effective.

«It's coming!» LeClerc hollered passionately.

The pathetic fallacy had done nothing to dampen the ardour of the revolt and, since the arrival and deployment of the army, the People's Division had managed to swell their ranks. The use of automatic weapons had only served to enlist more civilian sympathisers to the cause. What the actual cause was, was unknown but it was known that there had to be one and it had to be a *really* important one if the army was trying to oppress it. Probably something to do with civil liberties or principles.

At the centre was the Cathedral and around it was the clash and battering of fists against faces, bats against shields, swords against bone. Surrounding that was a barrage of almost ineffectual firing of rubber bullets and riot cannons. This attack had been slow in coming and, after it had started, quickly became weaker as witnesses on the outer circle were disgusted by the action and enclosed upon the army's defenceless rear. Beyond this perimeter, adding greatly to the confusion, were a large number of civilians with their own long range weapons who had taken sniper positions from a variety of windows around the island. Soldiers, police and rioters were being indiscriminately dispatched.

Brandon had managed to overcome his shock with the help of a shove to the floor by three smartly suited, silver sword bearing, murderous psychotics. Whatever was causing this was coming from the Cathedral and he had a pretty good idea that the artefact was involved so he was cautiously edging his way around Place du Parvis, hoping that his unrelenting faith would keep him safe and that someone would have left a back door conveniently open.

Within the melee itself, the Knights had come to a stand still; their area was saturated by people, they could not get a good swing of their weapons and had to rely on fists and the hilts of their swords.

"Only a few more feet, chaps," Jacques cried from a forward position. His suit had been ripped, his tie pulled open to one side, he had a large bloody gash down his left cheek but his hair was still immaculately styled.

"I … just … need … a bit … of space," Geoffrey complained. "Will you please move back so I can bring my sword down?"

"Je ne comprende pas."

"Is far too busy, ja?" a gruff Germanic voice agreed from behind him.

Geoffrey turned his head and saw a sweaty, hairy man wading towards him in a similar state; his sword arm and weapon wedged firmly above his head.

"Look, I'd love to engage in battle with you," Geoffrey called, "but this really isn't the best time or place."

"Nein! I am thinking we are on the same side," the man replied as he cracked open the skull of the revolutionary who impeded his progress. "Templars, ja? I recognise the insignia." He pointed at the crest on the base of Geoffrey's blade.

"Oh, I see. And you are?"

"Gottesfreunde. You know us?"

"I've heard of you. Jacques? Hugh?" Geoffrey called. "This gentleman says he's from the Gottesfreunde."

"Really, that's wonderful," Hugh shouted from beyond waving arms and sticks. "Never had the pleasure before. Pleased to meet you, er …"

"Henry," Henry replied. "This is good omen, ja? Providence? We can work together and find the purse."

The Templars exchanged conspiratorial glances between them and simultaneously shrugged their eyebrows.

"It sounds like a delightful idea, Henry," Jacques said and was interrupted by a spray of blood into his face. "Oh, for goodness sake, has anyone got a handkerchief?"

"No."

"I had to use mine, sorry."

"Nein."

"Anyway, as I was saying, it sounds like a good idea, Henry, but we do have a specific set of conditions attached to the return of the … purse."

"As do we," Henry acknowledged. "We can work out specifics later but concentrate combined efforts on getting the artefact?"

Again, the Templars had a quick discussion using only their eyes and came to some sort of agreement.

"An excellent idea, Henry," Jacques called. "We will move around to the rear of the cathedral while you continue your frontal assault, yes?"

"Ja. Good plan, Yack. We meet in between. Gottesfreunde! Schnell, schnell! Wir gehen innen!"

There was a surge in the crowd behind Henry and a few bodies were tossed into the air as The Friends of God pushed their assault forward, their wake pushing the Templars, law enforcers and defenders of the rights of the proletariat, alike, outwards.

Geoffrey had an expression of disgust across his face. "Did he just call me what I think he did?"

"Don't be so sensitive, Geoffrey," Hugh chided. "It means, 'to go.'"

A bullet ricocheted from Anjo's windscreen, shattering it into a fine mosaic of glass crystals, reducing visibility to zero. Suzette screamed, Anjo spun the steering wheel to rotate the car one-hundred-and-eighty degrees and the vehicle slammed into a wall.

He reached into the glove compartment in front of the hysterical woman and pulled out a 9mm Berretta. Suzette stopped screaming for a second.

«Not strictly police issue,» Anjo confessed, «but perfectly legal.»

A barrage of makeshift missiles hailed onto the roof: cans, bricks and bottles rained down the car's sides which renewed Suzette's palpitations and displeasure.

Anjo pulled at the lever beneath his seat and shoved it as far back as he could. He then fired a shot through the windscreen which caused the tightly packed shards to fall into their laps and scare off their assailants. It also made Suzette scream even louder.

He squeezed himself over his steering wheel, through the open windscreen and sprawled over the bonnet. Another shot into the air just to ward anyone off and then over to Suzette's door which he opened and then extracted her from her seat.

«Come, woman, get a grip.»

She stopped her noise to take account of her surroundings. It was early afternoon but as dark as midnight; the storm clouds above rumbled and sparked with menacing intent and mingled with thick plumes of smoke that rose from all around her; the rioting had spread deeper into the city and buildings were burning. She looked across the river to the anarchic violence there; she looked into the river to see it running red whilst lifeless bodies drifted downstream.

«Explain to me what there is to get a grip on, please,» she demanded stoically and Anjo had to accept her point.

«Just stop screaming, then,» he said and she nodded. «Let's go. Whatever is doing this, is over there.»

The darkness was interrupted only by the occasional mock candle that was lit purely for atmospherics in the daytime rather than any real practical use. They did nothing of value during the daytime but now, with no other light sources around, they cast really good shadows.

The two men were sitting in opposite pews, facing each other. The 90twos were out of reach at the far end of Cunningham's seat, whereas the tip of Professor's blade was pointed, unwavering, at the youngster's face.

"... and thanks to the grace of God, I was able to walk again," Cunningham said.

"And the eighteen months of physiotherapy probably helped a bit too," Professor added.

"I remember your rampant atheism, Professor. It was probably because of your teachings that made me embrace the path of the Lord even more. You never provided the answers that my faith has been able to."

"Yes, it's all rather too convenient for me."

"So, shall we return to trying to kill each other?" Cunningham enquired.

"No, I much prefer going back to the original notion that you tell me what is going on here or I'll kill you."

"This coyness is not at all like you," Cunningham purred. "Come now: the Da Vinci suite, the visit to *The Last Supper*, your return visits here? All too coincidental."

"Well, I assure you that's all it is. I'm completely out of the loop on this one."

"Very well, you will have to die an ignorant man."

Cunningham was very fast; he pushed all his weight on the back of his bench making it topple over, flipping his pistols across the floor.

Professor was faster, already leaping across the divide between them, ready to plunge his blade into the other's heart. He would have achieved it too had it not been for the emergence of two more of the Swiss Guards from the recesses firing indiscriminately around the room.

The clouds had had enough and struck out with furious vengeance against the sacrilegious heathens around the Place du Parvis. Huge forks of lightning tore the sky asunder accompanied by blasts of raging thunder that rattled windows, set off car alarms and made the rioters duck for cover. Unfortunately, the clouds forgot about Science 101 and that lightning is attracted to high points and metal so their smiting swords of electricity bypassed the revellers completely and hit the very building everyone was trying to protect.

The first hit was simply earthed by the Cathedral's conductor. The second, though, barely gave the metal time to recover and was able to escape into the building's wiring which instantly fused and extinguished what atmospheric lighting had been illuminating the gloom. The third had the lightning rod reduced to smelt and created multiple electrical fires throughout.

The lights went out and Professor hit the floor rolling for the cover of a nearby pillar; fragments of stone exploded around his head as well-aimed bullets vied for his vital organs.

As the third bolt of lightning set off a sequence of micro-eruptions around the great hall, the front doors caved in under the ministrations of a dozen burley German missionaries.

"We have -" one of them declared but was swiftly cut down by a plague of bullets. The others quickly scurried off into darkened corners.

Outside, the Heavens opened and flushed all their toilets at exactly the same time, blocking out the last vestiges of light that were sneaking into the city around the edges of the clouds. The occasional flashes of light took snapshot images of gargoyle faces of anger, aggression and pain. They caught glimpses of the surreptitious movement of a blackly clad figure as it weaved itself through the throng.

Although its hands never seemed to leave the pockets of its Fila hoodie, anyone who came within an arm's length of it in one shot of light, was felled in the next. This was the hour of the Black Monk.

Penny allowed the darkness to cover her. She had been in these situations too many times to go blindly running around in circles and end up bumping into the very thing she was running from. Especially in this case, considering she was the thing to be running from so she stood and waited to be bumped into.

The gun shots and muzzle flares were too far away to concern her and her quarry was of no match to her combative prowess, so what was it that did trouble her? Something about standing in the middle of a pitch black room made her feel quite vulnerable. She wondered if Jason Vorhees ever had these moments of self-doubt, thinking, 'Any second now and the lights will come back on and everyone will have legged it out the front door and I'm here all on my own; I'm going to feel like a right 'nana. Oh wait, here comes a teenager now. Phew.'

But she still waited, even beyond the comfortable time that it should take to get bumped into. And, during that time, she tried to get her eyes to accustom to the darkness, yet every time she started to make out some sort of definition in the darkness, the bloody lightning would go off again and blind her.

There was a movement.

*Good.*

Something almost glittery slithered along the outer wall, catching some light from embers that snowed from the roof.

*Erm.*

That irksome feeling returned as she watched the burning particles, seemingly, pass straight through where the shimmering body had been. After they extinguished themselves, she could see the silvery outline quite clearly again and follow its passage towards her. She adopted a defensive stance, ready to block or strike, and when the floating ball of water was within reach, she defensively backfisted the thing but made contact with nothing substantial.

"Hello?" she called out (and regretted it immediately; you never heard Jason do it).

The lightning returned and backlit a face, inches from hers: disfigured by nature or accident, twisted into a visage of malice and hatred.

"Shit," was all Penny had time to comment before the creature thrust itself into her psyche.

Penny's mind was in turmoil, a mass of conflicting opinions, thoughts and emotions. This thing was imposing everything that had happened in its life on her: such beauty that would attract the unwanted, unwarranted advances of men around it; such horrendous ugliness that would cause all to rebuke him without provocation; a naïve innocence forced upon him by entrapment from society; a street-wise savvy developed through learning to survive harsh living conditions and tolerating discrimination; a hatred for the punishments befallen her in life; an unrequited love that could overcome death; a shackle to the mortal world; the freedom to explore beyond the constraints of time and space; a need to exact her fury upon anyone she was given access too; a desperate need to find peace and forgiveness for all the bad things he had been forced to do.

Penny was doubled over on the floor, panting heavily, saliva pouring from her mouth, her teeth grinding together. «That's it?» she growled. «*That's what you've got? You're a bit pissed off that life has been shit to you? You've got a strop-on because the guys you fall in love with never fancy you? Grow up! Here have a taste of my life!*»

She stopped fighting and allowed the psychic entity full access to her deepest memories: oppression, repression, alienation, segregation, discrimination, sexism, ageism; she had been a victim of every possible form of negative attitude which had had serious detrimental effects on her social interaction abilities, id and ego. What was perhaps the most damaging aspect of this treatment was that it was all implemented and reinforced by the man she loved, respected and just wanted to be shown love and respect in return. The most infuriatingly frustrating aspect of it was that no matter how often she reminded herself of all his failings and the countless incidents of demoralising, the deprecation and humiliation, and no matter how angry these things made her, she still loved him.

«So get the fuck out of my head,» she ordered and the spirit spiralled from her body and across the floor.

Although it would seem to be a redundant action, the apparition panted heavily as it stared with malicious intent at its rebuker.

«Come on then,» Penny goaded. «If you think you're hard enough.»

The creature considered these words then decided to cut its losses by dissipating into the darkness.

When she was sure the thing was not anywhere near her, she curled herself up into a foetal ball on the floor and started crying. Although she allowed herself this moment of weakness, she was still in control enough not to allow her sobs to come out any louder than a pitiful whimper.

The gunfire had divided The Friends and ensured they could be easily picked off one by when as and when they were discovered. Henry, the more rotund one, was sidling along the walls with a slimmer, taller associate close behind.

„I did not sign up for this, Henry."

„Stop complaining, Ralf, your rewards will be great."

„What good are rewards if you are not around to be able to spend them?"

„I'm not talking about earthly rewards", Henry growled. „This is very unGermanlike behaviour, you know."

Ralf harrumphed with disdain as they progressed, then grumbled under his breath: „I'm Bavarian, you oaf."

They crept through the darkened, smoke filled-room, cautiously peering through the gloom for any indication of the chance for righteous smiting or being smote.

A solitary blade of light managed to pierce through the smoke and reflected against something shiny ahead of them.

"Was ist das?" Henry whispered and waved the tip of his broadsword at the glimmering enigma.

Ralf wiped the grime from his glasses with his beret then screwed his eyes in concentration. He relaxed his stance and turned to his partner. "Das ist ein candelabra," he stated.

Henry relaxed as the fallen lighting fixture became more apparent through the gloom. The light managed to lighten the murk and glimmered off the glass crystals and -

There was something else within the fallen light fixture; something like a large ball of translucent cotton wool but moving as if it were alive. It seemed entangled amongst the shimmering fragments and clouded rays of spectrum so Ralf took a couple of steps forward to get a better look and, perhaps, release the creature.

He stepped on a large splinter of stained glass which cracked louder than the rioters' uproar outside the building.

The thing started and pivoted to face him. It had the most serene face he had ever seen. Something akin to Michael Angelo's angels on the roof of the -

"Mein Gott!" Henry screamed as the creature's face screwed itself into a ball of absolute fury and hatred and threw itself into Ralf's body, the impact hurled him back down the aisle, clattering through the shattered pews. The sudden racket attracted the attention of a shower of random gunfire and Henry threw himself to the ground at Ralf's feet.

Henry stayed stock still, not sure whether any movement might attract the thing's attention, that of the variety of assailants around him or might distract his brain's attention from staying conscious.

"Ralf, ist alles in Ordnung?"

"Ich bin slimed."

"Was ist 'shlimed'?"

"Nien. Nicht '*SH*limed', 'Slimed'."

Henry sighed with relief that whatever it had been, had not been serious enough to upset Ralf's semantic pedantry. "Hokay. Was ist-"

There was something about the change in Ralf's facial expression that derailed Henry's curiosity from terminology definitions to empathy for his associate's plight. What had been a look comprised of disgust and confusion with a hue of relief had become a blank canvass, devoid of any discernable emotion. As if he had just been switched off.

"Ralf?"

Ralf picked up a sliver of glass and rammed it into through his eye socket until it wedged against the bone and split into his hand skin. He slumped forward as he went off to redeem his reward and the vaporous entity phased from his head, looking almost pleased with itself. It scanned its immediate vicinity for the other one but Henry's Beine hatten Abschied genommen.

The front doors had been opened and the people stormed the building: each one claiming to be liberating the Holy ground from the person proceeding and preceding; each one relishing in the moment of overthrowing the left-wing, fascistic, anarchic government; each one providing a new target for the Swiss Guards to have another pop at. Each one distracting everyone's attention from the backdoors.

Brandon flinched at every sound going: the gunfire, the shouting, the thunder and the beat of his heart which was desperately trying to do the sensible thing and get as far away as possible from this place – with or without him. Really, it looked like he was the calmest person there, striding boldly across the ambulatory when in reality he was convulsing so much, every muscle was in a perpetual state of rigid shock.

Then another, altogether different noise managed to pervade the horror. It was a sound that he responded to on an unconscious level, so slight it was almost ultrasonic but it tapped into his soul and called to that part of him that constantly tried to remind him why he dedicated his life to make life better. Someone was crying.

That should not have been so much of a shock, considering the number of dead bodies and dismembered limbs he had to traverse to get here, but it was not a cry of physical pain but that heart-wrenching wail of someone lost, without answers, needing help.

He meandered through the darkness to come across a girl's huddled body, lying on the stone floor.

"My child? What ails you?"

She stopped her sobbing, sniffed twice and turned her head to Brandon. "Are you taking the fucking piss?" Penny enquired.

The Templars had penetrated the inner sanctum via the rear offices. Silent hand signals were given by Jacques and the three men split up, circling around the perimeter of the great hall. They were more interested in keeping secluded rather than embroiled in the fracas; their focus was on locating the purse rather than scattering the heathen blood of the sacrilegious and disbelievers.

However, there were times when they could not help it and each smiting was performed with a fusion of merciless fervour, deadly precision and a soupçon of savoir faire.

Hugh was skulking through the wreckage of pews and bodies; turmoil ensuing all around him and none of it demanding his attention until he recognised the flash of colour of a Swiss Guard with the muzzle flare of his gun as he fired indiscriminately into the ruckus.

*A set up?* he pondered as he stood stock still, hoping that he could pull off an effective impression of a piece of wood.

After another couple of shots, it was evident that Hugh had not been noticed. A pause in the onslaught suggested the gunman was reloading so he moved – swift, silent and precise – and had his blade at the Guard's throat before he could glide his full magazine into place.

"Speak quickly and truthfully and your departure will be quick," Hugh whispered. "What is your purpose here?"

"An artefact," the Guard replied calmly.

Hugh angled his sword so the Templar insignia on his blade caught the Guard's eye. He was pleased to see a flash of surprise and drew the silver edge through his neck until it grated against his spine.

"Finocchio," a voice spat from behind him.

He turned slowly, knowing full well that he had foolishly left his rear exposed. "I don't know the word but I *do* recognise the tone all too well."

The guard sneered with the jubilance of being able to expunge a Sodomite from his God's green vales. His finger lingered with lascivious intent over the trigger, delicately stroking the figurative clitoris.

Then he turned the gun around, pressed the barrel to his eye and pulled the trigger. Blood ejaculated from his ear and the back of his skull but, other than that, made no real difference to his state of being. So he simply inserted the shaft into the open socket, the heated barrel sizzled against the moist cavity walls. He adjusted his grip for a more satisfying angle of penetration then thrust deeper, sighing with a sense of rapture, then emptied his load deep inside.

As the guard's head erupted in a climactic spray of blood, brain and bone, Hugh's sense of relief was tempered by confusion and singed with a disturbing air of eroticism. This moment was, of course, ruined when the guard's spent body fell backwards, hit against a pillar and rolled over, then released a backed up reservoir of trapped gases.

He pondered whether the body might complete the analogy and start snoring when it emitted a hazy substance from its back; a sort of heat wave gently rose from the corpse and hovered a few feet in mid-air. As mesmerising as it was, something instinctive forced him to edge away, putting a pillar between himself and whatever it was. He controlled his breathing and prayed that he could make himself, for once, completely unnoticeable. And it was while he was attempting to fuse himself with his stone shield that he became aware he was staring at an open Bible atop a lectern. The thing that really distracted his attention, and caused him to step away from his protection was the lustrous glint of delicate cloth on the book.

"That's it," he murmured hypnotically to the chaos around him. "The quest is over."

The Black Monk ducked beneath the horizontal arc of Professor's blade. At the same time, he pivoted on the spot and knocked the swordsmith's feet out from under him. Cunningham had managed a well aimed shot at his ex-mentor's head which passed through empty air as he fell to the floor. Professor quelled the impact with a deft tuck and roll, throwing sharp shards of shrapnel at his attackers, forcing them both to duck and cover.

Another barrage of bullets sent Professor and Monk scuttling for deeper sanctuary, trading potentially lethal blows with each other; lethal if it had not been for their equally proficient defensive training. Each failed attack was echoed by a barely audible exclamative from the religious Ninja which was, seemingly, having a greater effect on Professor than the physical assaults.

The Monk attempted a whirling backfist which Professor sidestepped and took full advantage of the rare opening with a hearty kick in the abstinent's back. They parted company as a spray of masonry erupted where they had been standing.

Professor dived into a deeply shadowed recess and took the opportunity to show how out of breath he really was. "One of them, maybe," he panted quietly to himself, "but not both of them at once."

The assassin had rallied the support of his compatriots and they were firing indiscriminately into the darkness, pinning Professor and Monk alike firmly in their place.

Professor could see the hooded figure cowering behind a very minimal piece of wreckage across the aisle from him. "Hey," he called out. "Why are you fighting me?"

The Monk attempted to support his weight on his knees and started making awkward hand gestures.

"Are you mute? I don't understand your sign language," Professor told him.

The Monk shook his head violently and began tapping at his fingers again.

Professor performed a mental double-take. "But I heard you swearing. What the hell is the matter with you people?"

The pent up frustration had become too much and the Monk raised his body, arms and fist to the ceiling and screamed, "...!" A plague of bullets befell upon him and drove him further into the depths of the building for cover.

Now that all the attention had been removed from him, Professor acted. He was a man of action, he was a man of bravery, he was a man of principles but, above all, he was a man of science which meant he needed to have answers. It was for all these characteristics which made his next move so vital for his peace of mind and continued existence.

Professor snuck out the front door of the church. "Fuck it," he muttered. He stepped out and surveyed the carnage still in full swing in Place du Parvais. "Fuck it all," he reiterated and began to wind his way through the riot. He gently shoved a wrestling couple from his path and was quite surprised that his careful manipulation caught both men's full attention. "Sorry," he said then corrected himself. «Pardon me. I'm just trying to get past.»

One of the combatants, a gendarme, could not take his eyes from the old man's face. «It is you,» he said then turned to his opponent. «It is him.» He removed his hold on the other man hand reached inside his torn jacket to retrieve a folded piece of paper. It was while he was hurriedly unfolding it and twisting it the around when Professor experienced an sense of impending doom. It was a feeling he had had on many occasions in his life; coincidentally usually when he was desperately trying to explain something in front of an irate mob.

The gendarme pressed the crude sketch into the other man's confused face. «It is him,» he stated while jabbing his finger on the image. «He is the one responsible for all of this.»

«What?» Professor screeched. «You can't seriously be ...»

But it was too late; the lull in the conflict had spread as had the information and Professor could feel the widening radial of eyes all turning to him.

He nodded his head with embittered resignation. «Place de Grève then, I suppose.»

Hands were upon him.

The Black Monk stopped scuttling across the floor when he was self-assured that he was no longer a target of blistering pellets of death. Right now, he really wanted to kill something but knew that was entirely wrong so castigated himself with a solid punch to his head. He knocked himself out and slumped against the pedestal he was hiding behind.

The twisted spirit drifted from mind to mind, imparting empathic revenge on each soul it touched. There was some sense of satisfaction but at the same time, in keeping with its dichotomous existence, a deep regret. There was also a heady relief that one had managed to spurn it that, in turn, was being overshadowed by a vindictive resilience to try again. So, instead of selecting random targets, it set its sights back on its original intent and began its search with renewed vigour and resigned disappointment.

The shroud of covering fire gave Cunningham the opportunity to circle around the perimeter of the hall in the hope of doubling back on his old mentor.

A sparkle of reflected light distracted him for the briefest of moments and he targeted the source with his pistols. A momentary beam of light had crept through the raging storm, filtered its way into the church and was bouncing off a small piece of glass embroidered to a delicate piece of fabric.

The light died but the image remained burned on his sensitive retinas; it was a sign.

From a shadowed recess, the last vestiges of a confessional booth watched the turmoil that desecrated the hallowed hall before it. It had borne witness to all manner of divulgences of indulgences of every sin known to man, woman and beast - and then even more so. Confessions from thieves, sexual deviants, murderers to oppressed children, repressed housewives and innocents who felt that if they sought forgiveness for the slightest of things then they might infer a reason for their existence.

Never had it been subjected first hand to the literal damnable actions of humanity, nor had it ever heard a confession such as the one it was enduring now.

«-will slaughter the fucking bitch and her bastard father. Drive a splintered wedge in their soul and rip them apart. I have done all this and soon will be capable of so much more - anything I want. I just need to fill my purse.»

LeClerc pushed his face up to the baize door panel and peered out across the Dantean nightmare. The applied force to the door knocked over a brass pot that had been hurled in his direction earlier, as well as dislodging a rosary necklace, a thurible and a small pair of finger symbols that had collected on the roof of the cubicle. They clanged noisily as they jostled across the floor but drew no attention; the reverberations were swallowed by the judgmental growls from the storm overhead and continued ruckus from all around.

But despite all that noise, one voice pierced through it all and dialled his psychopathic rage up to eleven.

"- and was pulling my brain apart at the seams," Penny explained.

"A ghost?" Brandon asked.

"For the thirteenth time, yes, a fucking ghost. A great big, ugly, bad tempered, head fucking ghost," she bellowed.

"But there are no such things as -"

"Don't you fucking dare," she warned through gritted teeth. "You bury your head so far up you liturgical arse and blinker out anything that doesn't conform to your idealistic, pious preaching so that when ..."

Brandon's grasp of the English language was fairly rudimentary and many of the expressions Penny used went beyond his understanding. His innate naivety and politeness almost had him stopping her in mid-flow to explain herself better, however, his instinctive sense of self preservation could tell that she was quite capable of, and probably more than willing to, kill him where he stood. He decided to use ignorance as his diplomacy. "I have no idea what you are talking about."

"You're about to find out."

It was there again, that subtle refraction of light in the shadows; like a silhouette of steam that vanished with every flare of backlighting. Light blindness and the contrasting darkness lost the spectre until pupil adjustment and its subtle movement disclosed itself again.

"I can see it but there is nothing there," Brandon stated with hushed awe.

"Do something," Penny pleaded and took a cowering step backwards.

"Me?"

"You're a priest -"

"Actually, I'm -"

"- an appointed representative of God and this thing is evil. Exorcise it or something."

The spirit calmly snaked its way along the walls, pausing momentarily at the wreckage of a confessional booth.

"Exorcisms are a thing of fiction," Brandon explained. "The Bible, it says nothing about exorcism rites."

As soon as it reached a perpendicular point to them it changed course towards them; directly and quickly.

"Try," Penny begged. "If there was any one time that made a practical use of your career choice then it is now."

"I don't -"

"At least tell it to 'Fuck off' in Latin."

'A practical use of his career choice.' That was what she had said and it had hit home hard. Had everything he had ever done in his life been about the soul, the heart or the spiritual within people? Had he ever done anything really real? Yes, he was able to make people feel better to give their lives purpose when they felt there was none. Yes, he was able to make people feel bad to encourage them to do good. But had he ever 'done' anything real in the name of his 'career choice'? And was it just that, a career? It certainly was not one when he started. He positively relished the martyrdom of poverty and pain in the name of a pure mind and soul. Then, later, when a path of progression became clear before him, he saw the opportunities of rank presenting the chance to spread his belief of goodwill to more people much faster. But then his advancement up Jacob's Ecclesiastical Corporate Ladder took him further and further away from the masses and closer to the elitist, Papal paper pushers who analysed God's words, looking for more ways to damn mankind than save them.

The thing was directly in front of him: something that should contradict the edicts of his company reference guide; something that should question the advice of those who had inspired him and those he had passed on to others; something that could symbolise the non-existence of his life's purpose.

So why was it that he felt reassured in his so called 'choice'? Why was it that he felt his Faith Meter swell to overflowing? Why was it that every doubt in himself, his 'career' and life in general suddenly washed away in a baptism of renewed confidence?

A test. It was all a test. Not specifically this moment but everything that had come before him and he had been failing. He had been brought back to primary level religion and was having to remember how to deal with the literal before he was going to be allowed to consider the figurative. 'Deliver us from evil,' was the motto and he had forgotten what evil looked like. His God had performed a miracle for only He was capable of returning life to the dead.

And the words came to him as naturally, and as calmly, as breath. "Et ait illis: Ite."

The ghost stopped in its vaporous tracks as if considering some deep thought. Then, as its features presented a rapid slideshow of conflicting emotions, its amorphous body bowed at its centre, elongated at both ends and split.

Two supernatural creatures stared at each other.

One was a girl. She was young and pretty. Her round face and high cheek-bones offset a large pair of dark eyes that flashed lightning when they looked at you. But these were not lightning bolts of malicious intent, more like invigorating sparks of excitement.

The other spirit stared at her. It was not much more than a huge forehead that overshadowed a pair of squint, recessed pits of eyes. Its nose was flattened against its face and its mouth drooped sullenly from its cleft pallet. But again, there was no vindictiveness in its expression; at its alter ego or its intended target. There was a look of relief and happiness.

Each had been bound to the other through a naïve sentiment of affection. The death of one had been unjust and been the fuel for her revenge; the death of the other had been through profound sadness and been the seed of his regret. Being forced to cohabit the same space had accelerated these emotions to their extremes and now they had been released ...

Their forms swelled and deflated as if sighing. Then they dissipated.

The remaining door of the confessional booth flew from its delicate hinges and LeClerc burst out. «Nooooo! What did you do?»

«I told it to fuck off,» Brandon replied with a shrug. «In Latin.»

«You have destroyed everything again, little witch,» the old man raged. «I should have killed you with my bare hands. It would have been far more satisfying.»

«No offence, Robert,» Penny soothed, «but you're over seventy years old and would probably have a coronary thinking about going one-to-one with me. Especially after last time.»

LeClerc's anger took a moment to consider this and recalled her fighting prowess from the other night. He also could not stop himself from remembering her astride him. He turned and fled for the nearest exit.

«Robert!» she screamed at him and vaulted the debris that had separated them. «You have a lot of explaining to do.»

Brandon would normally have stood alone, feeling, and looking, incredibly bewildered. Instead, he felt an overwhelming sense of pride and self-satisfaction; he had done some real good for a change. He looked around him in search of some other poor soul to save and saw an open Bible on a pedestal. On that Bible was a small piece of cloth.

LeClerc bounded up the stairwell to the observation balcony, two steps per stair. He held on to the railing with each hurried hobble and cursed his arthritic hips in between cursing his ex-girlfriend. Luckily, he had managed to put enough initial distance between him and her that it was taking Penny a few wrong turns to pick up his trail. That and the fact that his minimal movement was so silent he left no tell-tale foot thumps echoing down the corridors.

He carefully pushed the balcony door open and entered to, what looked like, the dawning of a brand new day. The sight was overwhelming; rays of blessed gold were slicing through the blackened skies. Piercing through the hearts of darkness above and below him. The tumultuous fervour was being quelled by this shower of pure heaven and everything was right in the world again.

The vision before him and physical wave of peace left him awestruck, drew a tear from his eye, sent him reeling backwards. He collided with a souvenir stand, which sold a variety of scale replicas of the Emmanuelle bell. They poured across the floor and peeled to Brother Jack that the morning bells were ringing.

«Robert!» he heard her scream from within and he backed away from the door.

She burst through, stepped directly into one of God's spotlights but, unfortunately for LeClerc, it did not have the same calming effect. If anything, it simply illuminated every facet of her anger.

Her white summer dress was stained and ripped, revealing pockets of flesh from her thighs, midriff and arms. Each section of toned body had been blemished with scratches, bruises or more filth. Her hat had been discarded or lost long ago and her fair hair had been darkened and ruffled around her head as if one of the storm clouds had symbiotically attached itself. Her face, equally grimy, served to accentuate the white violence in her eyes. She panted heavily through exertion and desperate self-control.

«You are responsible for all of this,» she told him and waved an arm in an attempt to encompass everything but had to give up because it was all too much to take in. «Why? Did I really hurt you that much?»

His fear lapsed. «This isn't about you, you selfish girl. You are something that came along. Nothing more.»

It was Penny's turn to derail. «Oh. Really? I thought …»

«Yes you hurt me and I had to claw my way through life from then on, but I forgot about you and your father and found … a greater love.»

«Oh. Well, good. I'm sort of happy for you,» she said, desperately trying to hide a shade of disappointment, «but why all this then?»

«Money,» he said resolutely.

Her expression changed again, this time to incomprehension - «You killed people for money?» - to disgust - «You've murdered hundreds for money?»

«Lots of money,» he said, smiled wickedly and unconsciously dry washed his hands.

She looked over the horizon of her home: fires were being extinguished but smoke still plumed into the atmosphere; bodies were being gathered in the courtyard below and the injured being tended to; in the distance she could see a mob trying to enact a last vestige of common law on a smartly dressed man with pure white hair and …

"Oh, for fuck's sake," she sighed and turned.

LeClerc was upon her. The smile had turned into a clenched teeth, murderous grimace. His sharp, bony fingers strapped themselves around her neck and attempted to squeeze the life from her. The locket jangled in her face like a psychotic moth and the Alice Band slipped down over his eyes like a knight's visor.

Penny frowned, grabbed his arms, released them from her throat and tossed him to one side without any effort at all. She advanced to the door but was surprised to hear him scream for slightly longer than was necessary for a stumble to the floor. Turning to see where he landed, she realised she must have undercompensated her strength and overcompensated his weight as she saw that he had gone over the side of the wall.

"Oh bugger."

Peering over the side, she could see he had got his robe snagged on the pointed ear of a gargoyle and was dangling above a free fall to the ground beyond her reach.

He squealed and tried to twist his body to get a grip of the statue but only caused the material to rip. A small piece of paper fell from the split and danced in an updraft before his face. He swung his arms around to grab it and caused his stone saviour to lose its grip more. In turn, more pieces of paper fell out.

Penny looked from her ex to her father and was torn between which she should try to save.

"All that I have ever loved," she mumbled.

«Fucking bitch!» LeClerc screamed.

"Well, that resolves that dilemma," she decided and looked around her. Her eyes fell on the felled souvenir stand.

LeClerc had managed to recover a few of the slips of paper that teased him and the rip in his robe had edged its way to a strong seam that could hold his light weight indefinitely.

«Oi, shit head!» Penny called from above him.

He turned and saw her silhouette wielding a football sized metallic object that glinted in the sunlight.

«You were a rubbish shag,» she told him and hurled the larger of the scale replicas of Emmanuelle at him.

It chimed righteously as it struck him square on his nose, bursting it across his face. The additional force was too much for his robe and the final seam gave way, sending him plummeting to the ground, closely followed by a deluge of dozens of slips of paper in his wake.

The riot had stopped, the storm had passed and the final localised groups of rebels were being disbanded through force or diplomatic words.

Anjo and Suzette had made it to the cathedral steps when they heard a door-bell like ring and a loudening scream of terror.

«Suzette,» Anjo called, «step back.» He pulled at her shoulder just as a dark figure whizzed past their eye line and slammed into the ground at their feet.

Things snapped, bits burst, a bell bounced off what was left of its head, butterflies of paper littered around it. The body wheezed as air seeped from its fluid-filling lungs, an eyeball rolled in its socket and settled on Suzette.

«Suzette,» it gurgled. «It is I, LeClerc.» Then it was silent.

Anjo looked at her for some sort of affirmation but she could only shrug with incomprehension through the reactions of shock and nausea.

«I do not know the name,» she confessed, «but the face does ring a bell. I think it might be Robert.»

«Another suicide,» Anjo cursed. «We were too late. What the hell is this?» He snatched one of the fluttering papers from the air and studied it. «A lottery ticket?»

*Illottonatti.*

He grabbed another; the numbers were near identical.

*Bits of code.*

Another had a combination of the other papers.

*Someone wanted all of the code.*

They all had variations of the same numbers and there were dozens of them.

«They are this week's numbers,» Suzette gasped as she gathered the slips. «This has five matching numbers, as does this one and this. This one has all six.»

«These must be worth millions,» Anjo deduced.

«And they're all mine,» she declared. «We were a syndicate. I have the contract. The signatures. Robert must have spent a fortune on mixing the numbers up in the hope -»

«And when the numbers came in, he wanted it all for himself,» Anjo concluded, staring blankly at the shattered doors of the Holy building. «He couldn't risk any of you being around to divide his wealth. All of this, just for a few Euros. A few Euros stained with the blood of hundreds of Parisians. I hope it will all be worth it, Suzette. Suzette?»

Anjo turned around but Suzette had disappeared from sight. She was lying on her back on the floor, a frozen smile on her face was slightly twisted by the pain of the sudden, fatal coronary she had suffered.

He scuffed his feet through the human detritus, went back to his car and drove to the hospital.

Case closed.

# BOOK 7

## Dénouement (*Maintenant*)

## The Bells

Penny was still running across the island when she saw her father talking on a public phone. He hung up and approached her.

"I thought I was going to have to rescue you from another hanging," she gasped.

"No, they eventually ran out of steam," he told her. "Mobs today just don't seem to have the same stamina, passion and perseverance of old."

"Who were you calling?"

"*I* just received a call from one of your vampire friends."

"What?"

"She has asked if we could lend a hand in some problem they've encountered."

"Good," Penny sighed. "Let's get out of here."

The couple linked arms and began a leisurely stroll through the city streets, avoiding as many human encounters as they possibly could.

"Is this going to be one little mystery that eludes us then?" Professor asked.

"I got some answers but not really the whole story," his daughter replied. "I think we'll just draw a line under this as some horrible mix up."

They were walking past the gates of the University of Paris when Penny stopped in her tracks to read a poster.

Professor halted and turned around after he realised she was not intending to catch up.

"What is it?" he enquired.

"I know this man," she told him. "He's here and I think he might be able to help us."

He walked to her side to inspect the poster: a Doctor Trevor Leavis was giving a guest lecture at the university; a presentation on secret codes throughout history.

"How can he help us?" Professor asked incredulously.

"He was one of my tutors at Leeds," she explained. "He knows things. He might be able to shed some light."

"He was in your secret order?"

"I can't tell you that," she replied.

"Which I will take as an affirmation," he concluded.

"I thought old Teabag must have died with everyone else," she mused to herself.

"I'm sorry, who?"

"Hmm?" she asked as reality seeped back. "Oh, him. Sorry. He was called 'Teabag' around the faculty."

"Ah," Professor acknowledged. "A term of endearment, I presume?"

"A self-entitled epithet, actually."

"A lifelong nickname derived from his name, T. Leavis - tealeaves?"

"Erm. Not quite," she hesitated. "I'm not sure that you actually want to know."

"After acquainting myself with your friends in Leeds?" he asked. "How bad could it be?"

Penny shrugged with resignation.

"Although he's practically pushing eighty, he did enjoy fraternising with the students and, after about half-a-dozen brandies would perform his party trick. Usually on an unsuspecting, young girl sitting down, minding her own business."

"And the party trick in question?"

She looked at him with confusion. "Well, he'd teabag her, obviously."

"Not obvious enough."

Penny emoted a mix of frustration, annoyance and severe discomfort as she tried to explain verbally and gesticulatory and kept having to scrunch her face up between attempts to either redirect her train of thought or erase the images she was conjuring.

"It's - ugh! Well, when - tsk! He would - aargh!"

Her hands would cup and she would tap them to her forehead. Her father just stared at her in complete incomprehension.

"No!" she finally decided. "I'm not ready to have this kind of conversation with you. Go *Google* it."

Professor took a step back in shock. "Penelope!" he gasped reproachfully. "Is that some kind of genital euphemism?"

"No, it's -" she started to respond then flapped her hands at her side. "You're impossible," she declared and stormed past him.

He was genuinely put out but followed her onto the campus grounds without another word.

Teabag was in his late fifties with mousy grey hair, interspersed with generous strips of white throughout. He had it brushed straight back from his forehead to display a mischievous pair of blue eyes that could switch from affectionate to menacing with equal levels of aplomb.

His face was soft yet craggy, allowing him incredible versatility in his expressions.

He greeted the couple in the foyer, wearing a pale blue dressing gown over plaid pyjamas, and spoke to them in a soft voice with perfectly enunciated Estuary Standard English.

"You will have to forgive my attire," he apologised. "I was torn between the ignominy of entertaining in my jim-jams or the rudeness of keeping you waiting while I dressed and freshened up."

"Thank you for seeing us at such short notice, Teabag," Penny said and stepped forward to embrace him, then planted a kiss on his cheek.

"Ah, my dear," he praised. "I thought you must have been lost to the ravages of the epidemic."

"I thought the same of you," she countered.

"How fortunate for us both," he stated. "I was invited to join this lecture and you escaped because …?"

Professor stepped forward. "I, too, would like to apologise for this invasion," he professed. "I did try to convince her that it wasn't necessary but -"

Teabag shook his head at Penny and tutted a few times. "I am sorely disappointed in you, dear girl," he admonished and leaned in to whisper in her ear. "You said *I* was too old for you."

Penny pushed him away. "Stop it, you lecherous goat," she spat. "He's my father."

"Ah, in which case, welcome to my humble, yet temporary, abode," he greeted and presented his right hand to Professor. He clasped it and they shook. Then they did not let go. They just looked into each other's eyes.

"Really?" Teabag asked. "And yet there's -"

His expression changed to one of awe and he retracted his hand.

"Your father is a man of the World, my dear," Teabag purred.

"I have been around the block a few times," Professor bragged.

"Some unusual blocks, too, I'd wager," Teabag pondered then remembered his manners. "Introduce us, girl."

"Trevor Leavis, this is my father who likes to be called Professor," Penny announced.

"A man of learning and irony, then," Teabag suggested. "To take such a notable name and know of its derivation implies -"

"It has always been my name," Professor interrupted. "I took it from no one, although others have attempted to take it from me."

Teabag pursed his lips in thought and then spun on his slippered heels.

"Come into the kitchen for some refreshments while you tell me what the devil is going on," he instructed and led the way through a couple of rooms and down a flight of stairs.

As they entered a large, stone walled room, Teabag lifted an electric kettle and filled it from the sink tap.

"So, Professor, how old do you think you are?" Teabag asked. "One hundred and fifty, perhaps?"

"Closer to two hundred and fifty," Professor replied nonchalantly.

Penny looked at her father in shock but he kept his eyes set on the lecturer's back as he continued with his tea ministrations.

"I have come across a few passages here and there that have referenced you," Teabag said. "Although it took some time to realise they were actually puzzle pieces and not just innocuous occurrences. Some of the references spanned a dozen decades so it was presumed to be nothing more than coincidence. I always thought it had to be more than that, so I continued digging and came up with this interesting piece of parchment."

He dried his hands on a tea towel and marched across the kitchen to a large suitcase. He opened it to reveal it was more like a huge compartmentalised box file. He deftly flipped his fingers through the various papers contained in the compartments until he came to a weathered and worn parchment which he pulled out and admired.

Teabag raised his excited expression to his wary audience and realised their expressions.

"Oh, don't worry. If there's one thing I know how to do well, it's keeping secrets," he assured them. "Sit down, sit down. This, I believe, was the start of your downfall."

Professor and Penny sat in the chairs around the large oak dining table. Teabag slid the paper across it to Professor who scanned it.

"It's believed that there was an entire journal at one time," Teabag narrated. "My great-great-grandfather made mention of it when he was living in Hamburg. He said he passed it on to a young academic who was doing a lot of research into European folklore. You may have heard of him. Stoker?"

Only Penny showed any signs of acknowledgement.

"I knew of the gentleman," Professor muttered disdainfully.

"Anyway," Teabag continued. "He swore blindly that it never got to him, which isn't completely out of the question. But after a couple of his novels were published it certainly made members a tad reticent about passing further information on to him. My ancestor retained this particular piece of the diary. You know the signature."

"Ferdinand," Professor growled.

Teabag barked a laugh of triumph and clapped his hands together with childish glee.

"This is truly amazing," he gushed. "I have spent a lifetime researching myths, legends and lore to come to undeniable truths that they were or were not real but to have one sit in my kitchen. To have the daughter of one study under me and never say a bloody word. You naughty girl."

"I wasn't in the mood to talk about him then," Penny muttered.

Teabag leaned across the table and tapped his index finger on the parchment. "It does say here that you and a companion were to be allowed safe passage out of Hungary," he stated. "If you don't mind, who were you travelling with then?"

The Professor did not return Teabag's earnest gaze but looked quickly at Penny before returning to the sheet of paper.

"Not you?" Teabag asked Penny.

"No, not me," she assured. "This is one of many parts of my father's history that I am not a part of. You probably know more about him than I do."

"It sounds like you may know more about my past than even I can remember," Professor said.

Teabag slumped back to his chair without trying to hide his disappointment. "Really?" he asked. "If it would jog your memory then I'm pretty sure it was a woman."

Professor could feel the inquisitional stares from Teabag and Penny trying to burn their way into his mind and so he laughed to deflect his rising emotions. "It was such a long time ago," he guffawed, "and there have been so many countries that I have been extradited from."

Teabag allowed his gaze to fall away back to the paper. "Yes, and I believe this particular death sentence should you return to Hungary is still binding?"

"They tried," Professor said flatly.

The excited gleam returned to Teabag's eyes. "I am sorry," he said. "I must stop quizzing you. I still cannot believe you really exist, let alone are here before me."

"Thirsty," Penny mentioned.

"Hm? Oh, the tea! Will the depths of my incivility know no bounds?" Teabag exclaimed. "Please, tell me your stories while I see to the brew." He leapt to his feet and turned his back on them. He was a flurry of movement as he juggled with chinaware and steaming water. "I'm afraid you'll have to excuse the quality of the leaves. This place has all manner of herbal and fruity flavours to cater for insipid hippies but discriminate against the true purveyors of liquid refreshment by providing only an English breakfast in a bag."

"We were in some sort of trouble," Penny said.

"Well, of course," Teabag concurred. "Unsolicited visitors very rarely come by to announce that all is well. And you have a family history of the stuff."

"But we're not entirely sure what kind of trouble," she continued, "and I was hoping you might be able to clear up a few details."

Teabag paused and turned slowly to them. "Vampires?" he enquired.

Penny shook her head.

"They are all wiped out," Professor said.

Teabag's eyebrows raised in admiration. "Good work, that man," he praised.

"It was a team effort," Professor replied.

Teabag's brow furrowed in thought. "It must have been a fairly recent thing, as I did hear of activities in Mongolia."

"Very recent," Professor said.

"Leeds," Penny added.

"I seem to be missing out on everything, don't I?"

"Anyway," Penny reminded.

"Yes, do go on," Teabag urged.

"We were wanted by a number of parties," she told him. "The police seemed to think we were involved in a series of odd deaths around the city."

"The suicides?"

"That's them," she said. "But I want to assure you that we had absolutely nothing to do with them. I think we must have been in the wrong place at the wrong time and since they didn't have any other leads ..."

"And you didn't declare your innocence to them because ...?" Teabag enquired.

"We seem to have been in quite a few wrong places."

"Victims of circumstance," Teabag pondered.

"There have been some," Penny had to search for the appropriate word, "men of the Church."

"Priests?"

"No, not quite," she said. "There was a Vatican Bishop and some bloke who was very religious. Very devout. Almost too devout."

"He is a Swiss Guard, I believe," Professor added. "And there's a monk of some kind. Very bizarre chap. I think he may have Tourette's."

"Oh dear, you attracted the attentions of some fundies, did you?"

"Some what?" Professor asked.

"Fundamentalists," Teabag iterated. "Although you could drop the 'funda' and have a more apt description. They're the type of people who know their Bible so well that they could justify anything they do to be under the sanctity of the eyes of the Lord."

"Quite," agreed Professor.

"Anyway, we heard that it might have something to do with Da Vinci's *Last Supper*," Penny continued. "They thought we had an object that was connected to it but we never found out what it was or did."

"Not this old chestnut," Teabag scoffed.

"It isn't much of a laughing matter," Professor rebuked. "This was what caused the riots. Hundreds of people died."

"Yes, fundies would be quite capable of killing under normal circumstances," Teabag said. "They certainly would not have any qualms about killing over this little puzzle. More likely that they would kill you after its resolution, though, just to ensure you kept quiet."

"You think you might know what it's all about?" Penny asked.

Teabag gave her a knowing smile and a wink, then returned his attention to the beverages. He collected cups, the teapot, cutlery and a bottle of milk then placed it all on the table.

"Help yourselves," he instructed then went back to his case. From there, he pulled out a laptop and small projector which set up on the table and pointed at a blank wall. After a second, the log-in chime sounded and a white square illuminated the wall. He tapped a few keys, glided his finger across the mouse pad and double clicked a couple of times.

"Well, if all the elements you have told me are related, then it can only come down to one artefact I can think of," Teabag stated as he negotiated his way through a myriad path of folders and document shortcuts. "Yes, it's been quite some time since the Vatican has been so proactive. Not since the great Templar 'outing' in 1312." Listening carefully to Teabag's report might have inferred a tinge of resentment in his voice. "Here we are," he announced as Leonardo Da Vinci's *Last Supper* filled the projection. "Supposedly, Leonardo was commissioned to knock up this little piece by Duke Ludovico Sforza and was given access to some of the original reference sources that were used for the final version of the Bible."

"Is this all to do with Jesus being married to Mary Magdalene and that's her -" Penny suggested.

"Oh, don't embarrass yourself with that piffle," Teabag scolded.

"That's fiction, then?" Professor enquired.

"Not at all," Teabag replied. "Absolute fact. Look at her, for goodness sake." He pointed at the figure next to Jesus with his cursor. "How can that possibly be anything other than female? No, that was all an attempted cover-up after publication. Not Leonardo's fault at all but a very sloppy suppression which was twisted into a clever misdirection."

No one said anything.

"Excellent, the perfect audience," Teabag purred. "It's the old magician's trick; look at this hand so you won't see what the other hand is doing. Everyone has been so obsessed with whether Jesus bore an heir that they never saw what secret Leonardo was actually revealing." He turned on them. "So, my dear. What did our little sect teach you to do?"

"Question everything," Penny recited. "But I don't …"

"What do you see?"

"People sitting around a table," Professor noted.

"'Around'? Interesting."

"Well, it's just been painted like that for dramatic purposes," Penny defended her father. "If it was drawn realistically then you would have disciples blocking others or with their backs turned."

"Perhaps. But what do you do when you're at a table and someone takes a photo of you?"

"Turn around, but that would look more unnatural for a painting than it does at the moment."

"Question everything. Even if the answer provides no additional useful revelations, everything must be questioned."

"Okay," Penny sighed. "Why was it called 'The Last Supper'?"

"It was Jesus' last meal with his disciples, when he would reveal his imminent passing and who around the table would betray him," Professor replied.

"So, where's the food?" Penny asked.

"What?"

"Where's the food? The supper? Where is it?"

"This was drawn at the point that Jesus was breaking the bread and sharing the wine; symbolising his body and -"

"They don't seem very interested in him, do they? Very involved in their own conversations."

"They are supposed to be shocked over the news that there will be a betrayal. They're arguing. That's why Jesus looks so disappointed with them. After everything he has tried to teach them, they still don't trust him or seem to have learnt very much."

"'Disappointed'. That's a good observation, Professor," Teabag commended.

"I don't get it, Teabag," Penny whined. "This is just what everybody knows."

"Why does 'everybody' know this?"

"Because it's what everybody has been told in the Bible."

"In a version of the Bible that everybody was privy to," Teabag explained. "So we have to see beyond what was told and what else might be involved. What do we know about Leonardo that might have inspired him to concoct this?"

"He was a visionary. An inventor. An artist. A satirist. A practical joker."

"Apply the context to the text," Teabag instructed.

"Very well," Professor puffed. "If this was to be a satirical piece then the mysticism of these people might be stripped away and them given very realistic lives. They are absolutely having a heated debate but not about betrayal they are arguing over ... how much Jesus costs their fishing business every time he walks on water."

Teabag applauded and laughed heartily. "That is excellent, sir. That's thinking outside of the box but too far in this case. We need to maintain the context of the setting."

"Wait a minute," Penny interrupted. "The food's gone. The meal's finished. Are they arguing over the bill? Who's had what and trying to split it."

"Bravo!" Teabag rejoiced. "I have always wanted to teach this one but would have been summarily executed for even suggesting such a thing."

"Jesus is upset because he knows he's going to have to stump up for the bill at his own leaving do," she continued. "Man, that's cold."

"That's just an interpretation of the piece," Professor added cynically.

"Leonardo was such an incredibly clever man," Teabag gushed. "Able to hide the most fantastic puzzles intricately within his works so plainly in sight." He pulled a marker pen out of his case and drew a rectangle around the frame of the projection. "You know of the Golden Ratio? Phi?"

"It's the natural focal point of a painting," Professor replied. "Dividing the image into half pieces leads to the natural points that attract the eye."

"Good. But knowing Leonardo as I do – that of a prankster, a rebel, a non-conformist – I would look at where he doesn't use it on this one. It's all over the place and 'experts' are so busy checking out the disciples, the ceiling, the table and the windows that they miss the really inconsequential stuff." He divided the rectangle vertically in half.

"Like?" Penny asked.

He turned around so abruptly that the couple jumped back in their seats. "The man painted transparent glasses for goodness' sake! Then? An historical continuity error from a very clever man who was allowed to see the actual menu? I don' think so."

Penny and Professor just gave each other glances of incomprehension.

Teabag returned his attention to the wall and halved the right side horizontally. "Leonardo obviously wanted us to see inside the glasses. The drink is nearly all gone and there are no more bottles on the table; another indication that the meal is over rather than in full flow. There are lots of things that he wanted us to look at, but where is the place that he didn't want anyone to notice unless you really looked?" He continued dividing rectangle across their opposite sides, then added a couple of corner to corner splits and then joined a number of points, creating a smooth inwardly concentrating spiral that finally settled on the table in front of Jesus.

Professor and Penny leaned in and scrunched their faces in the hope of making the image clearer.

"Jesus right hand is reaching for a bread roll."

"Rolls? Still on the table at the end of a meal? They're the first things to go. Here, let me show you one I prepared earlier," Teabag suggested and pressed a button on his keyboard. The vista changed to a high resolution close-up of the hand in question. "You won't see this in the public viewing section at the Louvre, I'm afraid. This was taken at the source before its unfortunate 'restoration'."

Quite evidently, under Jesus' hand, just out of reach, was a green piece of material. Shiny, like silk.

"Such a stickler for detail," Teabag narrated.

In its centre was a green, lustrous gem. Trailing away on either side of the material were two pieces of drawstring.

"I saw that," Penny gasped. "Robert had it on his Bible, just before …" She shuddered involuntarily.

"The Purse of God," Teabag exposed.

"Jesus had a purse," Professor harrumphed. "That's the conspiracy."

"No, dear boy. Now we look beyond the literal and consider the figurative. Leonardo was a non-conformist and enjoyed mocking the authorities who commissioned his works. Was Jesus a real person? Did any of this actually happen or was it just one of a series of cleverly devised morality tales put together to give meaning and impetus to the masses, the working classes, the uneducated, the restless, the demoralised?"

"The whole painting is about betrayal," Penny surmised. "They've all betrayed Jesus, he is having to pay the ultimate price somehow. Reaching for his money bag rather than them doing it."

"Who is 'they'?" Teabag enquired.

"They are his colleagues, his friends, his spokespersons. The church's representatives. They are all going to benefit from this; they are all going to continue to feed from his wealth."

"It's a bit girly, isn't it?" Professor added. "Surely he would have a plain sack cloth rather than something so ornate."

"Da Vinci's not suggesting Jesus was gay, is he?" Penny demanded.

"Well, the Liberatti would have you believe so but, no, not in this case," Teabag stated.

"Jesus was …" Penny fished for a connection.

"What if Jesus was also figurative?" Teabag hinted.

"Jesus represents the whole of Christianity, of God Himself, and He has a woman's purse which could imply … that God is a woman?" Penny deduced.

"Good work!"

"Is that it?" Professor asked incredulously.

"But that purse isn't figurative," Penny interjected. "I've seen it."

"Which might make you wonder what other inspirational sources Leonardo might have had access to in his time," Teabag supposed, "and how much of this theory is actually theoretical."

"But why would the church go to so much trouble over something so trivial such as God's gender?" Professor demanded.

"Well, consider that the entire ethos of Christianity is based on God being male -" Teabag started.

"Which has been the cornerstone for patriarchal dominance throughout history," Penny interrupted.

"- and the whole issue of 'thou should not really tell lies' kind of puts the entire faith into question as well as the validity of these men who have claimed so much power via the process of something potentially as credible and accountable as *The Hobbit*. Christianity would collapse, followed by every other blind-faith, god-dependent religion. People would lose hope and purpose to continue living righteously, society would collapse, anarchy would ensue, the end of the World would most certainly be nigh."

They sat in contemplative silence, considering the massive ramifications that such a seemingly inconsequential object could have on life as they knew it, the lengths some people would go to keep such an object away from public awareness and, perhaps, how the recent loss of human life had been a minor incident in relation to the potential worldwide calamity that could have happened.

"Fucking A!" Penny broke the silence. "We totally helped save the World again! Just wait till the others hear this!"

"Penelope!" her father admonished. "Language!"

# BOOK 8

## Épilogue (*Allors*)

## The Mother

It felt like it had been raining constantly for the entire week, although they knew that it had to have stopped occasionally. Neither Professor or Mary considered themselves to be particularly religious, even though they had been, once upon a time. All the things they had been through defied all religious texts and so they had to either completely disregard the possibility of the existence of God or, at best, assume that He was not everything the Church made Him out to be.

This rain, however, and their circumstances, could make even the most devout agnostic have second thoughts.

Their past did not need much more elaboration. Mary, being a vampire, had defied death and ecclesiastical judgement. That alone should be enough to cause doubt as to the Bible's views on the afterlife but their constant interaction with those creatures who were demons by any other name was the clincher. No deity in their right mind could allow such evil to walk amongst its children. That meant there could not be a God, or if there was then He had deserted this world and its people a long time ago.

That was their experience and as for their circumstance? They had been reduced to living on the streets and had been for almost a month. An encounter with an incredibly powerful vampire had them barely escape with their lives, had resulted in the destruction of their last safe haven and all their worldly possessions. Every one of their homes had been compromised as the vampires revealed themselves in an ever-increasing frequency. The family had no time to make preparations for a new home before they were running for their lives again.

He could not remember them ever needing to run as much as they were. The pair of them, before Penelope came along, had managed to get themselves horrendously outnumbered but very rarely ran from the battle. Those were the days when you knew that running was not really an option. Once a vampire had your scent then it would hunt you down relentlessly. To flee was just delaying the inevitable.

Of course they were no longer just thinking about their own lives any more. Penelope represented something worth being able to 'fight another day' for. But did they run, for her sake or because of it? After all, she was just a baby and despite the few parlour tricks she could perform, she was just a hindrance during a struggle. They were no longer concentrating on killing their enemy and preserving themselves but now having to keep an eye, and a free hand, out for her.

They would not be in this humiliating situation had she not been here.

He had learned a long time ago that this life often called for the sacrifice of others to ensure their safety. He was sure Mary knew that too but as he watched her shield her daughter's sleeping form under a sackcloth, he wondered.

She was risking everything for that child; risking all their lives and their relationship.

"It's not her fault, Abraham," Mary stated from under the blanket.

For the briefest of seconds he considered replying the defensive, 'I do not know what you are talking about,' but knew that was a dangerous path of secrets and deceit that would not help them.

"She should not be here," he told her.

"I know that," Mary snapped with an element of a snarl in her voice. "I'm just saying that it's not her fault that we're here."

"Who's fault might it be, do you think?"

She raised her head to glare at him.

"Don't patronise me, Abraham," she warned. "It was us who wanted this child. It was our decision to take her. She's our responsibility and just because things aren't working out how we'd like them doesn't mean we can just pass her to the first orphanage we come to."

"I think we may have made a mistake," he said.

"Perhaps, but it's one we have to live with," she countered. "Just like every decision that, in retrospect, may have been a mistake. Me being like this, you being like that and us being here. None of it's perfect but hopefully we'll get through it."

He stared dispassionately at her for a moment.

"Some mistakes are easier corrected than others," he suggested.

"It's called responsibility, Abraham," Mary told him. "You can't just dump her at the first sign off trouble."

"If that was the case then she would have been gone years ago," he interrupted.

"She's not like some of those boys you took under your wing," she continued. "They made a decision to get involved; she did not. We decided that and we have to stand by that decision until she is capable of changing it or the fates do it for us."

He allowed his severity to slip and placed his hand on her arm.

"I wasn't implying that we should give her away," he assured.

"Or drown her?" Mary demanded causing him to retract with indignation.

"Certainly not," he blustered. "She is our daughter and I have grown to love her as much as I do you and it is because I do that makes me wonder if she would not be safer under the care of someone else. Someone normal."

"It's because she's not normal that means we're the only ones able to care for her adequately," Mary said.

He slumped back against the wall and sighed.

"She's been a baby for so long now," he complained.

"And whose fault is that?" Mary asked teasingly.

They sat in silence, just staring at each other.

"I can get us out of this," she said.

"Don't remind me," he muttered. "The very idea is utterly abhorrent. I cannot allow it."

She raised her eyebrows at him.

"I mean," he stuttered, "I cannot agree to it."

"It will all be of my own doing," she said. "I don't see what part you will have to play aside from minding Penelope."

"You have no idea what the effect on you might be," he stated. "There is no way to determine any negative impact until it will be too late."

"Oh, come now, Abraham," she mocked. "What could the worse case scenario be? You must have considered it before now."

"I might have to kill you," he told her which knocked the smile from her face.

"You might try," she said coldly.

They continued to stare at each other until Mary suddenly averted her gaze. When she lifted her eyes again the stoic expression had been replaced with an irritated smile.

"I couldn't hold it," she confessed.

"You never can," he replied.

"It's not my fault that I have a sense of humour."

"It's not my fault either," he muttered.

"All right, you bloody misery," she growled. "I realise what the risks are but I think they are worth it given that all of this could be turned around before nightfall."

"There is no reward that could be worth the potential risk of losing you."

She shook her head at him and pursed her lips in abject resignation.

"This isn't healthy, Abraham," she told him. "For her or for us. Physically, mentally or emotionally. Something has to change and quickly."

He wanted this to be his definitive moment. He wanted the last words to be his. He wanted his to be the voice of undeniable logic and reason but the only rebuttal he could come up with was, 'But I love you,' and he knew that it was a very weak argument.

The worse part was, he did not even have the strength to say it out loud.

"I -" was all that emerged. He was saved the embarrassment of his voice cracking by her jumping on his supposed indignation.

"I have decided," she told him forthrightly. "We need to take the risk."

There were so many things that he wanted to say; anything that might make her change her mind or, at least, make her stay for a few minutes longer so he could cherish this untainted moment for as long as possible.

But she passed Penelope into his unresisting arms and ventured out into the overcast streets. Her diminishing figure was eventually completely engulfed by the sheets of rain.

He could only turn to the person left so looked down at his daughter.

He was taken aback when he saw that she was already staring up at him. When she acknowledged that his gaze was reciprocating hers, she smiled up at him despite the droplets of cold water that dropped on her forehead.

Could he really do that to her? Could he really do what was 'best' for everyone even though it would probably break his heart in two?

Even though it was only mid-afternoon, the heavy cloud cover made it as dark as evening. That would keep most people off the streets at the best of times. Paris may have been a city of decadence, civility and ostentation but the brighter the beacon of progressiveness was, the darker its shadow of poverty, contempt and exploitation would be. This city's shadows contained a varied crop of dangers; mortal and otherwise.

It was not Mary's intention to be hunted but sometimes the quickest way to lure your prey was to present yourself as bait. And, despite being an undead bloodsucker, she actually prided herself on her moral principles; she never fed upon innocents. Unless she really had to.

No, when it came to the point that she absolutely had to feed then she made sure it was feeding on someone who deserved to die. She could usually go about a week between meals unless she had been exerting herself, then it was more frequent.

She would try to leave it as long as possible because she had gradually come to abhor that side of her existence. The feeding. The taking of other people's lives. It was murder and she was still in touch with enough of her humanity to know that murder was wrong.

She supposed it came back to the whole religion dichotomy. Her religious upbringing had drummed in, 'Thou shalt not kill,' and even though she seriously doubted God's existence, it seemed unnecessary to incur His wrath just in case.

But as that seventh day came around, she could not help herself. That was when she completely lost touch of her humanity and she remembered what it was like during those first few hours of her rebirth.

She was not particularly educated - most of her knowledge and understanding had come from being with Abraham - so she sometimes found it hard for her to express herself. Even harder to do it without swearing but she thought she had nailed it perfectly by saying she turned fucking animalistic when the hunger really kicked in. Every element of her being cried out for blood and did not stop until she had some. And it did not matter how she was going to get it or whom it was from. Even Abraham was not safe when she got like that.

She wished that she could say she was not in control of herself when it came. She wished she could pretend that the pains would come and when they passed she found herself over the butchered body of another victim. She could then defer some of her guilt onto that more violent, unconscious persona. But, no, she knew all too well of the things she did during the pain; she was in complete control of her actions and motivations. It was a simple case of the urgency of one need outweighing that of another. The need for blood came before her need for a clean conscience.

Abraham had called it her 'blood lust'. It was a useful phrase to use in conversation or in the midst of a battle - all vampires suffered from the condition and although it did make them incredibly vicious it also made them very careless - but by naming it so simply sort of belittled the condition.

"GRAAAAAAARGH! I demand sustenance! I NEED BLOOOOOOD!"

"Are you having your blood lust, dear? Cup of tea?"

But, as explained, she did not have the vocabulary to put the feelings into words so left it to him.

It seemed to be quite the norm for men to create names for things they did not understand just so they could undermine the importance or power that they held. Sex, politics, ethnicity, religion; the list was probably endless and ranged from one extreme to another but all shared the bound of having been tamed by men's words.

Mary had always been dominated by men, in one fashion or another. Ever since she could remember, she could not remember ever having a father as such. She certainly had never used words like 'Papa' to call any of the disciplinarian males in her life. Her mother seemed to have brought a string of men into the household although she was under no delusion as to why she brought them in. Mary knew that they were not there for hers or her mother's well being, apart from maybe a financial one. In fact she remembered that she had not long turned into her teens before the dominant male at the time encouraged her to supplement the household's income.

Of course, she was not unfamiliar with sex. The size of their room prevented the most basic premise of privacy let alone any form of discretion. Mary had been an observer of her mother's craft for many years and it was inevitable that one of the men would look to educate her formally. In doing so, turning that learning into a profession was a logical and easy transition. She could look back now and think how horrible it had been to be her as a child but knew at the time that she had not given it much thought at all. The sex was generally unpleasant but, more often than not, over quite quickly. If her client became too rough with her then she soon found ways to dampen his ardour. Sometimes it was a permanent result.

When her mother was murdered, there were not many tears shed. Although she was not that old, the years of excesses had diminished her economic value considerably and their manager at the time, Mr Glendrick, encouraged the woman to go freelance and ultimately to her grave.

It was Mr Glendrick who came upon the idea of altering the business association. It became far more profitable (and physically comfortable) for her to act as a distraction so Mr Glendrick could mug the enamoured gentleman. That way they got all his money, it saved a lot of time and allowed for a greater frequency of them. It meant she was in less physical and biological danger; she was no longer the potential target of abuse, her customers' diseases or their offspring.

Then everything changed when she became a vampire. How much more different could things have been had Abraham not been there? She would have been absolutely dead rather than in this perpetual state of not-dead, that was for sure. Would that have been a better situation? How could she comment? Perhaps she would have been cast into Hell upon her demise and she would rather that not happen.

Ha! How odd it was that she would doubt the existence of God but still presume Hell to be a possibility.

If she had died then she knew her life would not be a constant battle against other vampires. That was something she would gladly exchange. It was not so much the physical fighting that she minded - the years of 'practice' had made her very proficient in hand-to-hand combat - no, it was always the feeling she got when they were around. It was sickening. Not so much the blood lust itself but an irritating itch at her conscience that she could quite as easily have been like them; victims of their desires, slaves to their cravings, more animal than man.

They came as a sharp cramp in her stomach as if trying to catalyse those death pains again and send her to her grave. Trying to get her body to reject the artificial life it had been transplanted with.

It was nothing like the feeling she had when mortals were around. They could make her feel like she was truly alive again. There was something about their existence that would rub off on her and exhilarate her. It was like an opiate just to be close enough to brush against their auras. And then, sometimes, it made her feel like she was a starving child standing in a bakery. Especially if she was approaching her next mealtime. The sweet scent of their bodies could make her head spin, make her feel ravenous and -

Oh.

Mary had forgotten herself. She had allowed her introspection to get the better of her and her thoughts had started to muddle with her reality.

Something had caused her to snap out of her private musings and she could tell there were about a dozen humans around her.

The air was suffused with the scent of blood, so much so that it had caused her thinking to wander towards pondering its luxuriousness and started to intoxicate her. But now her attention had been brought back to her immediate surroundings she could tell that something was very wrong.

A dozen mortals hanging around this alley at this time of night was wrong. One or two might wait in the hope of catching a lowly, lost wanderer. This many implied that there was something more organised afoot, that she had stumbled on a den or that they were waiting for something bigger to come their way.

Then there was this smell of blood. It was not like the normal scent of humans – their flesh, sweat and hormones - it was the smell of blood outside of its normal vessel. There was a lot of it too; so much that it had effectively thrown her thoughts off balance and disguised the presence of the mortals around her.

That could only mean one thing; they were waiting for a vampire to come down here. She could presume that it was purely a coincidence but that would deter her from being on her guard for another couple of potential valuable seconds. No, it was always best to fear the worst case scenario and that way you could never be disappointed by its resolution.

The worse case was that they were specifically waiting for her. But how did they know she was here? Vampire hunters weren't an uncommon occurrence around the world but they tended to be solitary workers, spurned on by vengeance and vendettas. They certainly never acted as a team. That meant they were mortals working for vampires.

Ever since she and Professor had disconnected her link with - what had he called it? - the collective consciousness of every other vampire on the planet, she had become a target of their attentions. They wanted her dead, for some reason. They had set traps before but, because she could sense them from half a mile away, they had never succeeded. This was something new.

Generally speaking, vampires were stupid. When humans are alive they seem to think of themselves as being immortal; death never becomes a consideration until it comes visiting. When humans die and become vampires then that reckless sense of immortality heightens and they give very little consideration for their personal, physical safety which actually makes them incredibly dangerous. They strike without thought of the consequences, they continue to strike even though their brethren may have fallen before them and, even though you might rend their limbs from their bodies, they will still try to strike.

And why? Because they'd been told to.

That was quite a sweeping generalisation. There were a few vampires who were not so instinctively irrational. They were the generals, if you like, the ones who would do the telling what to do. And they were not to be underestimated, they were incredibly dangerous. Usually educated and still in touch with enough of their humanity to be logical, charming and incredibly underhand. At least when you faced a drone you knew it was going to try to rip your head off. You could have been wined, dined and taken to the theatre before you realised one of the leaders wanted to rip your head off. And then it would be too late to do anything about it because your head would be ripped off. But even after all of that, they were still subservient to those above them. If their masters told them to impale themselves on the spire of the cathedral then they would go out and do it.

The humans were something else altogether. Even worse. They were not dead so had no excuse to throw themselves under speeding horses. They were not gifted with abnormal strength, speed or reflexes so had no reason to go wading into fights where the odds were inherently stacked against them. They were not a part of the collective consciousness so they still had a choice but there was this minority who revered the undead and would do whatever they asked.

Vampires tended to indiscriminately choose their victims. They seriously considered themselves to be above mortals in every way, so to even consider a fondness for any particular one with the intention of immortalising them was absolutely preposterous and, to be perfectly honest, downright disgusting. That would be the same as falling in love with a cow.

Humans were food and not much else. Sometimes they were amusement; vampires could derive much pleasure from inflicting as much physical and mental pain on a human before he or she would be driven to taking their own life. And then there were these people who would willingly offer their lives in the hope of being blessed with their own immortality. There were no acts of depravity that these people would not consider for that slim chance, no one they would not betray or murder.

Of course, the good thing was that they were quite easy to pull apart.

The vampires wanted her and they sent in humans to do the job. This meant she was probably being watched and that they wanted her alive.

The scent of the blood had already fired her up and she had pinpointed the location of each of her assailants. One had managed to get close enough to her to drive his dagger into her back. He must have been a relative new pet to the broods. He probably did not even know what she was or what his employers were. He had probably been dragged along by one of the real serviles to bolster their numbers on the promise of a big reward. He was relatively innocent, a pawn in the proceedings but that did not make him any less of an immediate threat to her.

What was it about theatrics that worked so well? Why could she orchestrate a melee with humans with but the slightest inflection of an eyebrow? She could remember back to her own mortal days when no amount of tears or begging could generate an iota of mercy or ease the level of abuse yet with a dramatic swirl of her petticoats, she could cause a horde of drunken thugs to take a cautionary step back.

The knife was driven just below her shoulder blade and it hurt but she did not make a sound nor did she flinch. The man let go of the handle and she turned slowly and gracefully to face him. Yes, she could see the fear in his eyes, she could tell that he was completely out of his depth and that if he survived this encounter then it would serve as a reminder for the rest of his life.

If.

She swung her arm out and slapped him across the side of his face with her open palm. The impact caused his head to spin around two-hundred-and-seventy degrees, snapping his neck. His body collapsed to the floor.

They had used him. He was just a diversion. If he could inflict some severe damage upon her then so much the better.

She heard a gentle twang of taught string being released and she stepped backwards the instant before the arrow zipped past her face. There followed another twang from above her so she moved, then another so she began to run. With every step she took, an arrow sliced into the ground where she had stood.

Surely they could not be that poor of marksmen not to get her once? But perhaps they were such proficient marksmen that they were not trying to hit her, just keep her moving along the alley.

Instead of continuing her path along the narrow street, she leapt up the sheer wall beside her and landed on the roof. The look of fear on the face of the thug next to her delighted her as it meant she was going against their plans. She grabbed him by the collar and forced him to the edge of the roof. There followed a series of muffled thuds and a forced exhalation from the man as multiple arrows ripped into his back. She let go of him and allowed him to fall into the alley.

She jumped the gap to the opposite roof and collided with her next victim. The silence of the night had started to fill with occasional cries of confusion; too many of the men had lost track of where she was. It meant they were no longer in full control of the hunt.

She sat on the stomach of her latest victim and decided she could afford herself a few seconds with this one. Only a few, though.

She jabbed her index finger into the side of his neck, rupturing his jugular and sending a spurt of blood out in a high arc over the edge of the roof. He was about to holler with the pain until she slapped her other hand over his mouth then angled her head in anticipation of the next discharge which she caught in her mouth without spilling a drop.

She threw him off the roof and scampered swiftly across the tiles. The man was allowed a very short scream of alarm and suffering before all of that was taken from him with the impact of the ground. Five men gathered around the corpse and shouted up to their colleagues, giving their target's approximate location.

An archer edged his way across the roof to stand above their point and looked down to the street in time to see Mary battering the fifth man to the floor with the bloody stump of fourth man's rent arm. The archer pulled an arrow from his quiver and aimed at her. Although he had not removed his attention from her, she was no longer there. He immediately redirected his attention behind him and fired his arrow; it thumped into a silhouette that had been approaching him. The shadowed body crumpled to the floor.

He drew another arrow and slipped it into place. He listened carefully but could only hear the furtive movements of his compatriots on the cobbles below or on the opposite roof.

He cautiously approached the prostrate body until he could discern that it was adorned in dresses. He gave her foot a kick but there was no reaction. He knew vampires and knew that none of these signs were indicative of her being dead, unconscious or no longer a threat. It was always better to be safe than sorry so he pulled his arm back and released the arrow.

Mary caught it before it could pierce her chest. She leapt to her feet and glared at him. She tried to glare but could only manage it with one eye; her other still had the shaft of the first arrow sticking out of it.

«That was a good shot,» she commended and snapped the feathered flight from the end.

He was experienced with vampires but she could still unsettle him. Theatrics.

She put her hand around to the back of her skull and felt for the arrowhead.

He fumbled his hand over his shoulder, searching the quiver for another arrow. Each time his desperate fingers touched one it seemed to dance out of his grasp.

She pulled the arrowhead and the remaining shaft slipped into her socket and out the back.

His fingers found purchase on a quill and he pulled it free.

She winced as the murky hole in her head slowly filled with substance and the gentle crackling of fusing skull fragments tickled her inner ear.

He brought the arrow forward and slid it into place on the bowstring. The string sliced into his fingertips, breaking the skin.

She blinked her eyelids as her new eye focussed itself.

He squinted one eye as he raised the bow to take aim.

She took a menacing step forward.

He took a quick step back and plummeted down into the alley.

There was a thud and a twang from the darkness below and a sliver of wood flew up past the rooftop into the night sky.

She was almost disappointed; all that effort had gone to waste. If she had wanted him to fall to his death then she would have just pushed him over the edge. That arrow in the eye had really hurt and she wanted to see how much he liked the sensation.

That particular measure of retaliation would have to be saved for someone else.

She had cut their numbers in half but it meant she would be up against the more proficient pets; the ones who had survived more of their masters' challenges to better understand how vampires worked.

Well, how *their* vampires worked, not her. They could never hope to understand how she worked. She was the best of all worlds: still in touch with her humanity, proud of her femininity and in full acceptance of her vampirism. She knew how humans thought and how the other vampires behaved. She was in control of this skirmish, not them.

She ducked further into the shadows of the roof and sensed the last of her hunters' movements. There were only three left, two on the opposite roof and one in the alley. Yes, they knew how a vampire worked and were trying to keep as quiet and still as they could. The slightest movement would give their position away, but they forgot that the mixed rhythm of their hearts resounded down the alley like the rattling wheels of a steam train. She knew exactly where they were and how they were feeling.

The one in the alley was the obvious first point of attack. It was obvious to her and it was obvious to them. His was the most rapid heartbeat; expectation and fear. The two on the roof were quite calm. They were probably marking his position with their bows, but how strong were they? How long could they hold the tension in their strings before their muscles would give up? She could wait. She had all night. She -

One of the rooftop assailants' heart rhythms stopped. She listened carefully trying to differentiate between the two remaining beats. There was the alley bound man still thudding along on the verge of arrest and there was the last one on the roof. No, not calm but weak. Fading. Gone.

Had they committed suicide? Why would they kill themselves?

She concentrated again for the slightest indication of any one else present but there were no other heartbeats and no cramping sensations. If there were reinforcements then they were too far away to prove to be any immediate threat.

She pounced across the gap again and landed deftly on the opposite roof ledge. She silently crept along until she reached the first anachronism. There was a body tied, upside down to the roof. It had its arms over its head and its wrists were slashed allowing its blood to freely trickle down the walls. Inspection further along revealed a similar state with a second body. They had been the bait, the smell of pure, fresh blood that had distracted her enough to allow them to get the drop on her.

Something was wrong. This was more than just a hunt. With no vampires around in wait to clean up and these assaults seemed to be nothing much more than diversionary games.

Her stomach cramped, but it was not because she sensed the proximity of vampires.

Without hesitation or consideration of traps, she threw herself off the roof and landed with a sickening crunch in front of the last human. She straightened her body as dislocated joints popped back into their sockets, fractured bones reset themselves and torn fibres stitched back together.

The last human was a middle-aged man and, although she could still hear his heartbeat hammering away, he looked quite calm.

«Tell me,» she snarled and stepped closer to him.

«Away with you, foul mongrel!» the man declared and lunged at her with a sharp, wooden stake he had held behind his back.

She caught his wrist in mid-swing and then caught his other arm as he brought another stake up from below. She braced both arms against the wall, lifting the man off the ground.

«Tell me,» she ordered.

«You are a blight in the heritage of our Lords,» the man spat. «You are a walking desecration of their holiness.»

«And?» she demanded.

«You and your family will be delivered from this earth. You will all be cleansed from -»

She pulled his wrist down, thrust his stake into his open mouth, through the back of his head and pinned him to the wall. He dropped the other stake and she relinquished her grip allowing him to tug futilely at the stake.

She watched him for a second ensuring that he was still able to breathe and that he was in no immediate threat of drowning on his own blood. There was a chance that someone might come by and free him but she was willing to take it; she could not afford to waste any more time here. She had not been the target.

«Pray for death,» she whispered, «for if you live, I *will* hunt you down.»

She ran back along the alley as fast as she could, not caring if her unnaturally rapid pace should draw attention from any passers by. She had been foolishly confident and egotistical to think that she had been worthy of all that attention when, really, she was just being kept out of the way.

She got back to the gutter they called home to find it was deserted. It was difficult to say whether there had been a fight or not but since all of their possessions were still there then she had to presume they had either been abducted or had to flee in a hurry.

She could feel an irrational sense of panic creeping up her spine, trying to force her to run through the streets screaming their names but she knew that would serve no purpose. She was going to have to become the hunter. She was going to have to either track them to their new hiding hole or find out where they had been taken.

She ripped her soaking, shredded petticoats from her waist and pulled on a pair of Professor's trousers. They would provide her with more manoeuvrability. She contemplated loading herself with an array of weapons but did not want to waste any more time and considered that they would be redundant. In her current mood, she was as much a weapon as she was going to need and there was a very good chance they were not expecting her to have returned quite so quickly, if at all.

She had to presume her enemy was still human; despite how overcast the day was, no vampire would risk the chance of a break in the cloud and their instant evaporation. To successfully take on her husband meant there had to be a lot of them. A mass of men, out and about on this day, would be hard to hide.

She checked the main road that ran perpendicular to her alley. There were no signs of horses, which meant they were hobbling along on their little mortal legs. That meant they would not have been able to get too far. It would also mean they should keep themselves less obtrusive by sticking to the back alleys.

She had been accosted in the east, the river lay directly to the south so she should head to the north-west.

She scanned the immediate vicinity but the rain had successfully washed away any airborne scents that might have left her a trail to follow so she was going to have to do it the hard way. Three inhuman leaps gained her access to the rooftops, which she unceremoniously bounded across. Each step on the tiles resounded through the residence below, making the occupiers think that the heavens were falling upon them.

She had barely travelled a mile before she discerned a heavily discordant rhythm of heartbeats through the incessant hammer of rain and headed straight for its source. After traversing a few more alleys, she spotted a group of twenty men rushing along the narrow causeway, carrying, what looked like, a rolled rug.

He always had criticised her impetuous nature. He always tried to instil a notion of caution, a moment to ponder her options before she dived headfirst into a confrontation. To strike with objective rationality rather than raw emotion. There were two problems she always had with that logic that he never seemed to grasp. Firstly, they never allowed you a moment to ponder your options; they always used raw emotion to make that first move, using uncompromising ferocity to shock their target that little bit more.

Then, there was also the issue of her heightened reactions. Just because it looked like she rushed into a situation did not mean she did not have time to consider every angle of a conflict while she was already thrusting her fist out the back of her first opponent's cranium. She, unlike him, was quite capable of thinking about lots of different things at the same time. She had noted that he was incapable of processing multiple thoughts at the same time, they all had to be dealt with one after the other.

She was silently free-falling from the rooftops, heading directly for the densest pocket of men who were close to the rear of the mob and handling the back of the rolled rug.

Sometimes the best theatrics were those accompanied by unrestrained, disproportionate violence.

Her collision sent a wave of falling bodies along their procession. The few men left standing at the rear looked on in stunned silence at the heap of writhing, groaning bodies. There was not enough light in the alley to discern one body from another and the fall had happened so suddenly that they presumed someone must have tripped.

Louis had warned them that something like that was going to happen eventually because of the speed at which they had been moving. It was dangerous enough to run along these littered alleys by yourself at full pelt in broad daylight let alone a group of you, in poor lighting conditions with a large heavy burden.

Of course, no one had listened to him. «Shut up, Louis,» they had ordered and then his friend, Jean, had looked at him forlornly and said, «Why have you got to be so negative all the time, Louis? Stop looking on the bad side all the time. Cheer up. You're so self-absorbed, it's depressing.»

And then they all fell over.

Louis was just getting over the initial shock and was about to launch into a, 'Je vous ai dit ainsi,' lecture when the general complaining was drowned by a scream of agony and he was hit in the face with something very hard. The impact knocked him to the ground where he hurriedly checked his face for damage. His fingers traced over his features and came away dripping with, what looked like, blood. He panicked, sat upright and performed a more intricate examination hoping to determine the seriousness of the rupture. His narcissism blocked out everything around him and made him only dimly aware of heightened shouts and commotion coming from his associates ahead of him.

Aside from his nose being slightly more wobbly than usual he could not find any cuts to indicate where the blood had come from...

A call of alarm was cut short -

...There were no points of intense points of pain to suggest any internal damage...

- Something wet splashed against the wall behind him -

...Perhaps it was not blood after all, but a residue from the object that struck him. He reached down to his side for the cylindrical missile as something nudged at his foot. He picked the object up and studied its end; it was like a club that had been wrapped up in cloth and soaked in this bizarre fluid. But unlike a club, it had a flexible middle that allowed it to fold in half. He moved his hand down to the hilt to find someone else trying to grab it. He withdrew his hand reflexively and looked for the other person but there was no one there. He looked at the base of the club and found the other hand. The whole object had been someone's arm. He cast it to one side and noticed a huge spray of dribbling blood on the wall behind him. He then looked down at his feet to see what it was still resting against them and saw Jean staring forlornly back at him. But only Jean's head. Jean blinked at him.

He looked further along the alley and hoped to see his comrades standing there, about to berate him to within an inch of his life. Instead he saw his comrades lying across the ground, having run out of their own inches. The light made it difficult to identify one body from another but it was quite obvious to see they were all dripping wet and either had limbs missing or had limbs with too many joints.

There was movement from the shadows ahead and a person emerged from the darkness. It was a woman wearing trousers. She silently walked up to the rolled rug and nudged it with her foot.

«Who is in there?» Mary asked.

Louis could only stare.

«Who *was* in there?» she reiterated.

«Is it you?» he asked and noticed her aggression falter for the slightest second.

She was one step behind. They had been waiting for her in the alley, luring her there with the blood of their own, and now this overt group had decoyed her. Everything Abraham had ever said was right, even with her speed, strength and heightened reactions, she had just impulsively waded in without any real thought as to why they had been so easy to track. And so, with all this time wasted she was pretty sure that whoever had taken her man and child had them exactly where they wanted them. But with that notion came the premise that, maybe, it was still not too late. Why go to all this trouble if whoever it was just wanted them dead?

«Where are they?» she demanded.

«I cannot believe it is actually you,» Louis said.

«Tell me, before I -» she started but he cut her short.

«There is no hurry,» Louis said. «Nothing will happen until you get there.»

«Where? Who has them? Why have you done this?»

«You have to ask? Really? You have been a thorn in the masters' sides for decades.»

«Us? A thorn in *their* sides?» she squealed. «Where are they?»

«I told you, there is no rush.»

She was on him in an instant. She pinned his shoulders to the ground with such force that the back of his skull cracked on the cobbles. He just smiled at her.

«I am prepared for death,» he told her. «I have offered my life to my masters. Death is all I can offer them, yet they can offer me eternity.»

«Fucking fundamentalists,» she growled. «There is only one way to deal with you bastards, and that's to show you life through the eyes of those you victimise.»

Louis's confidence slipped.

«They are not the only ones who can offer eternity,» she said and smiled.

He had been assured that this mission would bring only death, but it would come in one of two forms; he would either be slaughtered by one of their targets or be rewarded with living-death. No one said anything about becoming an offshoot of this degenerate. If she infected him then he would become as much of a target.

«No, wait,» he yelled.

«You were given your chance to speak,» she said. «This is really going to hurt.»

She shifted herself to pin his arms by his side, then she clamped her hand over his mouth and pulled his head to one side. He wanted to scream for help but the restrictions over his mouth and stretched windpipe made it impossible. It was hard enough to draw a breath. All he could do was watch her from the corner of his eye.

She returned his gaze and slowly descended upon his neck. She opened her mouth and gently pressed her fangs against his flesh then drew her jaws together. The earlier battles had completely sated any blood lust she may have been experiencing; at this very moment, she was in complete control of her actions.

There is a common misconception concerning the sharpness of vampires' teeth. It his held by mortals and even some vampires. They seem to think that a vampire's fangs are as sharp as a surgeon's scalpel and can cut through skin just as deftly. This is not true. A vampire's canines only look a lot sharper than they actually are because of their extension and the bluntness of the surrounding teeth. The razor sharpness myth comes more from the speed and force of the bite itself.

Your average human jaw is able to exert around 100 psi of pressure which, on its own, is able to break the layer of skin. If you have been at the receiving end of such a bite then you will know it really hurts. Multiply that force by the increased strength and speed that a vampire possesses allows it to puncture the flesh more effectively. For some reason, they like this false impression that they could draw blood by just one touch of their teeth when, in reality, given the appropriate application of force, it's actually more like stabbing someone with a book.

Some vampires have tried to perpetrate this myth by filing their teeth to a point, only to have their natural healing return them to normal. A few have been known to wear caps.

So, should a vampire bite you really slowly then it would hurt as much as anyone else biting you really slowly. Then factor in that it would not stop until it wanted to because it had the strength to render you completely immobilised.

Louis's pain started before Mary had broken the surface. She had pinched a portion of skin between her teeth and he mewled like a new-born kitten. She pressed harder and his squeals gave way to desperate breathing and then a perfunctory grunt as his skin finally gave way.

Her canines had done the hard part so it was relatively easy for her incisors to tear further into his weakened skin. She pulled off a large chunk to expose the musculature beneath that quickly became swamped by haemorrhage.

Louis had his eyes screwed shut, trying to block out the pain but completely unable to block the stream of agonised tears rolling down his face.

Mary lunged again, biting harder and faster to chew through the thicker muscle and tougher artery wall.

As she felt the flesh rupture, she was rewarded with a more forceful eruption of blood which filled her mouth. As she swallowed it, she was very aware of the transference of her saliva into his open wound; a natural anticoagulant that stopped the blood clotting and ensured a constant flow beyond the body's normal volumes of expulsion but not so much as to drink him to death.

She withdrew her head and inhaled with rapture. Despite not needing it, damn, it still made her feel good. She dismounted Louis's body and watched it spasm as it instinctively struggled to retain its mortality.

Yes, he still had to have enough of a heartbeat to circulate her saliva around his body, to percolate it through his dying cells. Neither she nor Abraham knew how or why it happened but she carried something in her system that could stop a body from completely dying. The slightest injection could be carried by a person up until the time of their death when they would awake again.

She could drink them to death but that was never a sure thing. Even if she was absolutely certain her victim had been drained to death, there was still a slim chance that enough of her saliva had infected enough of the body to revitalise it.

But there was always one absolute way to know if her victim was going to be reborn or not. She just had to be patient. Soon enough, she started to remember things that had never happened to her. It was a commonly regarded belief to have your life flash before your eyes at the time of your death; it could also happen during a near death experience. It is a humbling experience to have everything you have ever done laid before you so you can evaluate your own worth. It is all too disturbing to have someone else's life flash before your eyes. Embarrassing, really. But that is what happens when vampirism spreads and a link is made between the sire and the spawn.

She remembered the pain of his death; the feeling of his flesh being breached. There was his confusion during the fight, which had surpassed his smug satisfaction when everyone had gone for a tumble. There was his flight through the streets and his group's divergence from a larger pack. And there was their mass assault on her family.

They must have known what they were doing and who they were after otherwise they would not have sent thirty humans to do one vampire's job. Abraham would not have known they were there until they were on him. Mortals were Abraham's one weakness. He had been dealing with vampires for so long that he could smell them from a mile away. Figuratively speaking, of course.

Ultimately, it was not even the mortals' strength that overpowered him but their sheer weight of numbers. One vampire may have been stronger than all these men put together but it would only take one precise incision to end its assault. With the gang of men, he would have to have made one incision and then another twenty-nine after. The other downside being that mortals do not have the decency to evaporate at their demise to clear a path to attack the next. No, a mortal's dead body could still encumber one's defensive strategy.

She had a fairly obstructed view of the assault itself as Louis kept himself to the back of the pack. She could just make out Abraham flurrying at the aggressors but it seemed that he did not have time to arm himself.

She needed to remember further back to when the plans were being made. There she found the men being split into three groups by a female vampire. By the look of her, she was an Apostle. They were a special breed of vampire who answered only to the Lord Vampire, himself. They carried this status because their turn to undead created more positive changes than negative. They, like her, could control their blood lust and so, very rarely reverted to their animalistic nature. Also, they tended to have been given more than one power. Nearly all vampires became stronger, faster and were able to regenerate their bodies when damaged but some gained extra abilities.

Abraham had been cataloguing the different types of vampire and their abilities as they encountered them. Some were so fast that they could move across a room within the blink of an eye. There were those who could hear your thoughts as if you had spoken them aloud. There were some who could put their thoughts into your head, to make you do their bidding. Some were able to manipulate the elements and there were even some who could fly.

Apostles usually had two of these abilities, sometimes more.

Mary had always found their name to be the most disturbing aspect of their existence and believed that was the true sign of why they carried the position; they thought the title was ironic and clever. They set themselves akin to Jesus' disciples as if they were their Lord's next in command, whereas the truth was more likely he gave as much responsibility to them as he would the normal rank and file. No, they were a self-serving, self-aggrandising group of elitist snobs whose self-constructed reputation actually pulled some weight with lower drones and mortal followers.

She knew they were powerful but the obvious thing that set them aside from normal vampires was their aloofness. They carried themselves knowing that they were better. They dressed ostentatiously to deliberately stand out and had no qualms about flaunting their unnatural state in public, displaying their red eyes and fangs as a fashion statement.

They were collected at Place du Parvis and the Apostle instructed the men to bring Abraham and the child there.

There was a brief sensation of falling and then Louis was awake. It was not that he had been asleep and awoken, more that he had not been awake and now he -

He saw the wooden stake flash before his eyes, preventing him from further existential analysis. The sharp point plunged through his breastplate and skewered his heart.

During the iota between being and not, he was able to identify his killer and immediately recognised the face of his raison d'être, his god. He was instantly enamoured and knew that he would do anything for her.

But he was not going to be given the chance to prove himself.

He expunged with a blast of light that slapped into Mary's body. She inhaled sharply as if having had something cold dropped down her back. Louis's necromantic power strengthened hers and, for that moment, she could understand the desire to sire as much as the other vampires did. Not only did you get yourself an unquestioning slave but also an investment of growing power that could be reclaimed upon its demise.

So many good reasons to slip down that path of corruption. She wondered if it was a path she could turn back from if she ever decided to take it.

They were thoughts of idle fancy at the moment; she needed to get to the cathedral as quickly as she could. The evening was drawing in and if there was an Apostle in the city then it meant she had followers with her and they would be preparing to leave their havens.

She vaulted onto the rooftops again and pounced across the streets and alleys like a cat chasing a panicking frog.

If she was lucky, she might get there before the vampires had risen and organised themselves. She did not hold on to that hope with too much optimism because, generally, her luck never did swing that way.

She stopped when she reached Pont Neuf and tried to scan the small island for any indication off the dangers that might be waiting for her. Her sixth sense stretched out but discovered nothing.

That was bad. There should have been something. When she concentrated, she was able to sense all kinds of life types, which meant there was always something there. Even if it was just a blade of grass or an insect. There had to be something. Even if it was just a space of no life types, it would still register. Whatever was there had such a negative force that it negated the islet's existence. The only thing she could think of that was capable of doing that was a veritable battalion of vampires. There probably was not enough area to hold the number needed.

What was her next move? They knew she was coming and there were elements involved that were outside of her field of experience so she had no way of knowing what her best course of action should be. She wished that she had not been so hasty to dismiss Louis and could have used him to assess the situation. She toyed with the idea of siring someone else to do it but the pink clouds on the western horizon reminded her that she was running out of time. There was something else at the back of her mind that warned her how easy it was to come up with excuses to create acolytes and less reasons to be rid of them.

So, a full frontal attack was out of the question and using stealth would just make her look foolish when she discovered they would be watching her all the time.

She sighed with resignation and suddenly became aware of how incredibly tense she had been. All these decisions that she had been forced to make, thinking that her family's lives were in the balance had been more stressful than she had realised. She acknowledged that she had been led through a maze and that any path she had taken would have brought her to here. It was a tremendous relief to know that, even if their lives were still in jeopardy, there was nothing she could have done to alter that. Maybe there still was nothing she could do.

She jumped down from the rooftop, dusted herself off and did her best to tidy her hair. She strolled resolutely across Pont Neuf as if keeping a dinner appointment rather than walking into an elaborately-conceived, well-executed and potentially fatal trap.

As she crossed the bridge, she could feel herself wading deeper into the darkness she had sensed. It was like walking into a freezing lake, she could feel herself gently immersing with every step. She tried to resist the increasing oppressive atmosphere as it inched up her body; it felt like the icy pressure was going to squeeze the undead life from her and she caught herself holding her breath as she became fully submerged.

She relaxed and allowed the dark death to swamp her. It was easier to acclimatise to the sensation once she was fully immersed in it. She could sense the raw power that the being who generated this aura must possess. She could hear the minds of the thousands of vampires this being must have sired to generate such power. Again, there was another reason why she should have come equipped with a battalion to combat this force.

She strolled across Place du Parvis whilst ignoring the scuttling bodies that constantly circled her like pack wolves. Perhaps, though they were more like sheep dogs, leading her toward her pen, ready to snap at her heels should she dare to stray off course.

She regally ascended the stone steps and the grand doors swung open upon her approach. She did not falter in her pace, even when she caught sight of Professor, unconscious, being held by the Apostle at the side of the hall. She only stopped when she saw the man at the pulpit and recognised him as the epicentre of the darkness. Even though candles had been lit all around the Cathedral and focussed their glare to the front, it seemed as if he was stood in a deep recess.

"Dearly beloved," the shaded figure hailed, "forasmuch as our Saviour Christ saith, *None* can enter into the Kingdom of God."

"I want my family back," Mary demanded. "Now."

"Ah, Sister Mary," the man growled with an East-European accent, "at last you have returned to the fold. Although you weren't with us for very long, you have been incredibly conspicuous by your absence."

"You are Zorga?" Mary asked.

"So you *do* remember me," he purred. "I am flattered."

"Why are you doing this to us?" she asked. "Why can't you leave us alone? We make no quarrels with you or your kind but you all constantly hound us."

The shadow receded around his face to reveal taut, feral features and a shiny, brown mane that flowed down his ears and over his shoulders. "You really don't know, Mary?"

"We thought, at first, that you wanted revenge for those we had killed, but soon learned you care for your drones as much as you care for mortals."

Zorga shrugged his shoulders and allowed the blackness to completely fall from him. For what purpose could not be seen because he was completely dressed in black velvet anyway. He stepped down from the pulpit and wandered to a font. "Probably even less, I would say," Zorga corrected her and rinsed his hands in the holy water. "At least mortals have something to offer."

"So then I thought it must be something to do with me escaping from your control," she said. "That my insubordination should be punished."

Zorga expelled a barking laugh that echoed around the cathedral. "I never held you responsible for that, Mary," he told her and nodded toward Professor. "It was the unfortunate result of ill-conceived tinkering. But you never fully left us."

"So the only thing left was the idea that I must have been some sort of abomination that had to be destroyed."

"What?!" Zorga bellowed. His turn of temperament was so sudden that it caught Mary and the Apostle off guard. "Had I heard anyone say that of you, I would have made them eat themselves until they were a festering puddle of self-consuming shit!"

"Oh," was all Mary could manage. She had not expected that at all and needed a moment to regain her composure. But, in that brief moment, her brain decided to act on its own. "Well, that's what she called me," Mary's mouth said without any real impetus from her. Her arm quickly realised where her mouth was going with this and pointed a finger at the Apostle.

She was only just recovering from Zorga's eruption and now had a double dose of shock piled on top. Not only from the outrageous allegation but also from being brutally made the centre of attention.

"She lies, Lord," the Apostle declared. "I never even saw this asshole before."

Zorga sighed wearily. "When will you people start to show some degree of faith in me? I know who she has and hasn't met. I know she hasn't met you before, Elizabeth. Simply because you still live."

The Apostle called Elizabeth flashed a red-eyed glare of anger at Mary that was fuelled more by jealousy and embarrassment than anything else.

Mary shrugged her shoulders and grumbled, "It was worth as try," then returned her attention to Zorga. "Then what? What the hell *is* all this about?"

He languidly swirled his fingers around in the font and ducked his head in mock shyness.

"I sometimes wish you had completely broken away from us, Mary, but you did not. You have always been there, at the back of my mind. You may have been able to block me from your thoughts but I have not been so fortunate. The others are there as a constant, festering, noise of greed, hunger, licentiousness and disregard. Disregard for everything around them and even themselves. And I have had to listen to this noise since the day of my first creation. The incessant keening of spoiled children for so long that I was eventually able to block it out and pretend it was not there. And then you were taken from me and, even though your voice was naught more than a ripple in the storm, because of your voice it shone through the darkness like a beacon."

"My voice? What the hell are you talking about?"

"You spoke of love," Zorga told her. "While all my others screamed of hatred and death, your whispering passion for life was what touched me and has enamoured me to you."

"Enamoured? You speak of love when all you have ever sent me are threats of violence?"

"No! They were just envoys sent to bring you to me but your over zealous nature made them defend themselves and forced me to send stronger envoys the next time."

"Next time? Try sending flowers and a note," she advised.

Zorga laughed loudly. The echoes bounced back off the church walls to add to the resonating laughter until it sounded like he was laughing at her from every corner of the building. Even the stained glass window reverberated with the waveform.

Mary saw, that even though the echoes of amusement were still bouncing around the walls and columns, Zorga was by no means amused.

"If anyone else ever dared to talk to me in such a manner then I would have their -"

"Heads stuffed into their own stomachs so they could slowly digest their own brains?" Mary asked. Again, her mouth had operated of its own accord and it took all her remaining will to stop herself slapping her hand over her mouth.

Zorga's eyes were ablaze with red fury. She could not work out if her insults were actually having a positive effect or not. She was fairly certain that she was going to die anyway, so it gave her some small comfort to be so defiant to make him spit blood.

"Do not overestimate my feelings for you," Zorga warned. "You have become an obsession to me. One that I must possess totally, or remove completely. You would be well advised to keep a civil tongue."

Mary needed that dressing down to remind her of the seriousness of the situation. For a moment she had allowed her impertinence to take over. It was probably her one trait that she really did try to curb, because Professor hated it so much. He had always said that it was incredibly unladylike and drew unnecessary attention towards her. He said that it was an incredibly unattractive habit that had followed her from her previous life. It reminded him that she had been a whore and that other men had used her.

She had not been absolutely sure that it really was a nasty habit – speaking your mind – or whether it was just another of Professor's empowerment things. There was something about him that was always uncomfortable with her physical strength and so he had to keep reminding her of her societal strength; that is, of course, none. She was woman and therefore a second class citizen. Nothing much more than an *object d'art* and propagator of the species.

She tried to keep her mouth in check, for his sake, but there was something about Zorga that made her want to mock him. There was something about his hair that she did not like.

But she was making him angry and there were still too many random factors involved; Professor was at the mercy of the Apostle and Penelope was nowhere in sight. Perhaps her insolence was not the answer to this problem.

"Now what?" Mary asked.

"You have something I want," Zorga said. "Something that we all want. Something that we have all wanted since the night of our rebirth."

"Why the riddles all the time?" she demanded. "Why can't you just say what it is you want? Why do we have to have this constant banter and never get anywhere?"

"It's almost like a lover's spat, isn't it?" he chuckled.

"No!" she growled. "Because I do *not* love you and I never will."

Zorga stared at her dispassionately and flicked the holy water from his fingertips. He then walked back to the pulpit and flipped through the pages of the Bible in front of him. He ripped out each page that he turned and tossed it idly over his shoulder.

"I exist," he declared whimsically while still discarding the pages and allowing them to flutter around his body like moths to the candle flame. They orbited his body rather than falling to the floor. "I exist with the taste of your love for your man and your child haunting my every waking minute. Then, when I sleep, it gets worse. I get peace during sleep. My children sleep too and their demands are silenced for those hours. But, because of that silence, your voice rings through even louder. I not only hear every resonation of your devotion but I also see through your eyes and I see the sunlight again.

"At first it was glorious. Even though it was only a diluted, second-hand memory it was still a glimpse of Nirvana for one who had presumed would never get so close. But all your beauty just put into context the squalor in which I had contented myself. You had given me hope that I might feel your love and that I might see the sunrise again, for myself."

"And that's why you needed this elaborate trap?" Mary asked.

"It got to the stage that I could not trust these fools," he waved his arm around at the shadows in the church and Mary could just make out slight movements from within them, "not to try to take your gift for themselves. You had to come here and want to give yourself to me willingly."

"You thought I would come here and fall in love with you? Just like that?"

"I hoped it could happen like that, yes, but then I also realised that it might not so I considered I might be able to persuade you." Zorga indicated to Professor's inert body.

"If I don't fall in love with you then you'll kill him?"

"I am not so naive to think that love works in that way," he stated. "I know it cannot be switched on and off just like that. It *is* something that can be encouraged and nurtured if worked at."

They stared at each other until Mary's frustration got the better of her.

"So why bring him?"

"If I kill him then you have one less reason not to give yourself to me," he said bluntly.

Mary looked worriedly between Zorga and the Apostle, praying that he was not giving her the secret signal to carry out the deed. She needed more time.

"But how will my affections help you walk in the daytime?" she demanded. "My surviving the sunlight isn't a result of my love for him."

"No, that's something that runs much deeper," Zorga concurred. "And perhaps it is a process that could be replicated. Perhaps it is a power that I might claim by feeding upon him, or..." His voice trailed off. "I am surprised that you have not asked after his daughter's well-being."

"I was hoping that if I did not mention her then she would not made an issue. I am hoping that she has just been picked up as an incidental to your plan."

"Good god, no!" Zorga barked. "She is probably even more imperative than your man, there. I am well aware of your levels of affection for both parties. I can feel them, remember?"

Was that her moment to do something? She felt her anger rising again, as soon as he had mentioned Penelope. He had openly threatened her daughter's safety, which meant she was perfectly at liberty to peel the front of his face open and scoop out the innards with a rusty meat hook.

Zorga snatched one of the twirling pages of Holy Scripture that danced in front of his face and read it to himself.

"How apt," he muttered and read. "But when Jesus saw it, he was much displeased, and said unto them, 'Suffer the little children.'"

It was if the sound had always been there but this was the first time she had noticed. It was as if there had been two layers of noise and the top one had been switched off, leaving only the sound of a crying child. Then a vampire stepped out of the shadows with Penelope in his arms. The child was in absolute hysterics with her face screwed up into a red ball of fear and anger. A steady flow of tears rolled down her cheeks and her constant screams of protestation had worn her cries down to a hoarse wail. The vampire walked calmly to the font.

"Exactly how much do you love the child?" Zorga asked. The fluttering tornado died around him and the pages fell to the floor.

"More than anything," she growled and was slightly concerned to feel her canines snag her bottom lip as she spoke.

"Mary?" a male voice called from the side. Abraham had regained consciousness.

"More than anything?" Zorga mused. "I might have to put that to the test. Tell me, Mary, the time has come to make a decision: whom would you choose to save when the lives of both your supposed loves are in jeopardy. Attempt to save one and the other will surely die. Deny both and come to me and perhaps I will let them both live."

There again, she was being given false options. How could she rationally allow one or the other to die? How could she really convince herself to 'love' this vile creature or believe that he would let them just walk out of there?

There was really only one thing she could do.

She kicked the end of the bench next to her. It was wrenched from the bolts that held it to the floor and rocketed into the Apostle and Professor. They both went reeling across the floor.

Mary raced forward and tackled the pulpit, taking Zorga down amongst a shower of oak and paper. This was the only thing she could do that would ensure it was truly her own decision. This was her free choice and not some option that had been laid out before her. And it seemed like it was something Zorga had not even considered might happen.

He had been Lord of all for so long that no one dared question his instructions, talk back and certainly not raise a hand against him. He had planned this operation in the mind that one of his spawn wase the target.

'Tell me,' he would ask, 'who would you save and who would you have me kill?'

'Er,' his minion would reply. 'I dunno. The man?'

Zorga had presumed she would have to take A or B. As far as he was concerned, he was the conductor of this Greek tragedy and not one of its players. He did not think to have sent his leading lady a copy of the script nor considered that she might leap off the stage, over the orchestra pit and try to stab him in the eye with his own baton.

He was caught off-guard and was probably completely out of practice with dealing with such a physical assault. It was even likely that he had not had to deal with a one-to-one fight for centuries, having always relied on his minions to throw themselves into any fray he demanded. He certainly would never have had to deal with an attack that was more than self-preservation but fuelled by a mother's protective instincts for her child.

Her arms were a blurring tornado of righteous vengeance; every blow was another retributive exorcism of indignant fury. Enough was enough. All Zorga could manage was bury his head in his arms.

Like her master, the Apostle was unprepared for anything other than the way he had predicted things would happen. Professor, on the other hand, had immediately noticed the corner they had been backed into and knew very well how Mary reacted in such circumstances. As the bench collided with him and the Apostle, she was sent sprawling across the floor while he was able to roll deftly and get to his feet quickly. He grabbed a sharp shard of the splintered bench in readiness for the battle.

Between the two scuffles stood the vampire carrying Penelope, again, caught completely by surprise from the sudden outbreak. All he had been instructed to do was carry the child to the water-filled font and be ready to drown it upon instruction. Now, he felt like he should, perhaps leap to the assistance of one of his betters. But who? His ultimate Lord and Master, Zorga who, really, in his opinion, should have been putting up a better struggle what with him being ultimate and everything. Or the Apostle, who was his immediate sire? Or was this all still part of the grand design? Had the woman made her choice? But which choice was it? Should he set the baby down or drop it in the font?

His internal deliberation was reflected externally by a blank expression and the gentle fluttering of his lips as if the inner debate was too much for his brain to deal with and the words were trying to escape through his mouth.

Professor lunged at the Apostle with the shard of wood but she easily stepped out of the way and countered his thrust with a swipe of her fist. Perhaps she was a more adept combatant than him, or perhaps he had not yet regained full consciousness, for where his strike missed, hers was spot on target. Her fist connected with his jaw and he crumbled to the floor.

"I am terribly disappointed," she muttered. "Perhaps your reputation has been built off the back of your woman."

"I would be nothing without her," Professor groaned and tried to raise himself up on his elbows.

The tide of Mary's attack had turned. Perhaps Zorga had not been so unprepared, perhaps he had just been waiting for her fury to wane so he could afford to react without her landing a fatal blow.

That was all it took, that iota of second guessing that allowed him to parry one thrust and return his own, striking her across the chin with so much force it felt like her jaw had been ripped from its socket. Her senses reeled and allowed him another clear shot at her head, a cannonball punch to her temple that reinforced the threatening delirium and forced her from her advantageous position.

Mary slid across the smooth floor and collided with a tall, ornate, iron candlestick, then slammed into the wall. The force was enough to break a few of her bones as well as snap the legs off the candlestick at its weaker, soldered joints. One sheered joint stabbed into Mary's side but she barely noticed; Zorga had deftly flipped himself to his feet and strolled over to her. Although his approach was quite calm and deliberate, his face was a maelstrom of rage. Oh, yes, she had been quite correct in her assumptions of his unpreparedness and inexperience but that had not made him any less of a real danger.

"How dare you rough-house with me!" he bellowed.

She tried to get to her feet but a fracture in her left femur had not yet fixed itself.

"Who the fuck do you think you are?" he continued. "I offer you a place by my side and you think you can turn it down and I'll allow you to walk away? I want you for your day powers and if I can't get them from you then I will take them from your man or your spawn."

"But she's not of me," Mary stated.

"There is enough of a mixture of blood between the three of you for each of you to hold the antidote I need."

"But she's only a child and -"

"I can wait until she's ripe," Zorga said.

"No!" Mary screamed and pulled the slither of iron from her side and threw herself at Zorga. He caught the metal stake before she could pierce it through his chest but was forced back against a concrete pillar. It cracked from their impact.

He was stronger than she was and she was not going to be able to fulfil her murderous intent but she felt that if she lessened her pressure in the slightest then he would be able to change his brace into a counter attack. She was stuck and could only pray that his strength might miraculously slip before hers. Or before more of his minions would emerge from the shadows that seemed to be becoming more defined.

The Apostle watched Professor's trembling back as he prized himself off the floor. "You are naught much more than one of our mortal neophytes. You cling to her for her power, thinking of yourself as an equal but you are just a parasite existing off the power of others. You've set yourself up on a pedestal spouting hypocritical morality and decrying my life as evil but at least I know who I am. At least the acts I perform are done so out of necessity rather than some self-constructed belief system."

Professor had gathered enough of his strength to upright himself to his knees. He had his back turned to the Apostle and his head bowed with defeat and, maybe, subservience.

She stepped forward and placed her hands on his shoulders.

"Do not be so hard on yourself," she soothed. "We all do what we must to survive. Some of us are able to accept those needs. What is important now is that you have made peace with yourself and allow your maker to judge you for the man you have been."

Apostles: narcissistic, egotistical and overconfident. It only took the slightest sign of submissive body language to turn them from raging ministers of bloody death into pompous snobs of self-conceit.

It only took the slightest movement from Professor's position to twist his body around and thrust the shard of oak into the Apostle's chest. She barely had the time to register the action before she had atomised into a fountain of light motes.

The babysitter had a few seconds to realise the consequences of Professor's actions. One of the downsides of being quite far down the hierarchy meant you had more chance of having your existence taken away by association. When your sire was expunged, quite frequently, you were too. He combusted and left Penelope writhing in mid-air. She toppled over, struck her head on the rim of the font and landed face first into the water.

Two bodily explosions should have been enough to draw anyone's attention but really it was the sudden cessation of Penelope's protestations that made the most impact.

The eye contact between Mary and Zorga related so much more than any words could; this was the moment he had given her. Now was the time to finally decide. But if she were to save Penelope then she would be undone in the process. Their only hope was Professor; he could save their daughter then help her overpower this devil, then everything would be at an end.

A movement caught her attention and she turned to see Professor making his way straight to her. If he did that then Penelope would surely die.

Again, eye contact that told so much so quickly. She was his everything, she was his priority and he would sacrifice anything and anyone to save her.

She came to a decision and let go of the metal bar.

That look she gave him would haunt him forever; disappointment.

Zorga did not really push, it was more that the sudden lack of restraining pressure made him fall forward and plunge the metal through Mary's chest, heart and out her back. He was probably more surprised by the action than anyone else.

Mary's body sparkled as tiny holes all over allowed her inner light to escape. Each hole widened and conjoined until her flesh and clothes were consumed by the brilliance. The two men watched in awe as the light wavered hesitantly, as if not knowing what to do next. Then Zorga came to his senses and embraced her, holding her ethereal form so tightly that it began to envelope his own until it eventually smothered him.

Professor was paralysed. Too many things had just happened that caused his brain to almost completely shut down. That look, the action, the reaction and now this. Was Zorga being consumed by her or bathing in her?

The light dimmed and Zorga's form became more prominent again, although he seemed as catatonic as Professor was. However, Professor was not so unaware of his surroundings to see the emergence of dozens of vampires from the deeper shadows.

Zorga turned his head and smiled at him, awakening him from his stupor and forcing his advance again. This time, with only bloody vengeance on his mind. But then his expression changed from smug satisfaction to pained confusion. Then to that same last look Mary had delivered; disappointment.

"What the fuck?" Zorga demanded whilst wrestling with himself. "What is that bitch doing to me?"

She was still there, an essence of her was still battling Zorga and Professor had let her down again. That was two chances he had to save Penelope but his selfishness had cast her from his concerns.

A line of vampires had sprouted from the corners of the cathedral, eager to take a more active role in the proceedings.

There was nothing he could do anymore. Too many things had happened too quickly and too many things required his immediate attention: the vampires, Zorga and Penelope. He was completely impotent and could only watch as the world unthreaded before his eyes.

"Bitch," Zorga growled again before it seemed like every pore on his body opened and erupted with a shaft of dazzling white, solid light. He was lost in its brilliance whilst his encroaching army was shredded into their component parts as the wave cut through them.

The blast knocked Professor and the font over, spilling the baby and water across the stone floor.

Darkness and silence flooded the cathedral. Professor remained motionless, awaiting an end to come. Any end would do, there seemed no reason to continue any more.

Then Penelope coughed, finally caught her breath and began to scream again. Professor was not sure whether she was protesting about the drowning sensation or directly rebuking him for his inaction. From that day forward, whenever Penelope cried, talked back or argued, his conscience would make him believe it was always because of the latter.

V—V

# **W**orks **I**n **P**rogress
*by Rhys A Wilcox*

## Blood Lust 2.75 – 4: Genetically Altered States

"Do you have a rogues gallery? You know? People you continually do battle with?"

"Most of the people I do battle with end up dead."

"So that's a 'no' then, is it?"

## Unfaer

Elsewhere. Between Hear and Faer.

"Aaaaaaiiiiiiiiiiie!" screamed Eldarigon, King of the Faerfolk as he suffered a fatal coronary and fell to the ground.

It was not the usual way to start the Festival of Faet and many of faeries thought it might have been some sort of elaborate joke.

Hispron, the King's seer, fluttered to the monarch's side and delivered the bad news to his people.

"The King is dead!"

The stunned silence around the amphithaeter quickly navigated through intense confusion to arrive at panicked shouting. The general query seemed to be along the lines of, "But what about the festival?"

## Like Father?

His father smiled at him and said something but Nathan neither returned the smile nor accepted the offer of assistance. He turned around, lowered himself on to the table then jumped down to the floor. He hoped this display of independent spite might put his father's nose out of joint but when he faced him he saw that his father's smile had widened even further. He called Nathan, 'a little man,' which made him very angry.

Nathan's father was the worstest in the World ever EVER at being able to take a hint.

www.ingramcontent.com/pod-product-compliance
Ingram Content Group UK Ltd.
Pitfield, Milton Keynes, MK11 3LW, UK
UKHW021318180426
11947UKWH00015B/1310